STAR WARS®

DARTH VADER AND THE NINTH ASSASSIN

THE RISE OF THE EMPIRE
(1,000–0 YEARS BEFORE THE BATTLE OF YAVIN)

AFTER THE SEEMING final defeat of the Sith, the Republic enters a state of complacency. In the waning years of the Republic, the Senate rife with corruption, the ambitious Senator Palpatine causes himself to be elected Supreme Chancellor. This is the era of the prequel trilogy.

The events in this story take place a few months after the events in *Star Wars:* Episode IV—*Revenge of the Sith.*

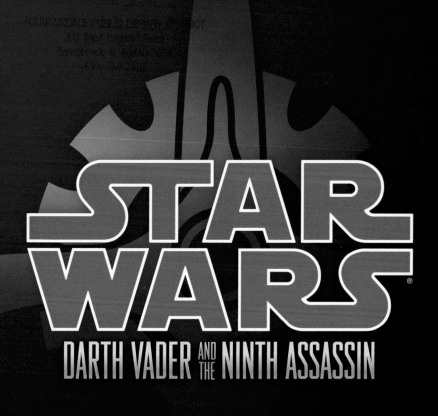

STAR WARS®

DARTH VADER AND THE NINTH ASSASSIN

Script
TIM SIEDELL

Pencils
STEPHEN THOMPSON **IVÁN FERNÁNDEZ**

Inks
MARK IRWIN **DENIS FREITAS** **DREW GERACI** **JASON GORDER**

Colors
MICHAEL ATIYEH

Lettering
MICHAEL HEISLER

Cover art
ARIEL OLIVETTI

DARK HORSE

LUCAS BOOKS

president and publisher
MIKE RICHARDSON

editor
DAVE MARSHALL

assistant editor
FREDDYE LINS

collection designer
JIMMY PRESLER

special thanks to JENNIFER HEDDLE, LELAND CHEE, TROY ALDERS, CAROL ROEDER,
JANN MOORHEAD, and DAVID ANDERMAN at LUCAS LICENSING

STAR WARS®: DARTH VADER AND THE NINTH ASSASSIN

This volume collects *Star Wars: Darth Vader and the Ninth Assassin* #1–#5,
originally published by Dark Horse Comics.

Published by Dark Horse Books
A division of Dark Horse Comics, Inc.
10956 SE Main Street
Milwaukie, OR 97222

DarkHorse.com | StarWars.com

To find a comics shop in your area, call the Comic Shop Locator Service toll-free at 1-888-266-4226.

Library of Congress Cataloging-in-Publication Data

Siedell, Tim.
Star wars. Darth Vader and the ninth assassin / script, Tim Siedell ; pencils, Stephen Thompson, Iván
Fernández ; inks, Mark Irwin, Denis Freitas, Drew Geraci, Jason Gorder ; colors, Michael Atiyeh ; lettering,
Michael Heisler ; cover art, Ariel Olivetti. -- First edition.
    pages cm
Summary: "One man has hired a deadly assassin to murder Darth Vader. While the assassin lurks, Vader
pursues a different threat to the Empire and encounters an ancient prophecy and a powerful weapon"--
Provided by publisher.
ISBN 978-1-61655-207-7
[1. Science fiction.] I. Thompson, Stephen, 1979- illustrator. II. Fernandez, Ivan, illustrator. III. Olivetti,
Ariel, illustrator. IV. Title. V. Title: Darth Vader and the ninth assassin.
PZ7.7.S482St 2013
741.5'315--dc23
                             2013026649

First edition: November 2013
ISBN 978-1-61655-207-7

10 9 8 7 6 5 4 3 2 1
Printed in China

NEIL HANKERSON Executive Vice President TOM WEDDLE Chief Financial Officer RANDY STRADLEY Vice
President of Publishing MICHAEL MARTENS Vice President of Book Trade Sales ANITA NELSON Vice President of
Business Affairs SCOTT ALLIE Editor in Chief MATT PARKINSON Vice President of Marketing DAVID SCROGGY
Vice President of Product Development DALE LAFOUNTAIN Vice President of Information Technology DARLENE
VOGEL Senior Director of Print, Design, and Production KEN LIZZI General Counsel DAVEY ESTRADA Editorial
Director CHRIS WARNER Senior Books Editor DIANA SCHUTZ Executive Editor CARY GRAZZINI Director of
Print and Development LIA RIBACCHI Art Director CARA NIECE Director of Scheduling TIM WIESCH Director of
International Licensing MARK BERNARDI Director of Digital Publishing

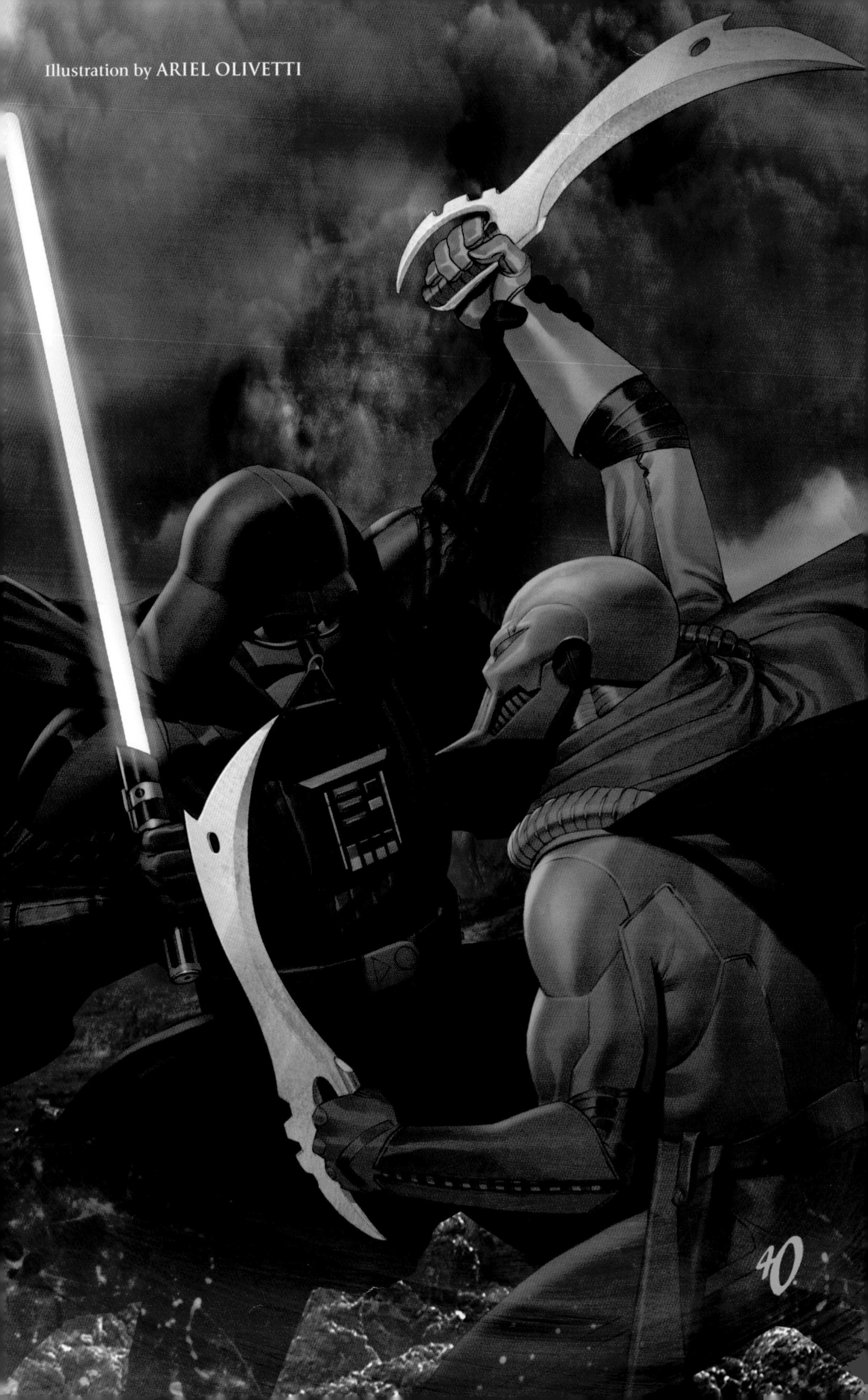

Illustration by ARIEL OLIVETTI

T HE CLONE WARS have come to a long-awaited end, and the
galaxy is now under the singular rule of Emperor Palpatine
and his mysterious apprentice, Darth Vader.

Under this new regime, still in the midst of consolidating power,
the entire galaxy is expected to bow to any and all dictates.

There are many who are not prepared for this altered way
of life, nor do they understand the already incredible reach
of the Galactic Empire . . .

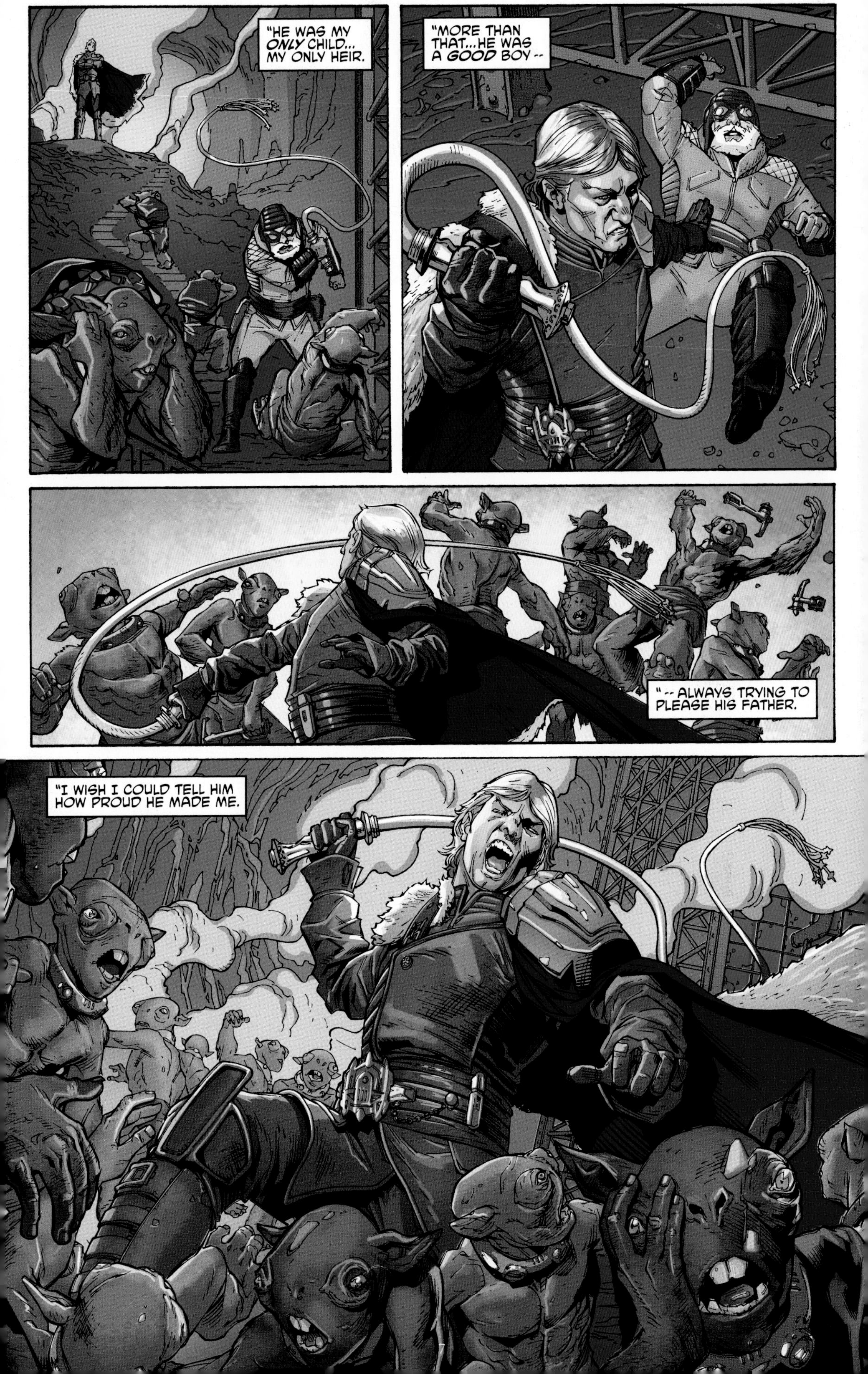
"HE WAS MY ONLY CHILD... MY ONLY HEIR.
"MORE THAN THAT...HE WAS A GOOD BOY --
"-- ALWAYS TRYING TO PLEASE HIS FATHER.
"I WISH I COULD TELL HIM HOW PROUD HE MADE ME.

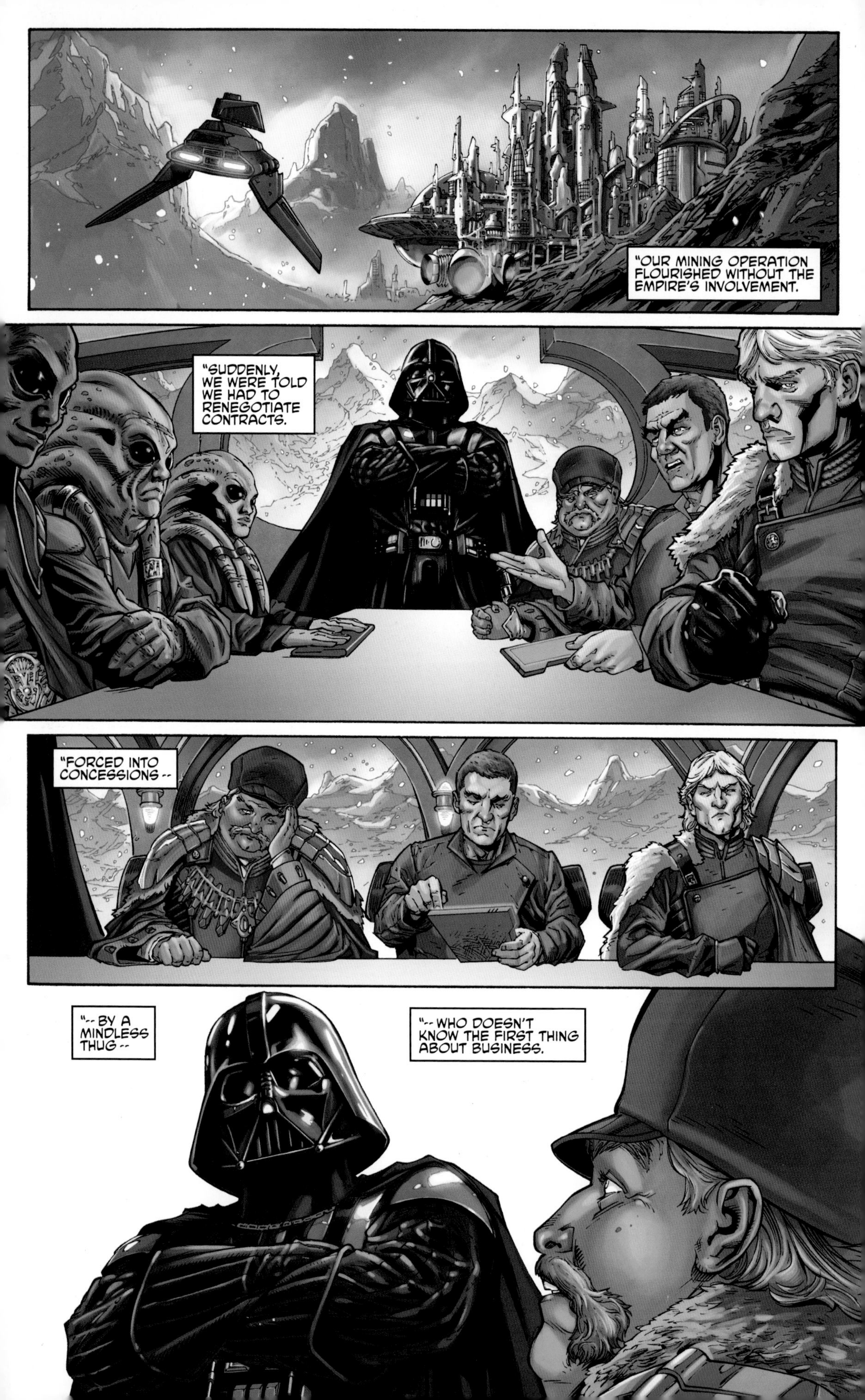
"OUR MINING OPERATION FLOURISHED WITHOUT THE EMPIRE'S INVOLVEMENT.
"SUDDENLY, WE WERE TOLD WE HAD TO RENEGOTIATE CONTRACTS.
"FORCED INTO CONCESSIONS --
"-- BY A MINDLESS THUG --
"-- WHO DOESN'T KNOW THE FIRST THING ABOUT BUSINESS.

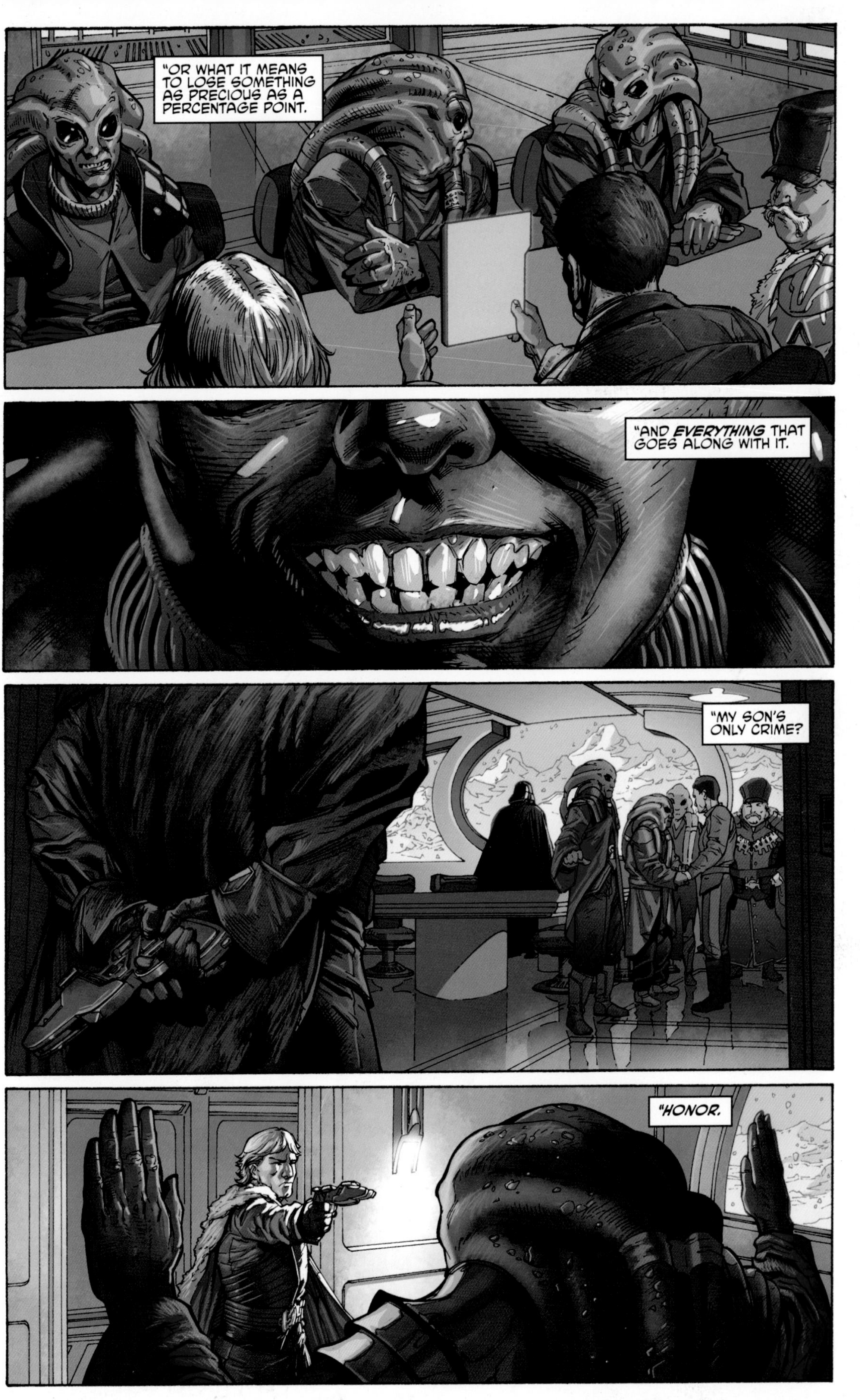
"OR WHAT IT MEANS TO LOSE SOMETHING AS PRECIOUS AS A PERCENTAGE POINT.
"AND *EVERYTHING* THAT GOES ALONG WITH IT.
"MY SON'S ONLY CRIME?
"HONOR.

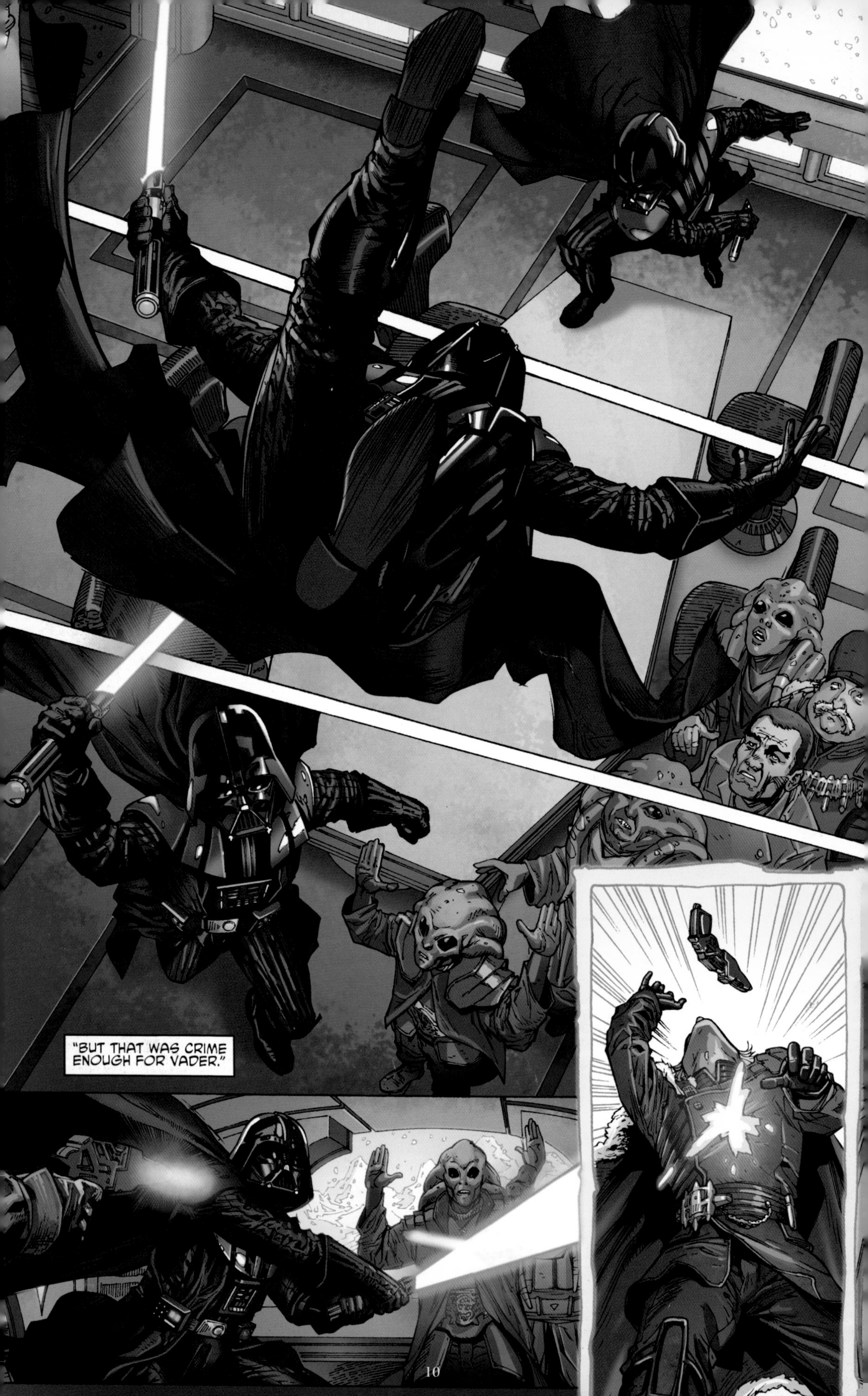
"BUT THAT WAS CRIME ENOUGH FOR VADER."

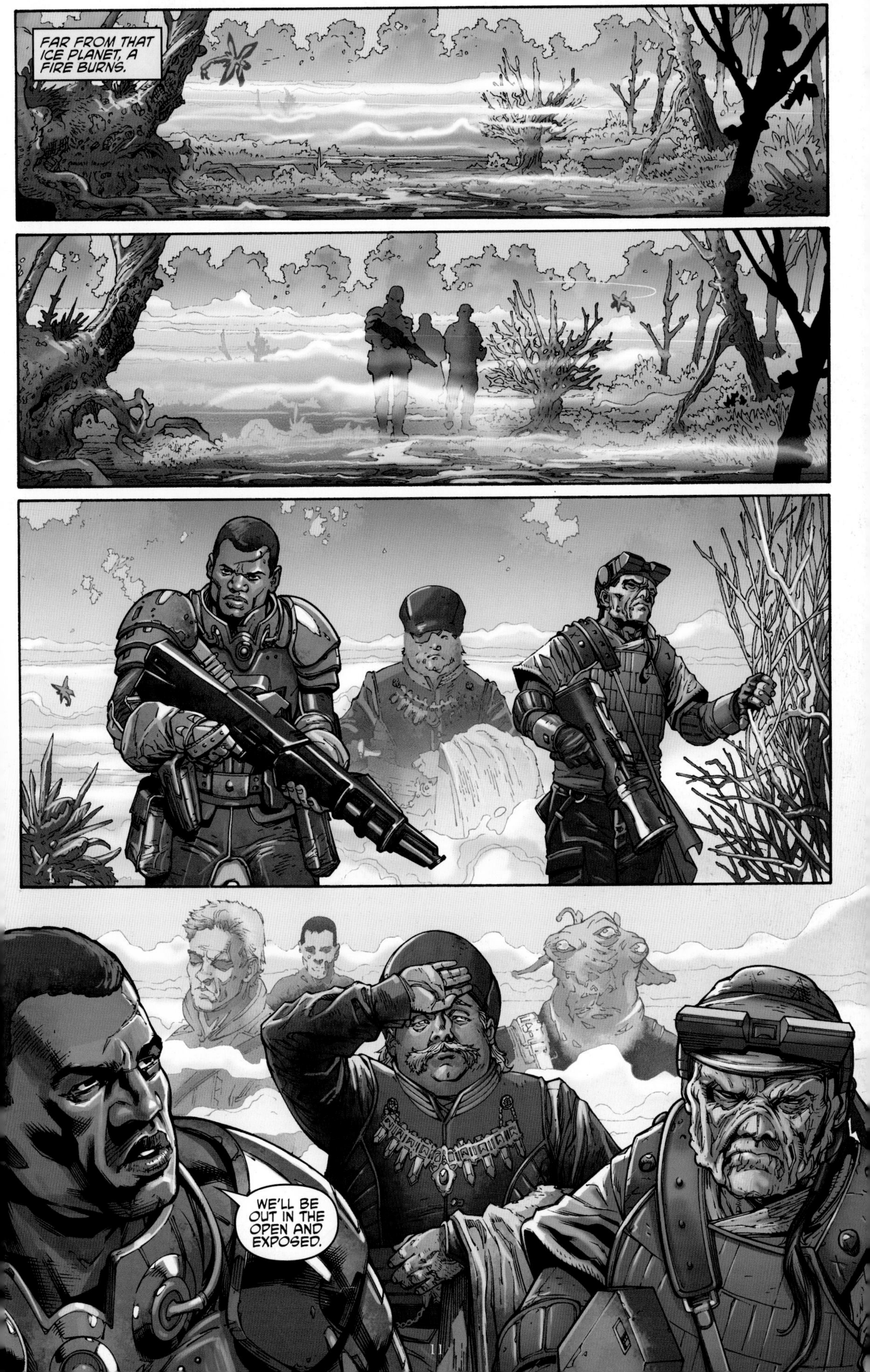
FAR FROM THAT ICE PLANET, A FIRE BURNS.
WE'LL BE OUT IN THE OPEN AND EXPOSED.

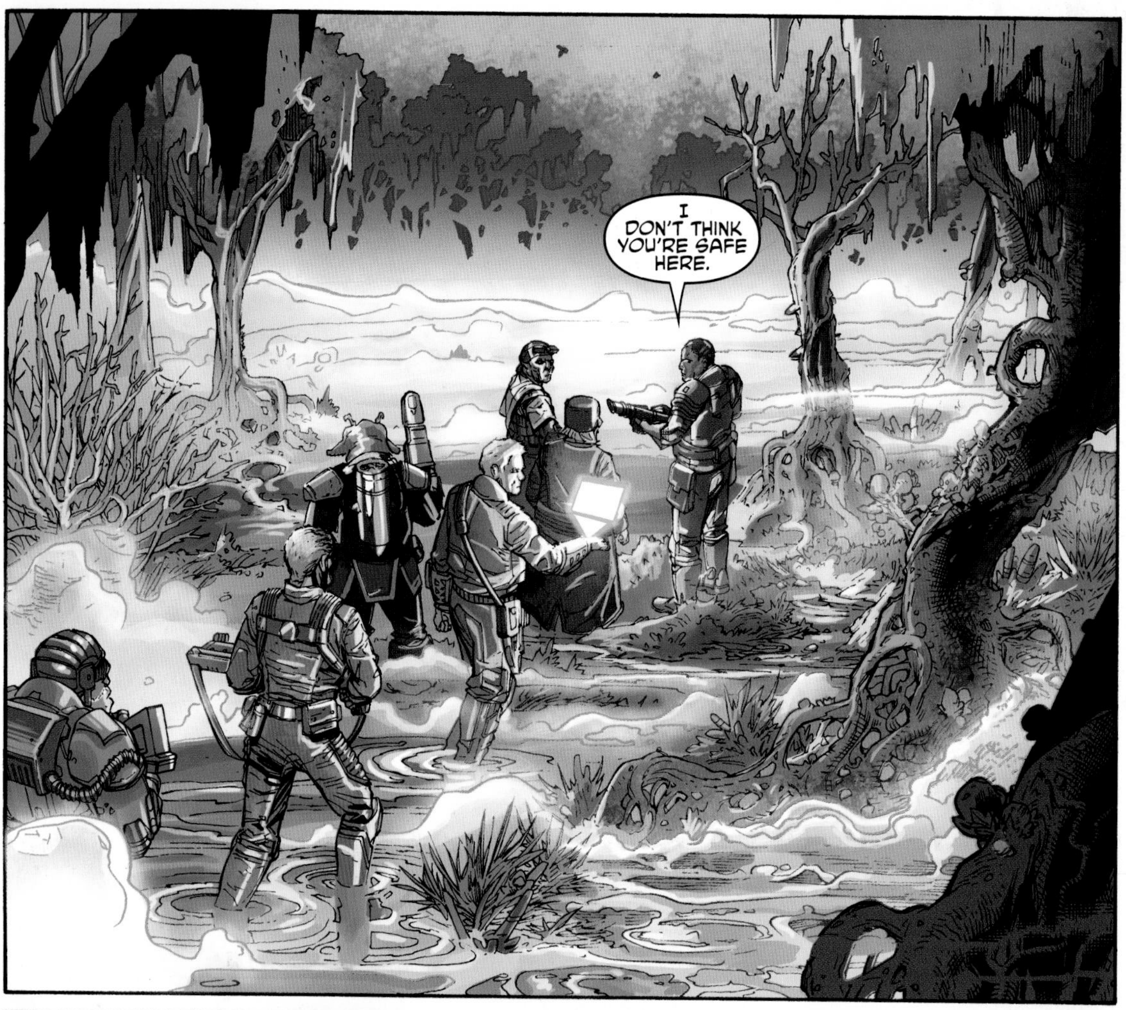
I DON'T THINK YOU'RE SAFE HERE.

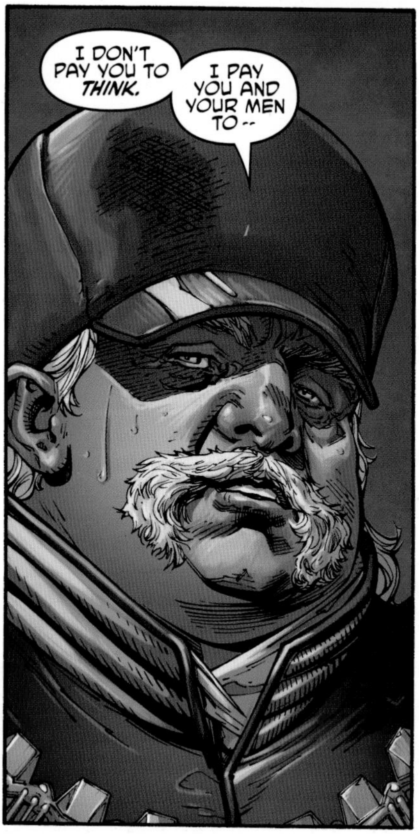
I DON'T PAY YOU TO *THINK.*
I PAY YOU AND YOUR MEN TO --

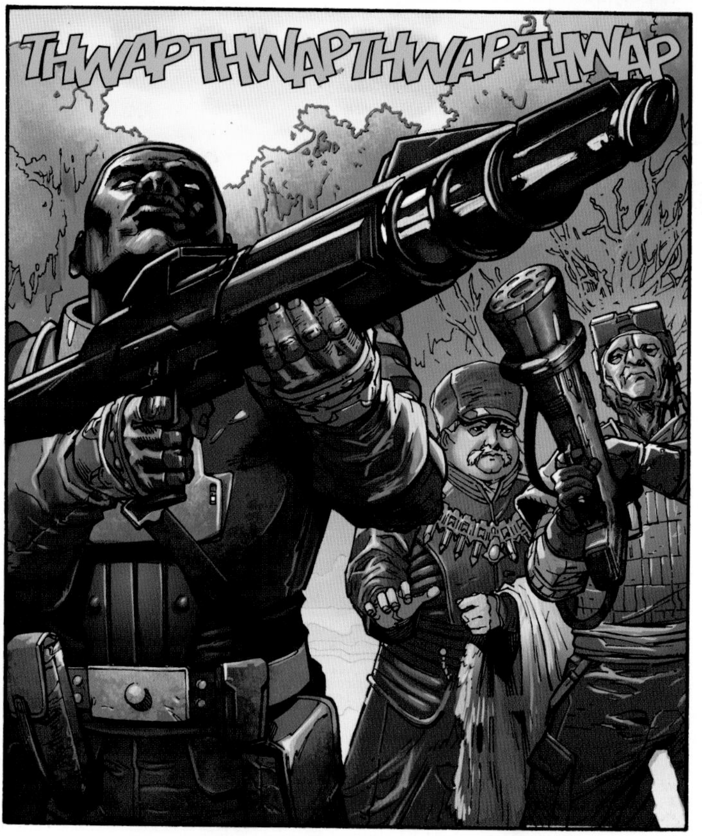
THWAPTHWAPTHWAPTHWAP

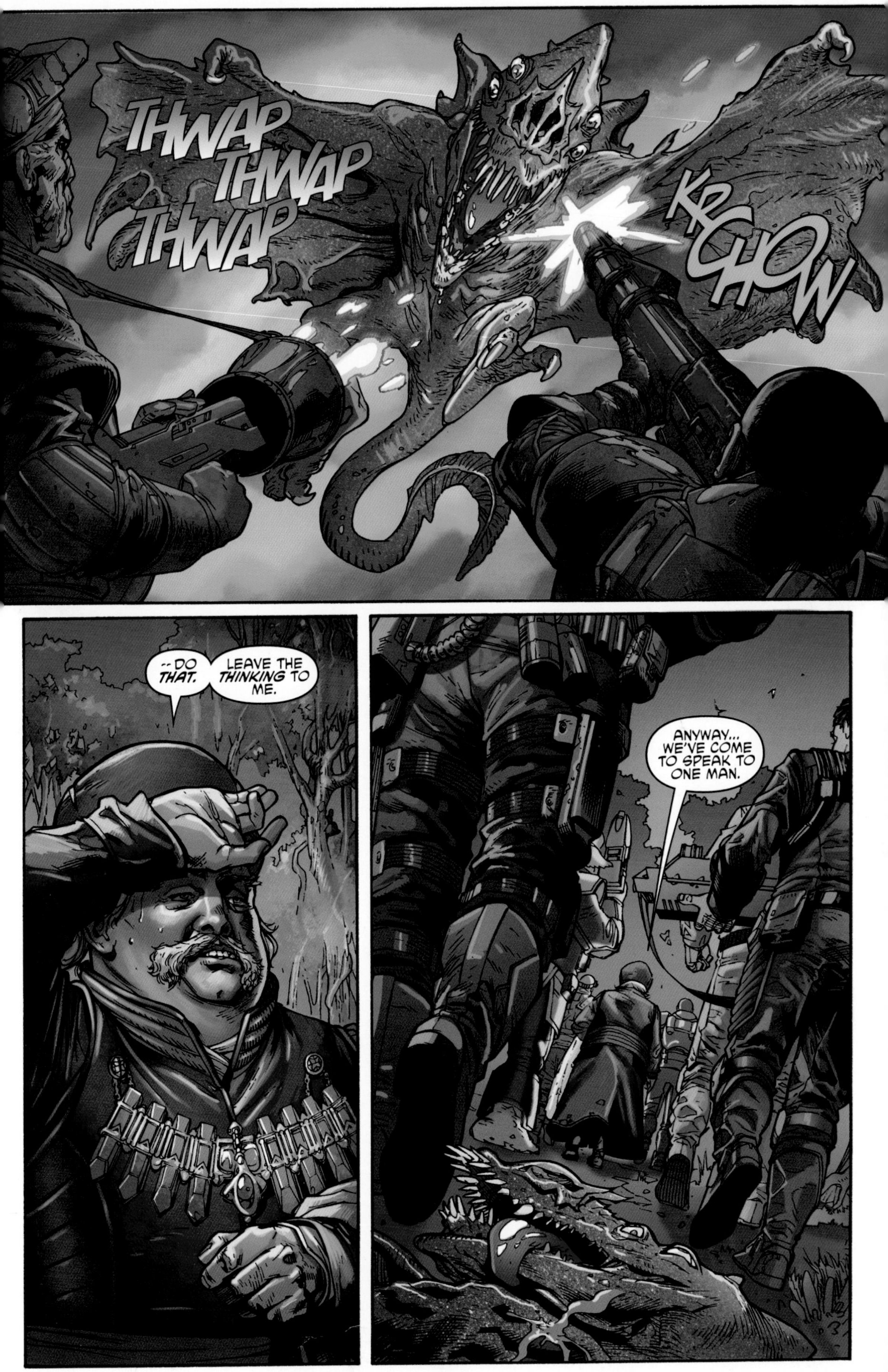
THWAP THWAP THWAP
KRCHOW
--DO THAT.
LEAVE THE THINKING TO ME.
ANYWAY... WE'VE COME TO SPEAK TO ONE MAN.

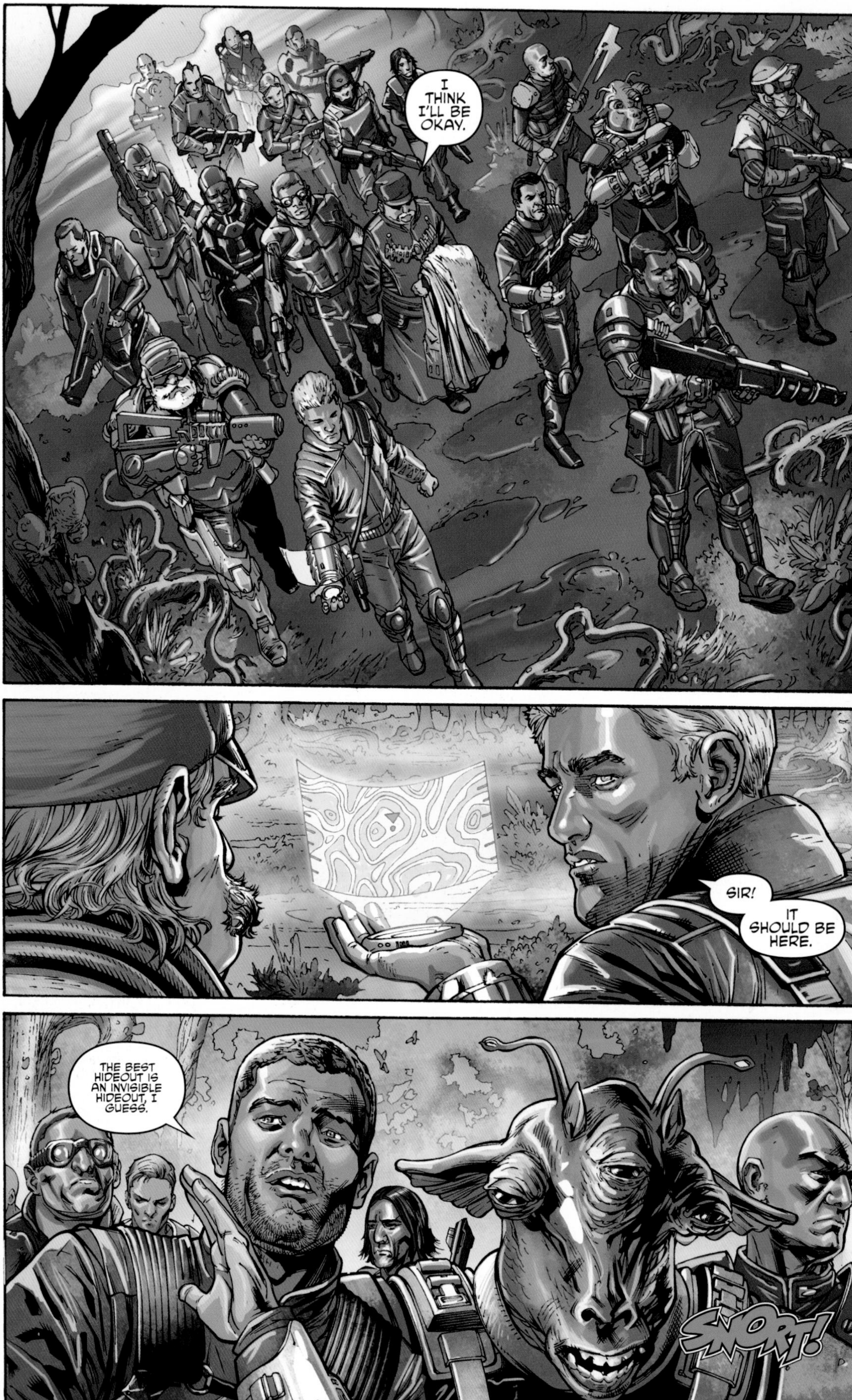
I THINK I'LL BE OKAY.
SIR!
IT SHOULD BE HERE.
THE BEST HIDEOUT IS AN INVISIBLE HIDEOUT, I GUESS.
SNORT!

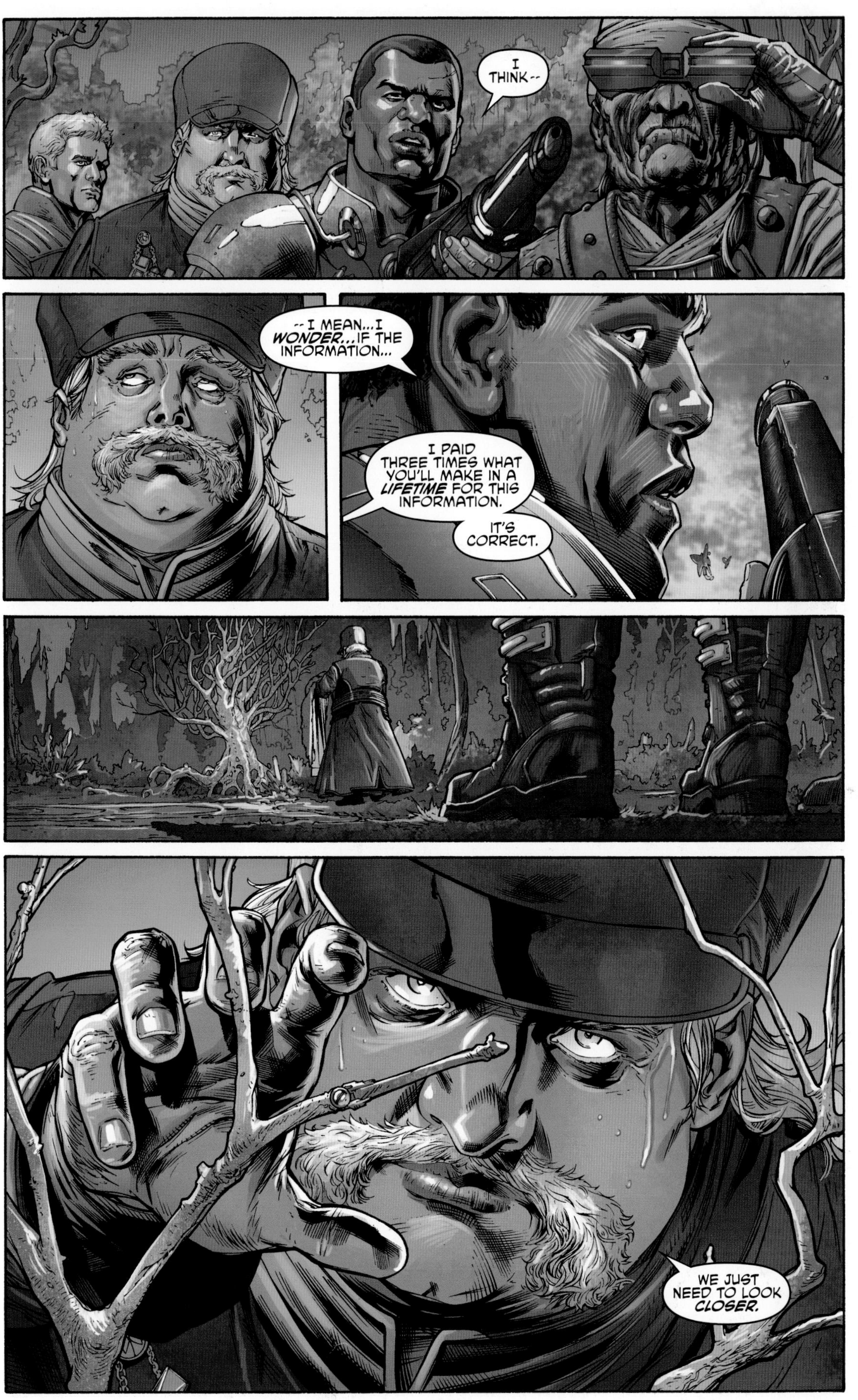
I THINK--
--I MEAN...I *WONDER*...IF THE INFORMATION...
I PAID THREE TIMES WHAT YOU'LL MAKE IN A *LIFETIME* FOR THIS INFORMATION.
IT'S CORRECT.
WE JUST NEED TO LOOK *CLOSER.*

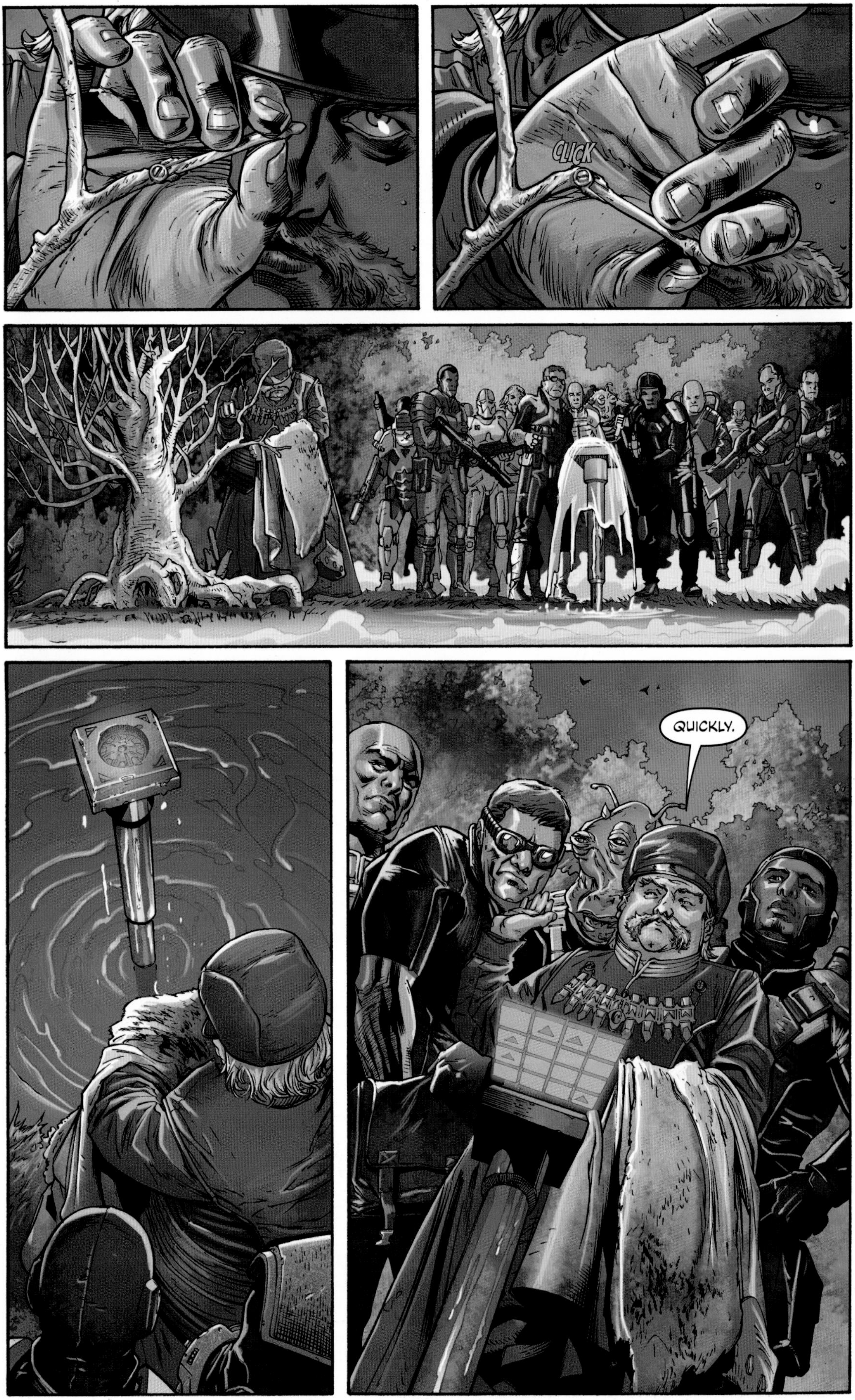
CLICK
QUICKLY.

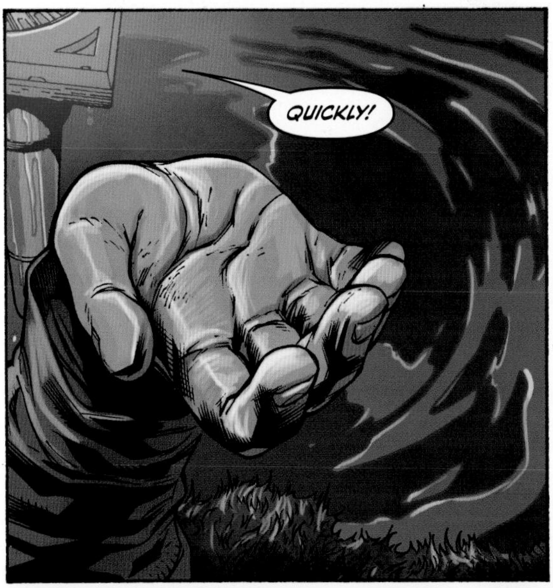
QUICKLY!

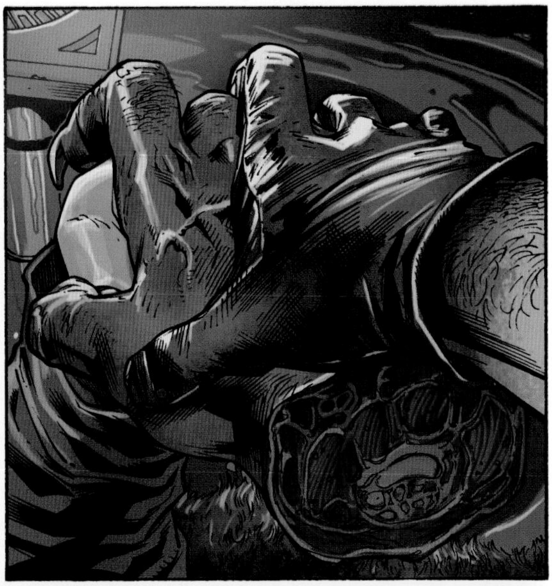

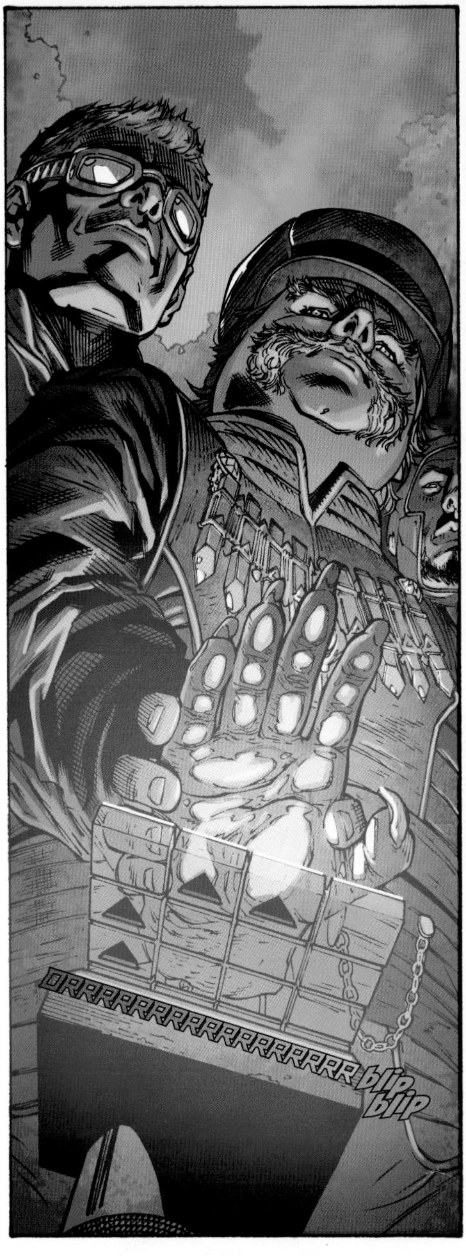
DRRRRRRRRRRRRRRRRRRRR blip blip

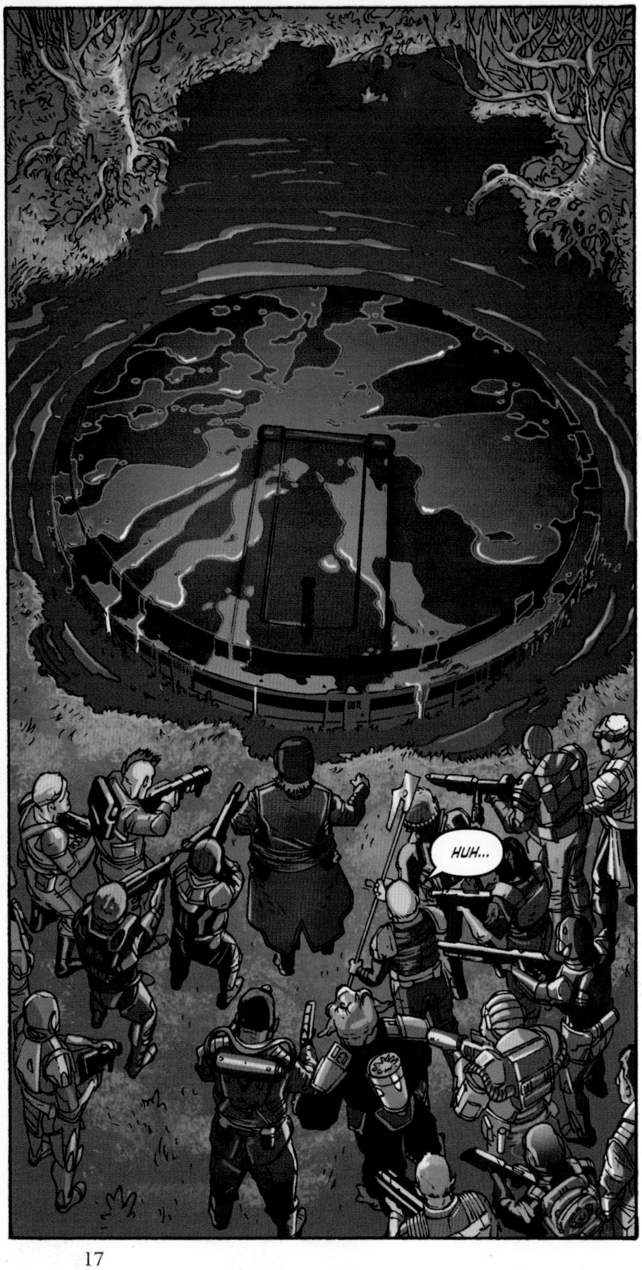
HUH...

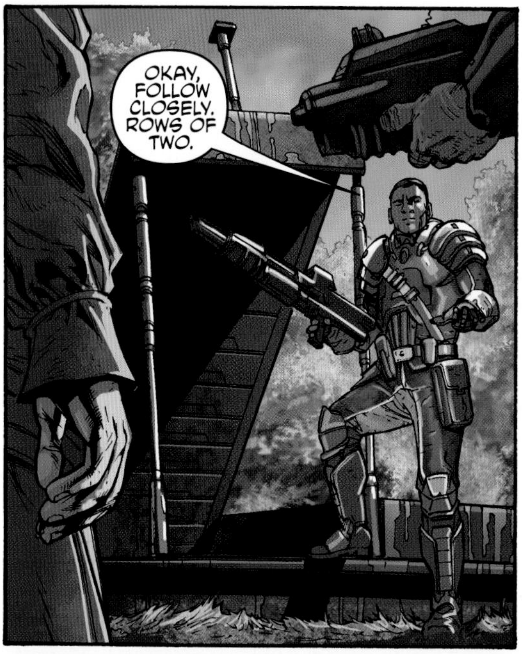
OKAY, FOLLOW CLOSELY. ROWS OF TWO.

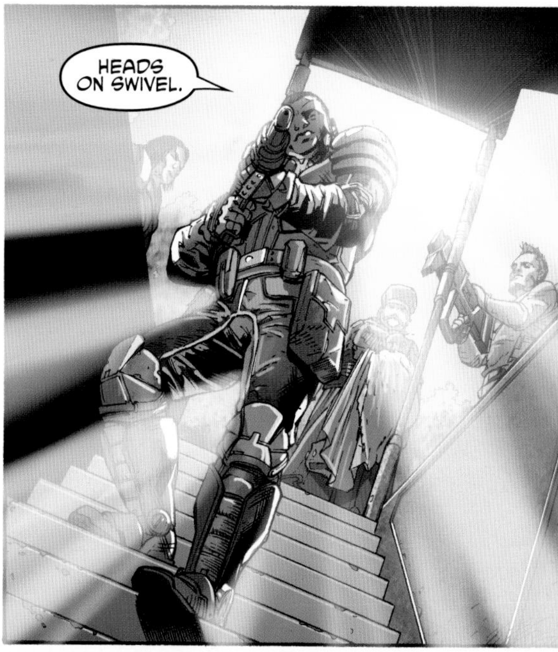
HEADS ON SWIVEL.

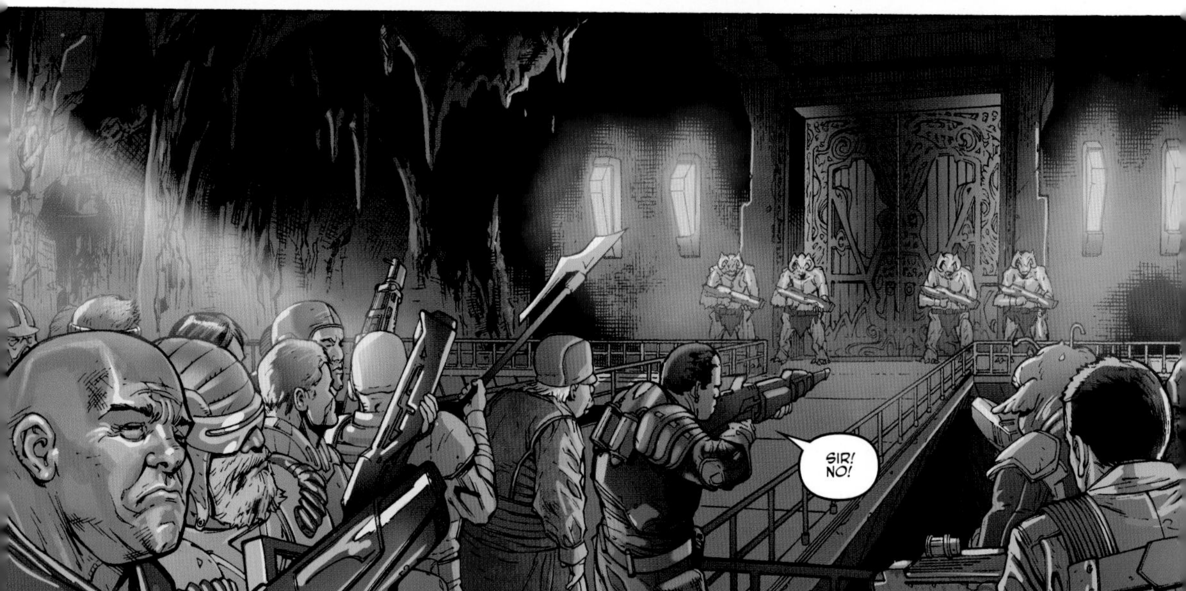
SIR! NO!

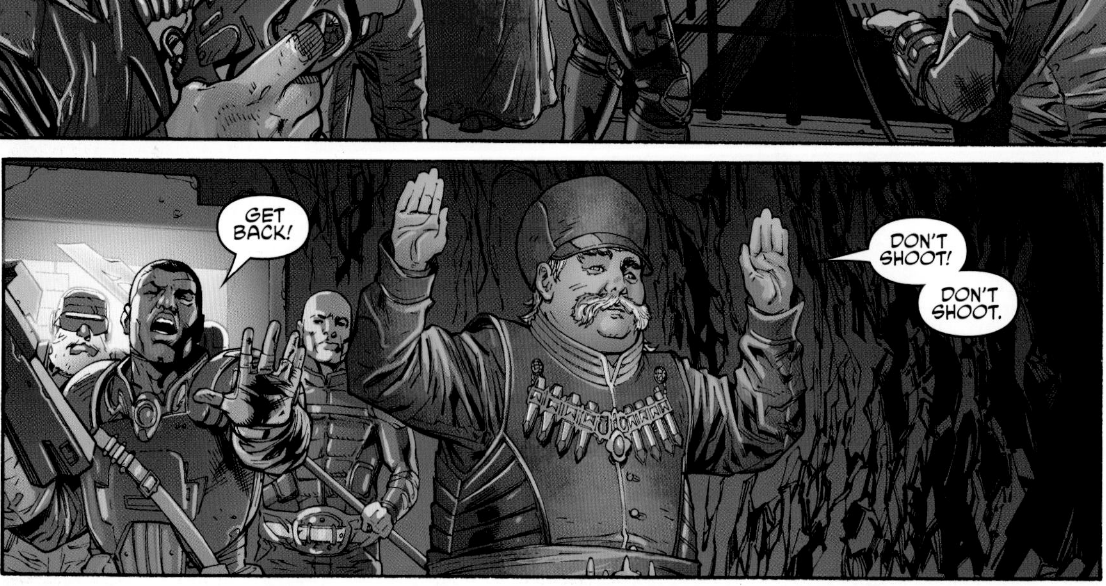
GET BACK!
DON'T SHOOT!
DON'T SHOOT.

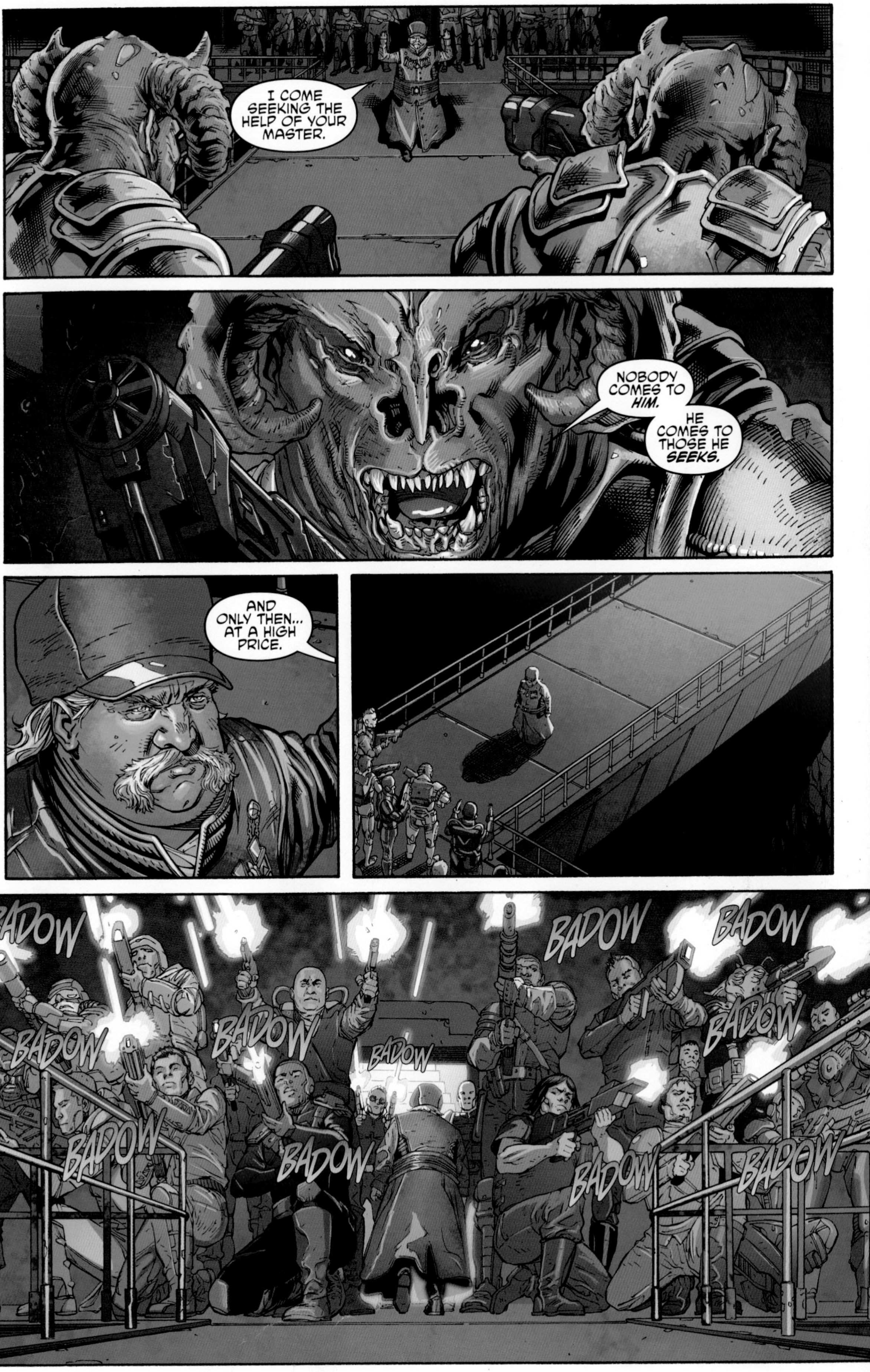
I COME SEEKING THE HELP OF YOUR MASTER.
NOBODY COMES TO *HIM.*
HE COMES TO THOSE HE *SEEKS.*
AND ONLY THEN... AT A HIGH PRICE.
BADOW
BADOW
BADOW
BADOW
BADOW
BADOW
BADOW
BADOW
BADOW
BADOW

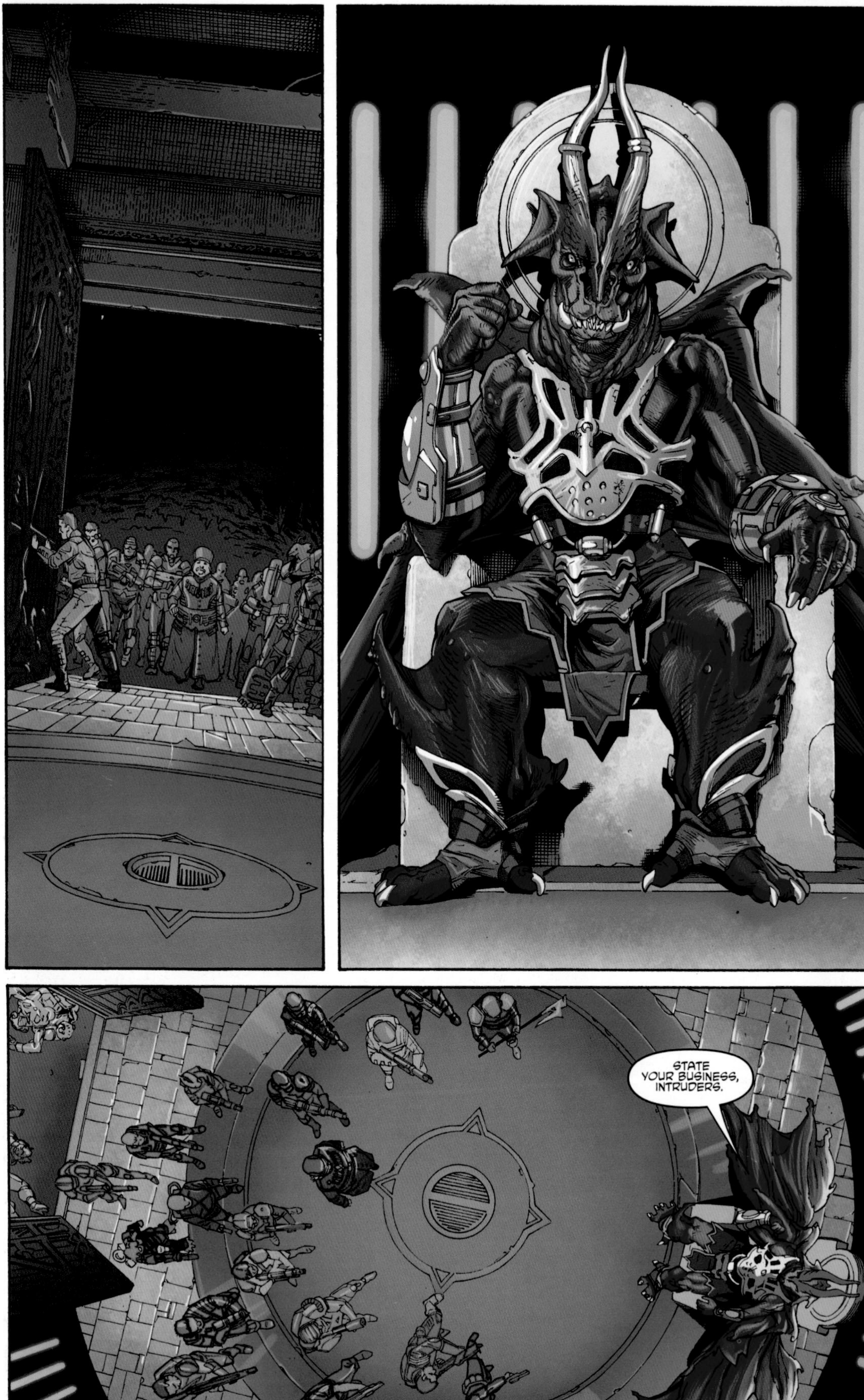
STATE YOUR BUSINESS, INTRUDERS.

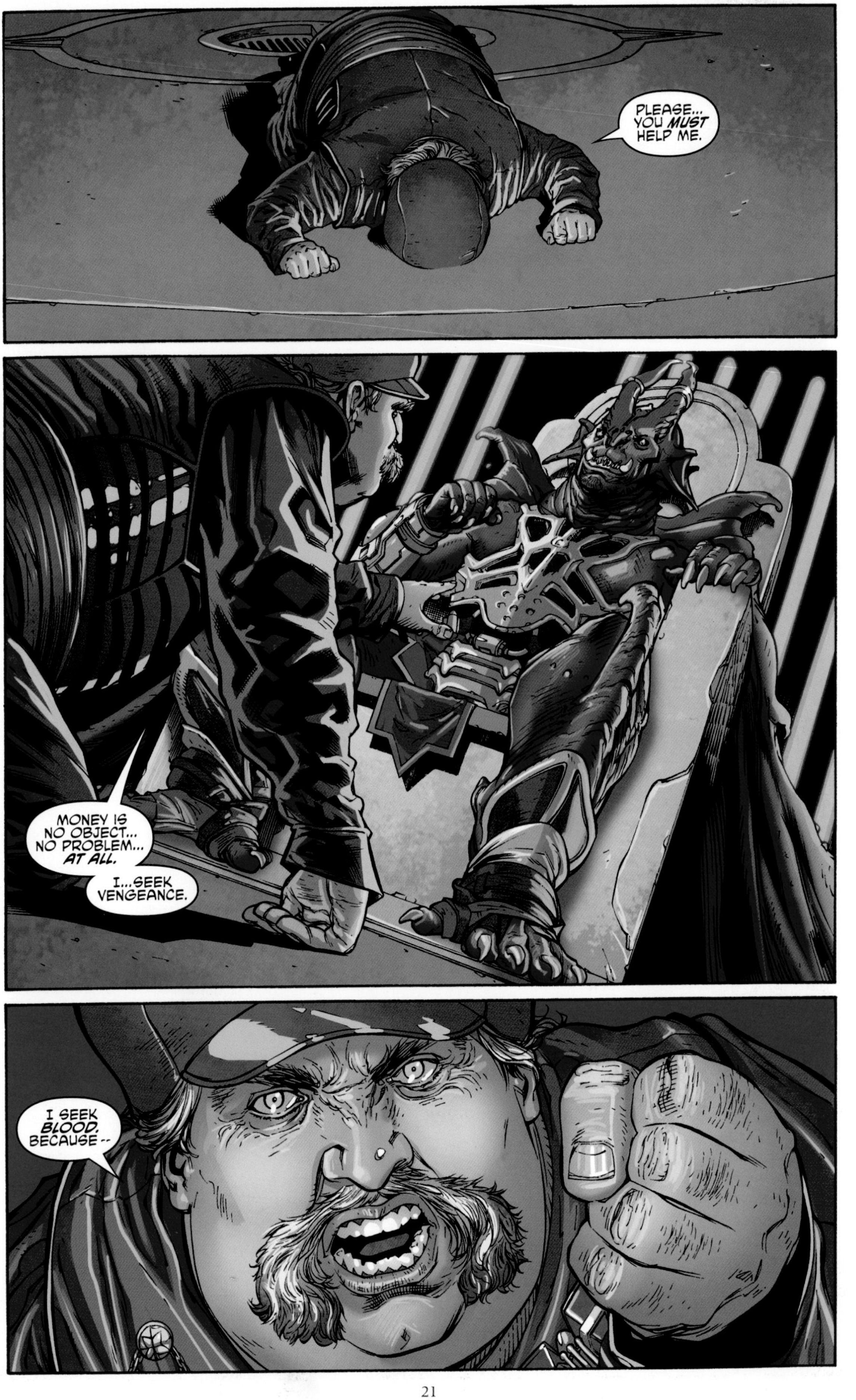
PLEASE... YOU *MUST* HELP ME.
MONEY IS NO OBJECT... NO PROBLEM... *AT ALL.*
I...SEEK VENGEANCE.
I SEEK *BLOOD.* BECAUSE --

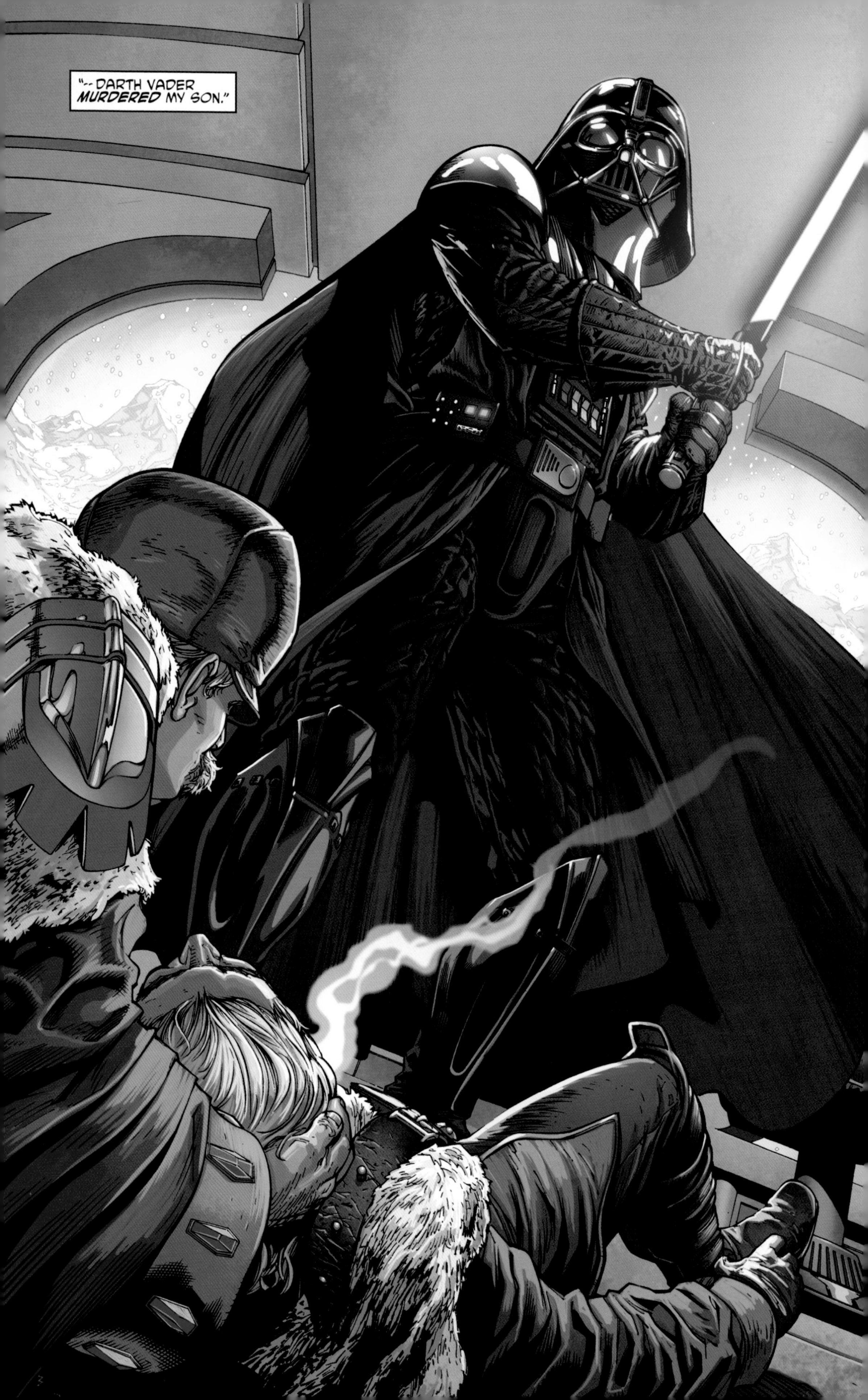
"-- DARTH VADER MURDERED MY SON."

I HAVE MADE THIS... *REQUEST*...OF OTHERS.

MY SOURCES TELL ME THREE WERE KILLED.

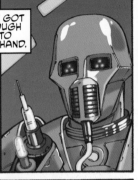

"ONLY *ONE* GOT CLOSE ENOUGH TO VADER TO DIE BY HIS HAND.

"I ASSUME THE OTHERS TOOK MY UPFRONT MONEY AND RAN."

I CAN *ASSURE* YOU...THE OTHERS ARE DEAD, AS WELL.

AN ASSASSIN'S CAREER IS NOT SUSTAINED BY HALF SALARIES.

WUH--?

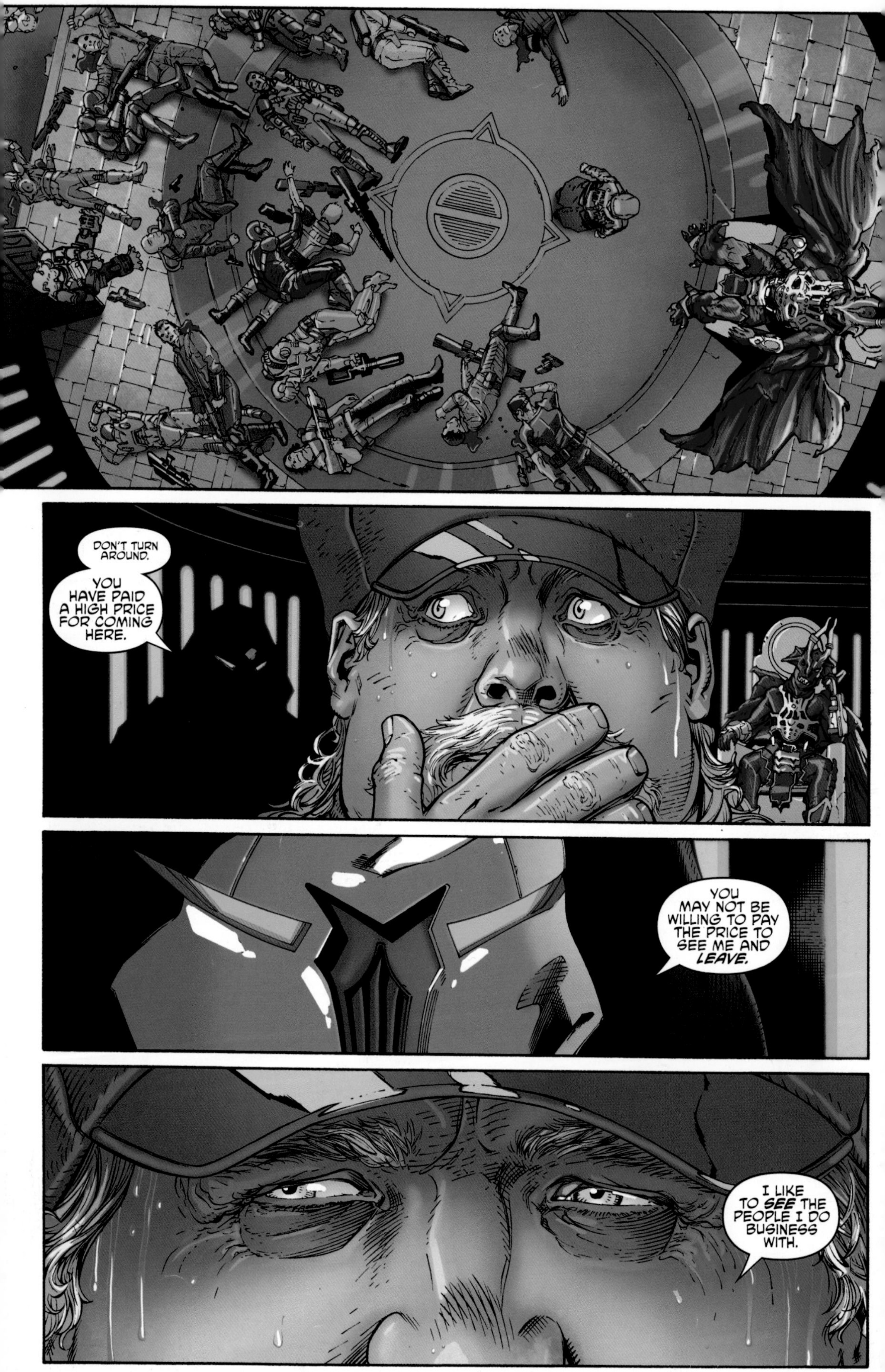
DON'T TURN AROUND.
YOU HAVE PAID A HIGH PRICE FOR COMING HERE.
YOU MAY NOT BE WILLING TO PAY THE PRICE TO SEE ME AND LEAVE.
I LIKE TO SEE THE PEOPLE I DO BUSINESS WITH.

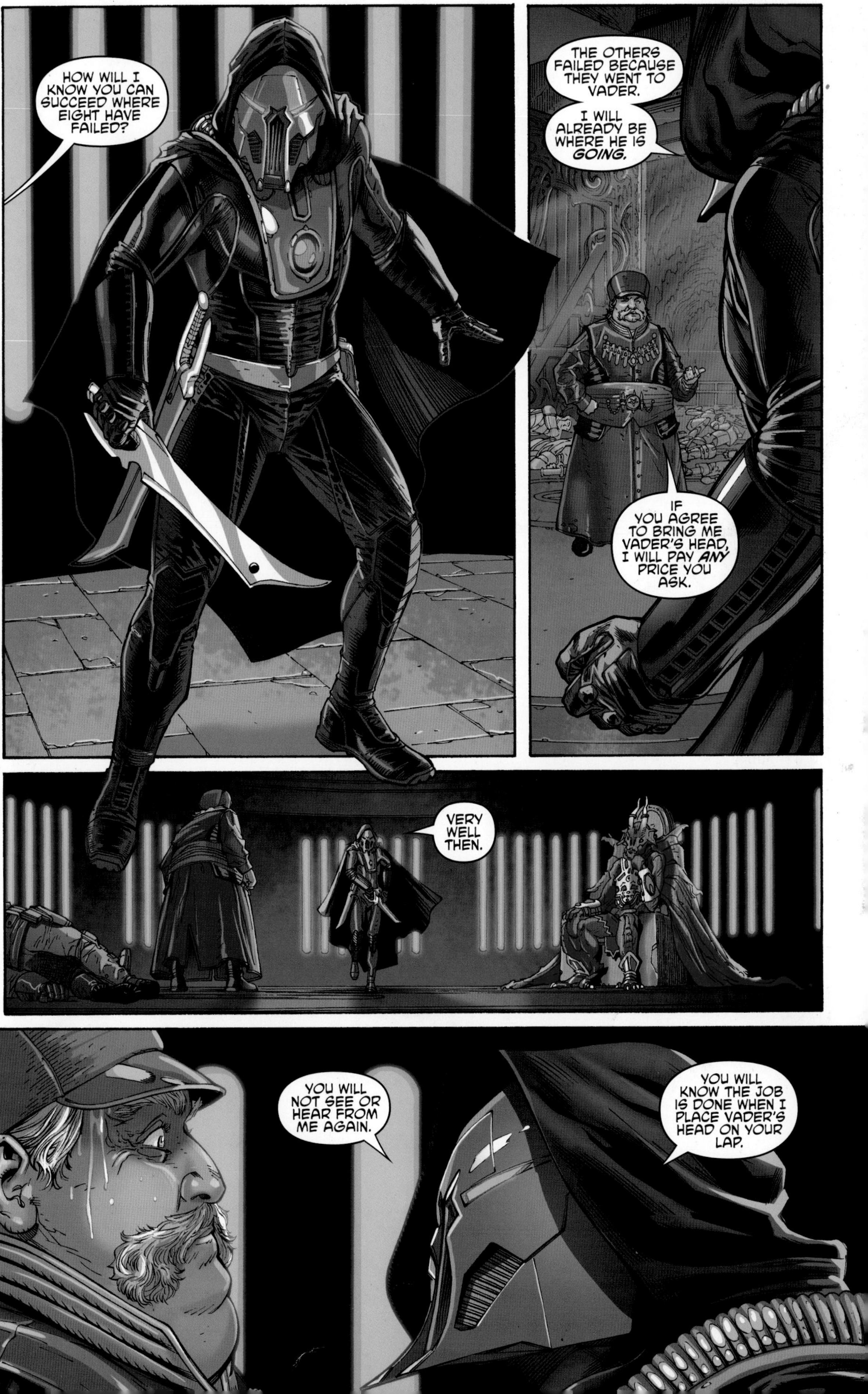
HOW WILL I KNOW YOU CAN SUCCEED WHERE EIGHT HAVE FAILED?
THE OTHERS FAILED BECAUSE THEY WENT TO VADER.
I WILL ALREADY BE WHERE HE IS *GOING.*
IF YOU AGREE TO BRING ME VADER'S HEAD, I WILL PAY *ANY* PRICE YOU ASK.
VERY WELL THEN.
YOU WILL NOT SEE OR HEAR FROM ME AGAIN.
YOU WILL KNOW THE JOB IS DONE WHEN I PLACE VADER'S HEAD ON YOUR LAP.

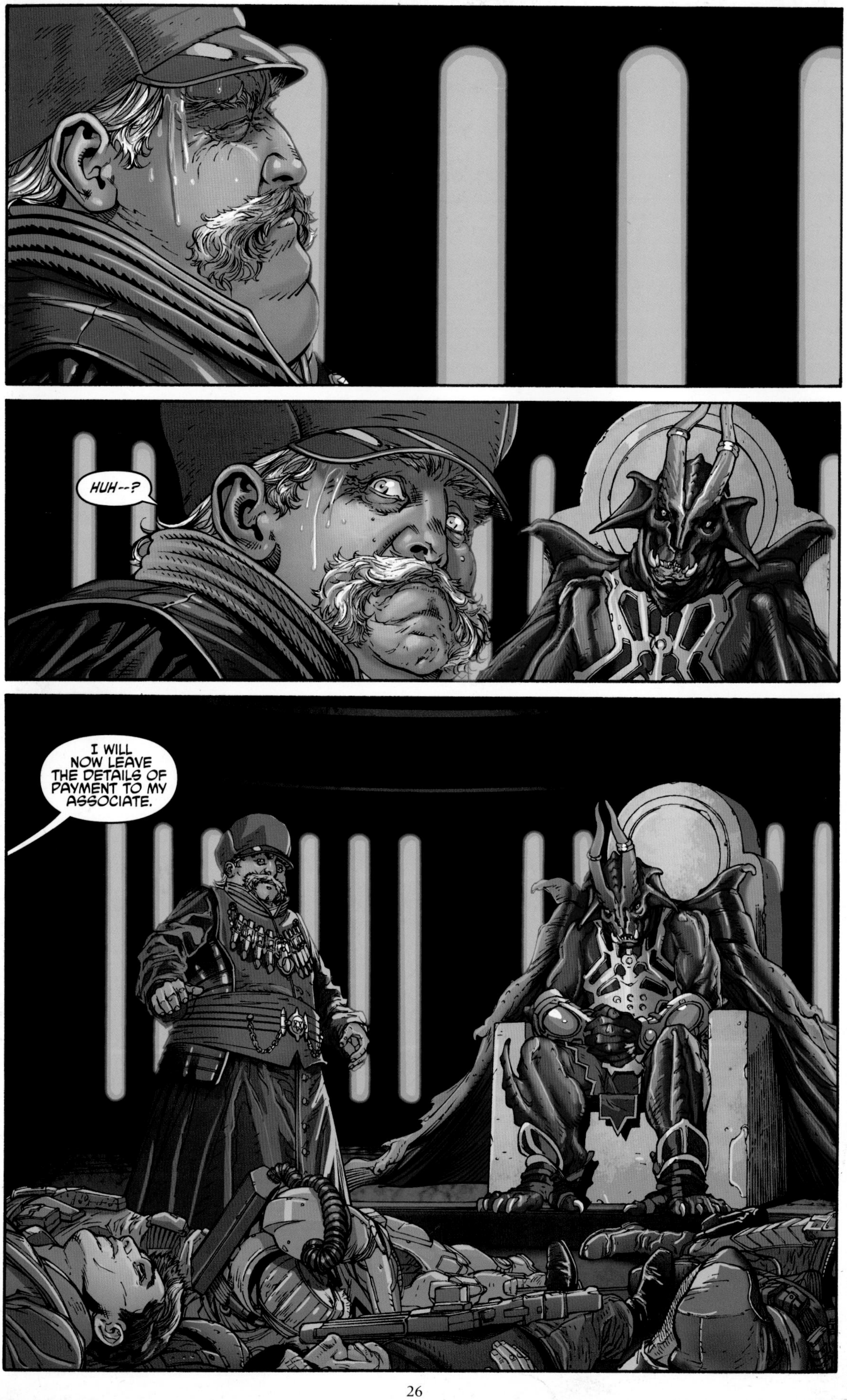
HUH--?
I WILL NOW LEAVE THE DETAILS OF PAYMENT TO MY ASSOCIATE.

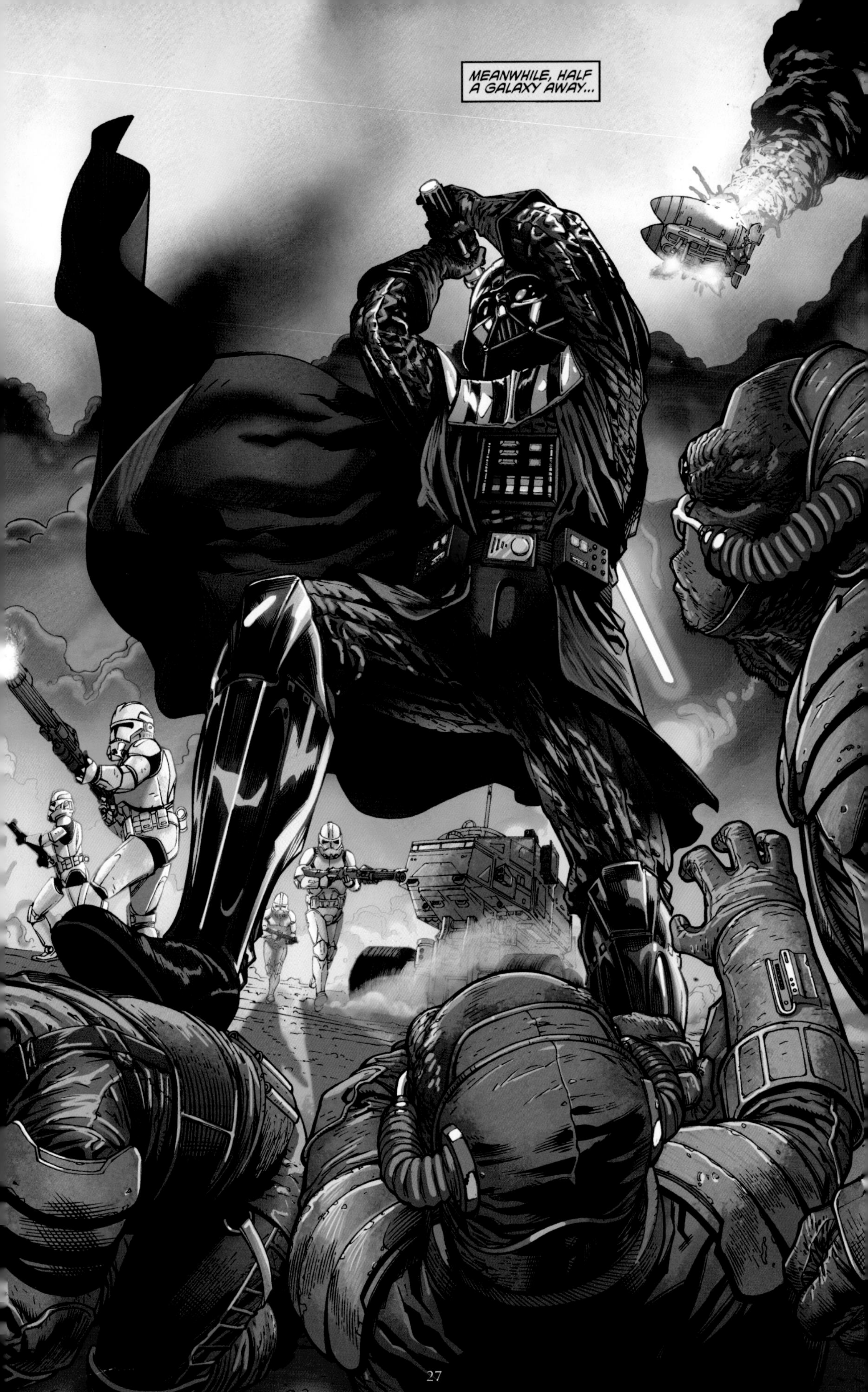
MEANWHILE, HALF A GALAXY AWAY...

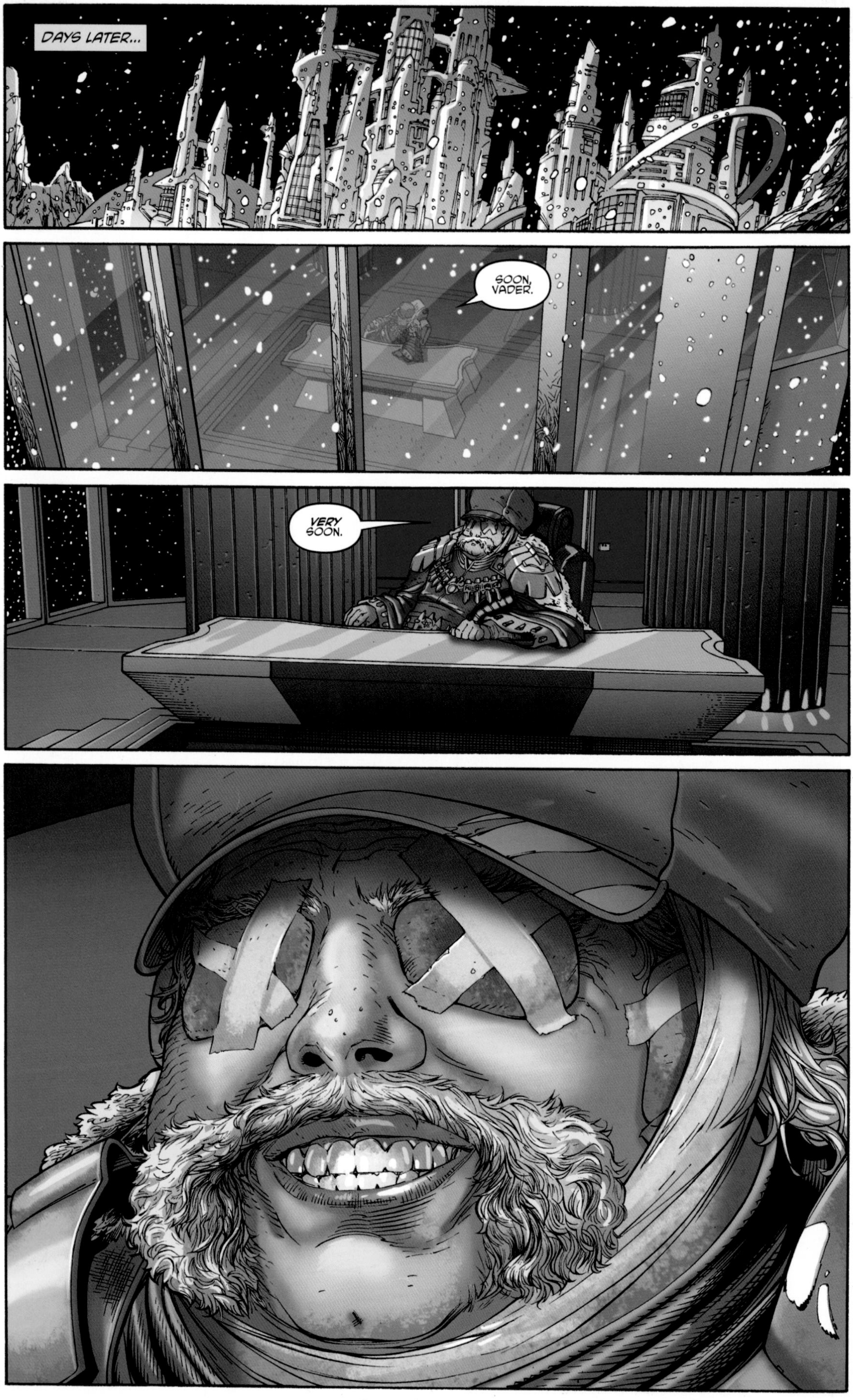
DAYS LATER...
SOON, VADER.
VERY SOON.

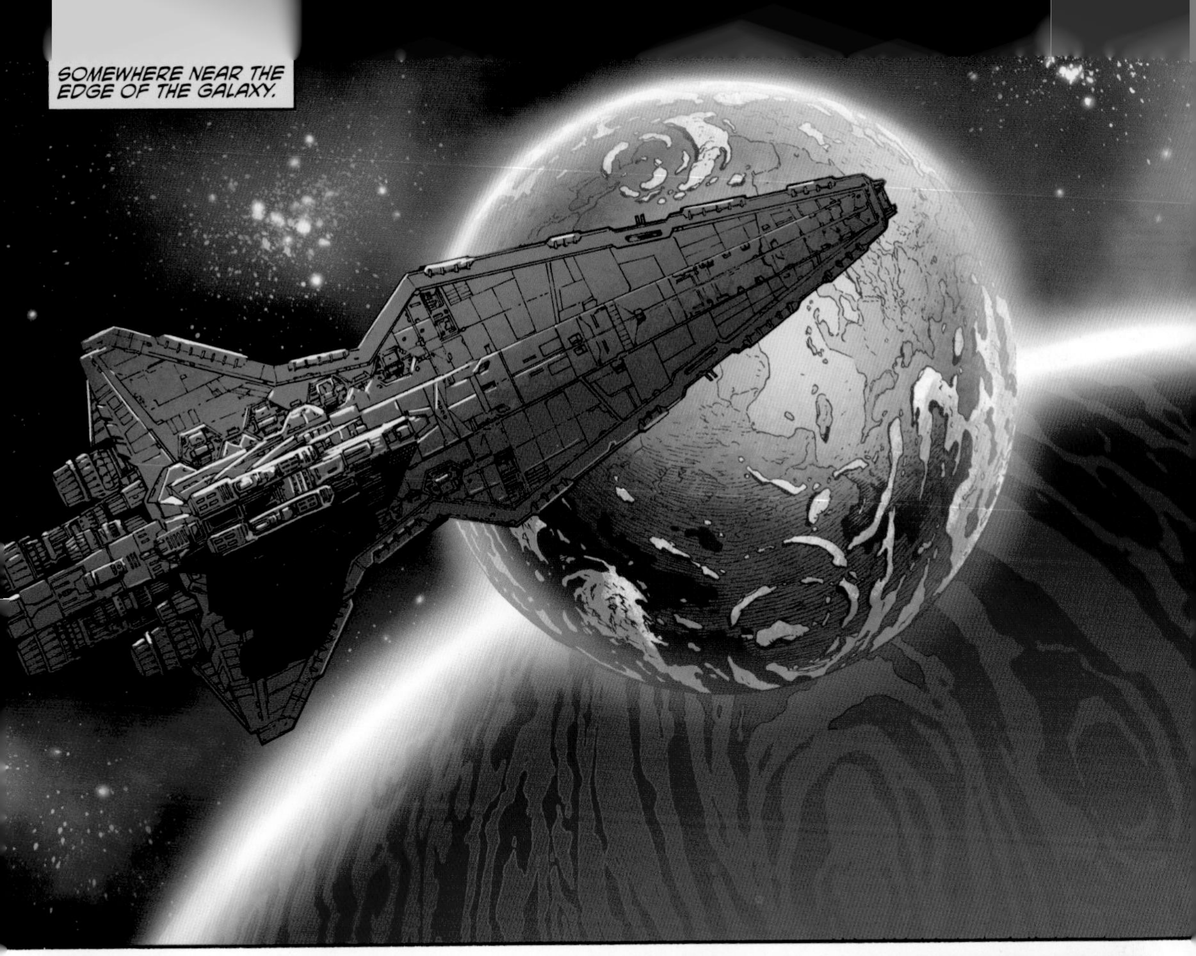
SOMEWHERE NEAR THE EDGE OF THE GALAXY.

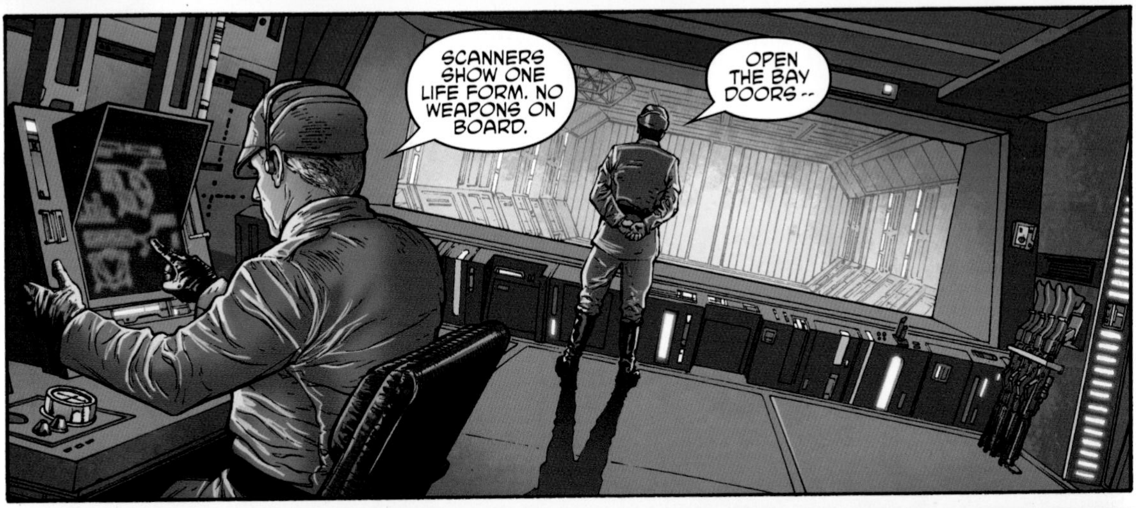
SCANNERS SHOW ONE LIFE FORM. NO WEAPONS ON BOARD.
OPEN THE BAY DOORS --

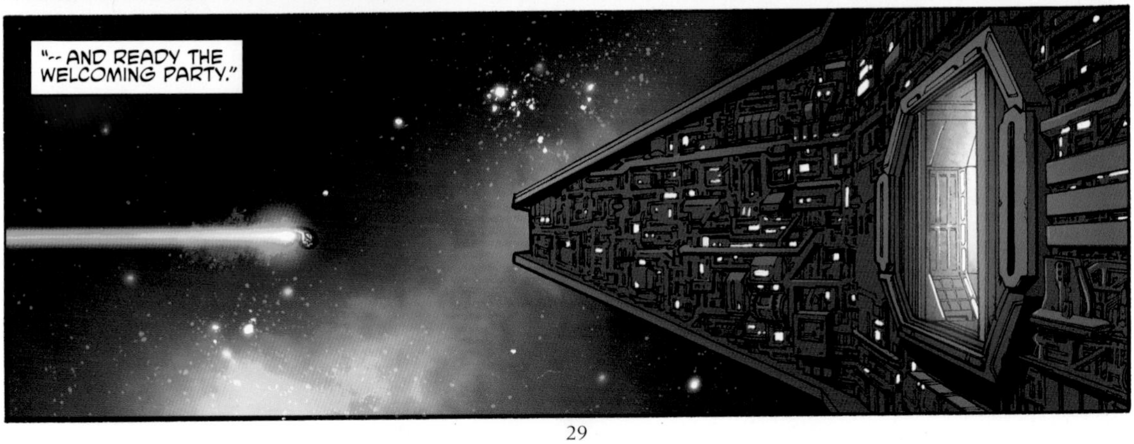
"-- AND READY THE WELCOMING PARTY."

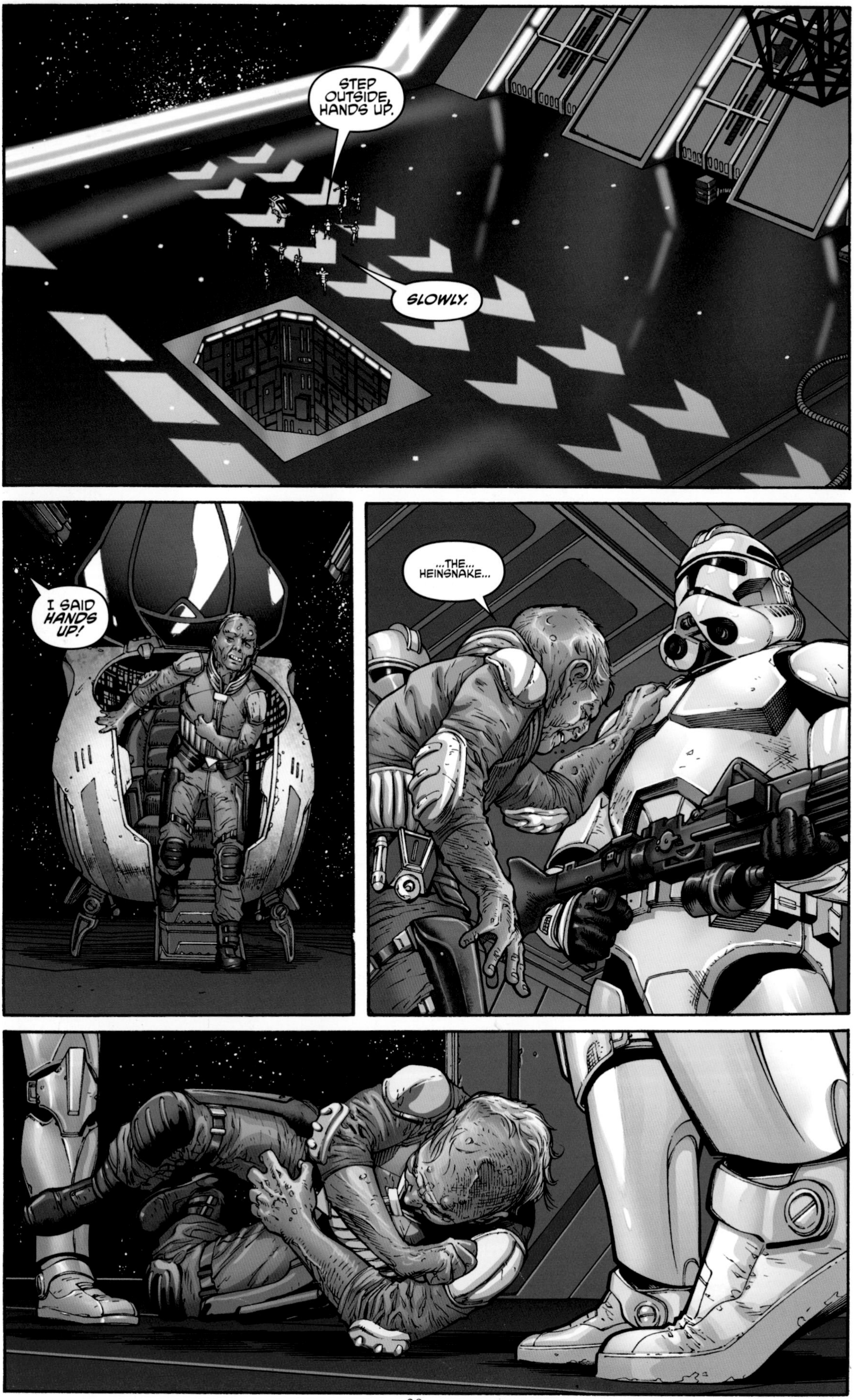
STEP OUTSIDE, HANDS UP.
SLOWLY.
I SAID HANDS UP!
...THE... HEINSNAKE...

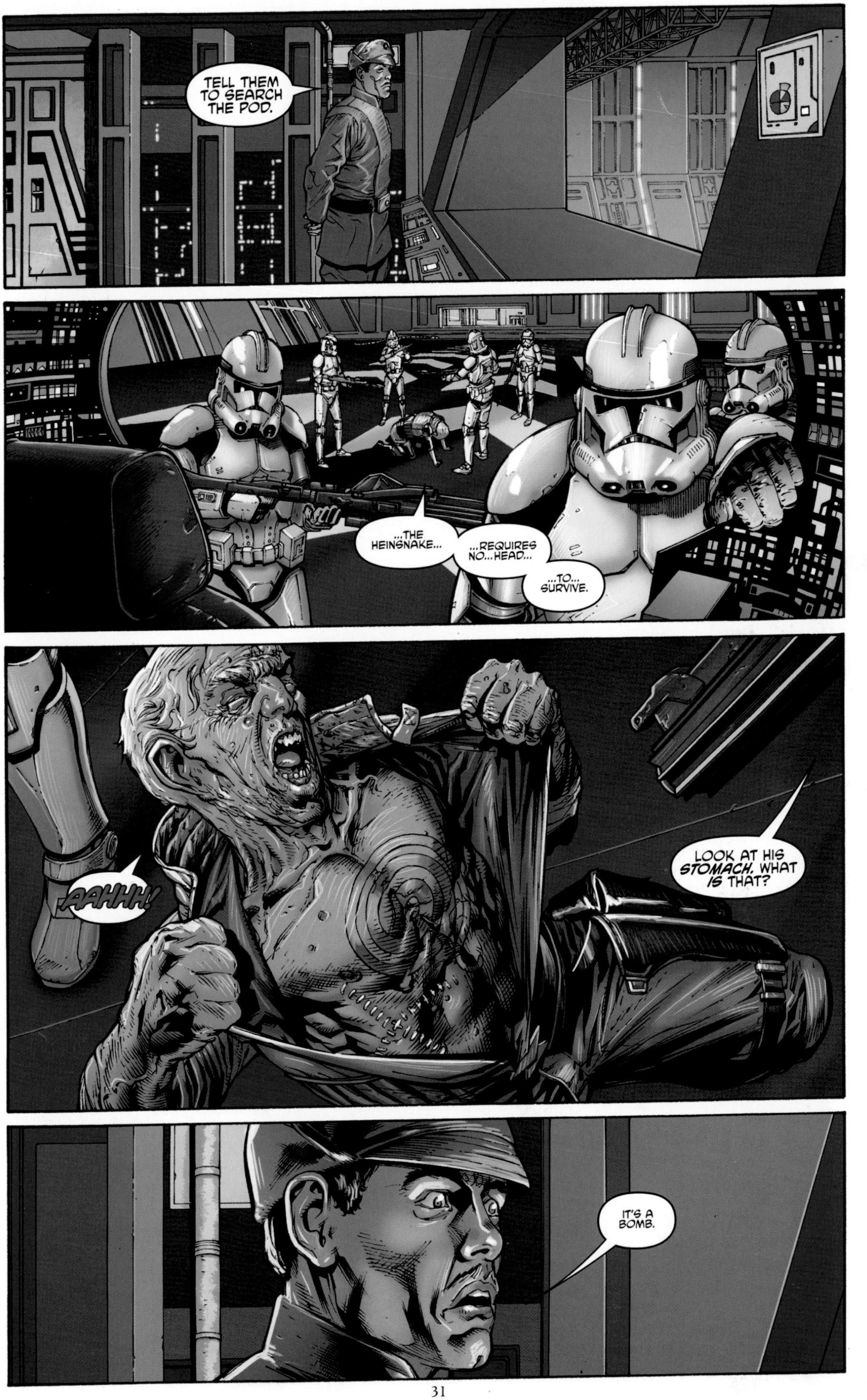
TELL THEM TO SEARCH THE POD.
...THE HEINSNAKE...
...REQUIRES NO...HEAD...
...TO... SURVIVE.
AAHHH!
LOOK AT HIS STOMACH. WHAT IS THAT?
IT'S A BOMB.

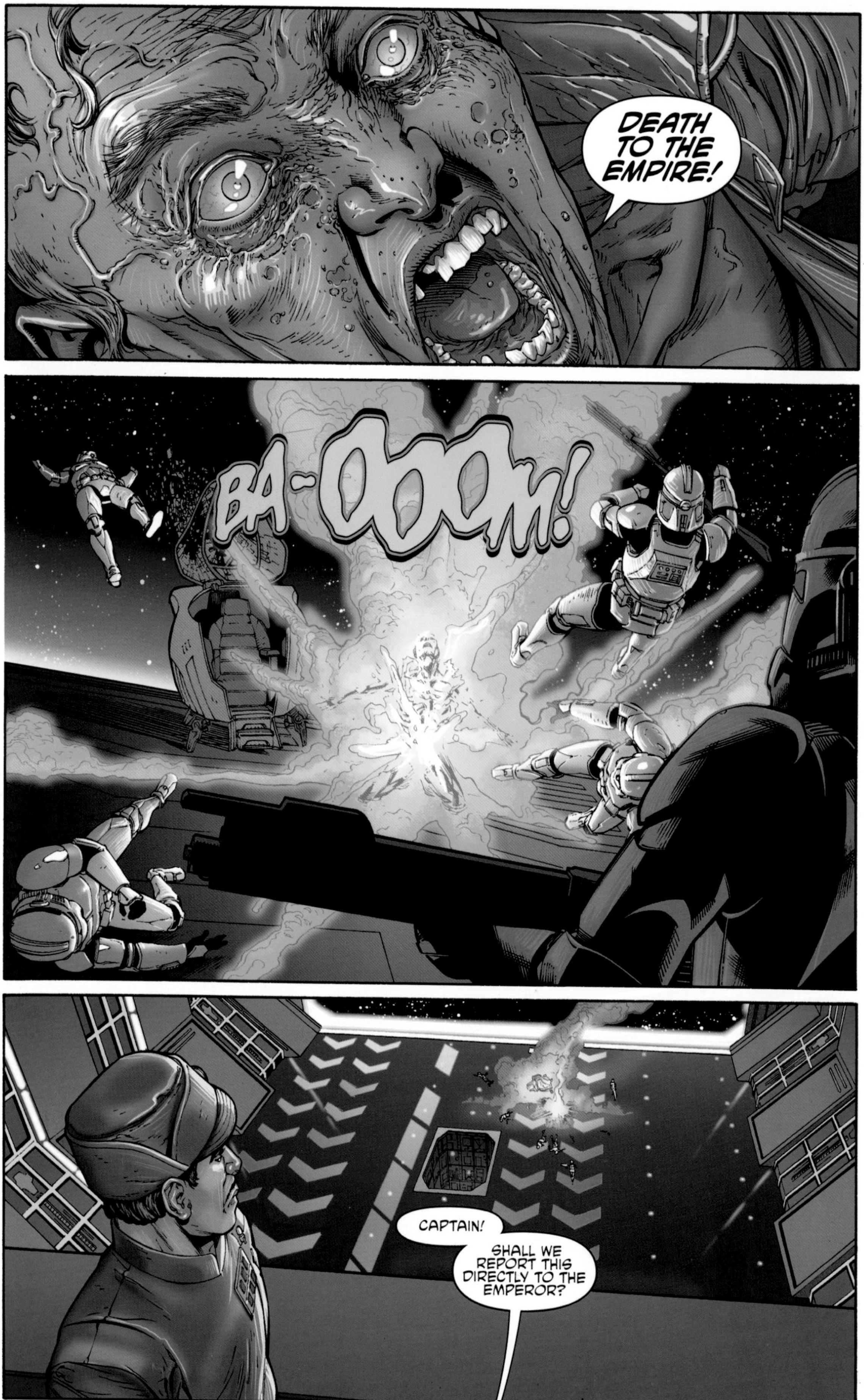
DEATH TO THE EMPIRE!
BA-OOOM!
CAPTAIN!
SHALL WE REPORT THIS DIRECTLY TO THE EMPEROR?

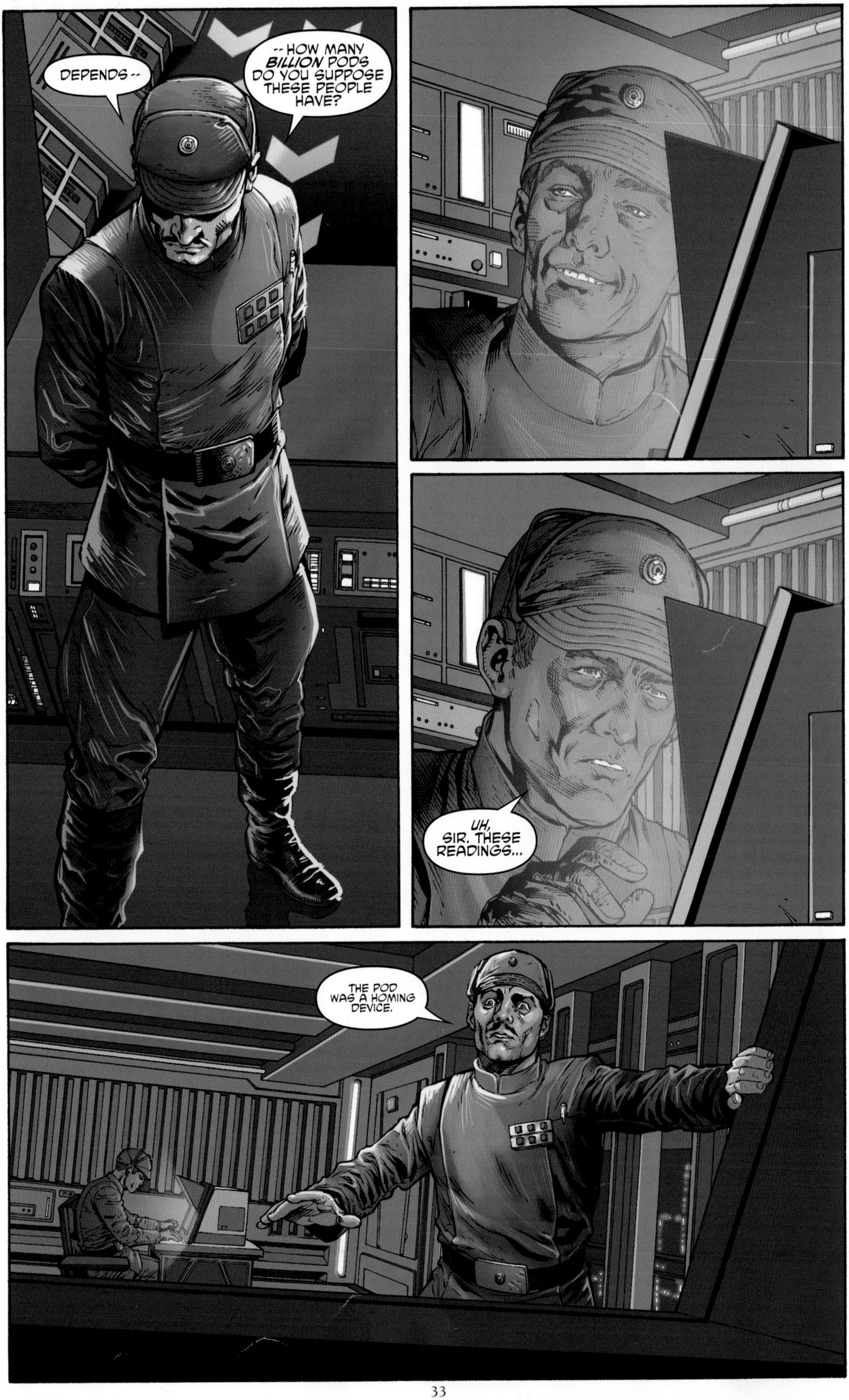
DEPENDS--
--HOW MANY BILLION PODS DO YOU SUPPOSE THESE PEOPLE HAVE?
UH, SIR. THESE READINGS...
THE POD WAS A HOMING DEVICE.

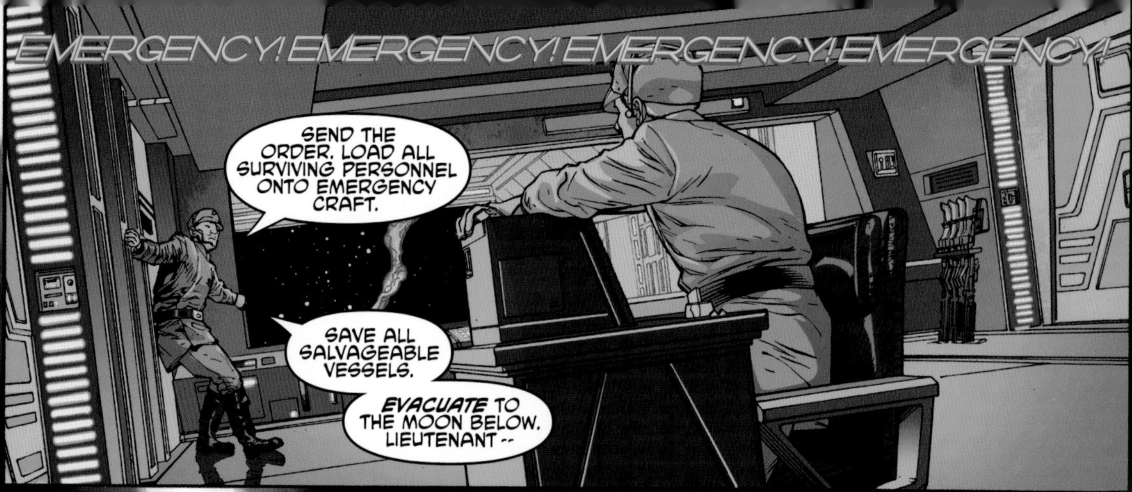
EMERGENCY! EMERGENCY! EMERGENCY! EMERGENCY!
SEND THE ORDER. LOAD ALL SURVIVING PERSONNEL ONTO EMERGENCY CRAFT.
SAVE ALL SALVAGEABLE VESSELS.
EVACUATE TO THE MOON BELOW. LIEUTENANT --

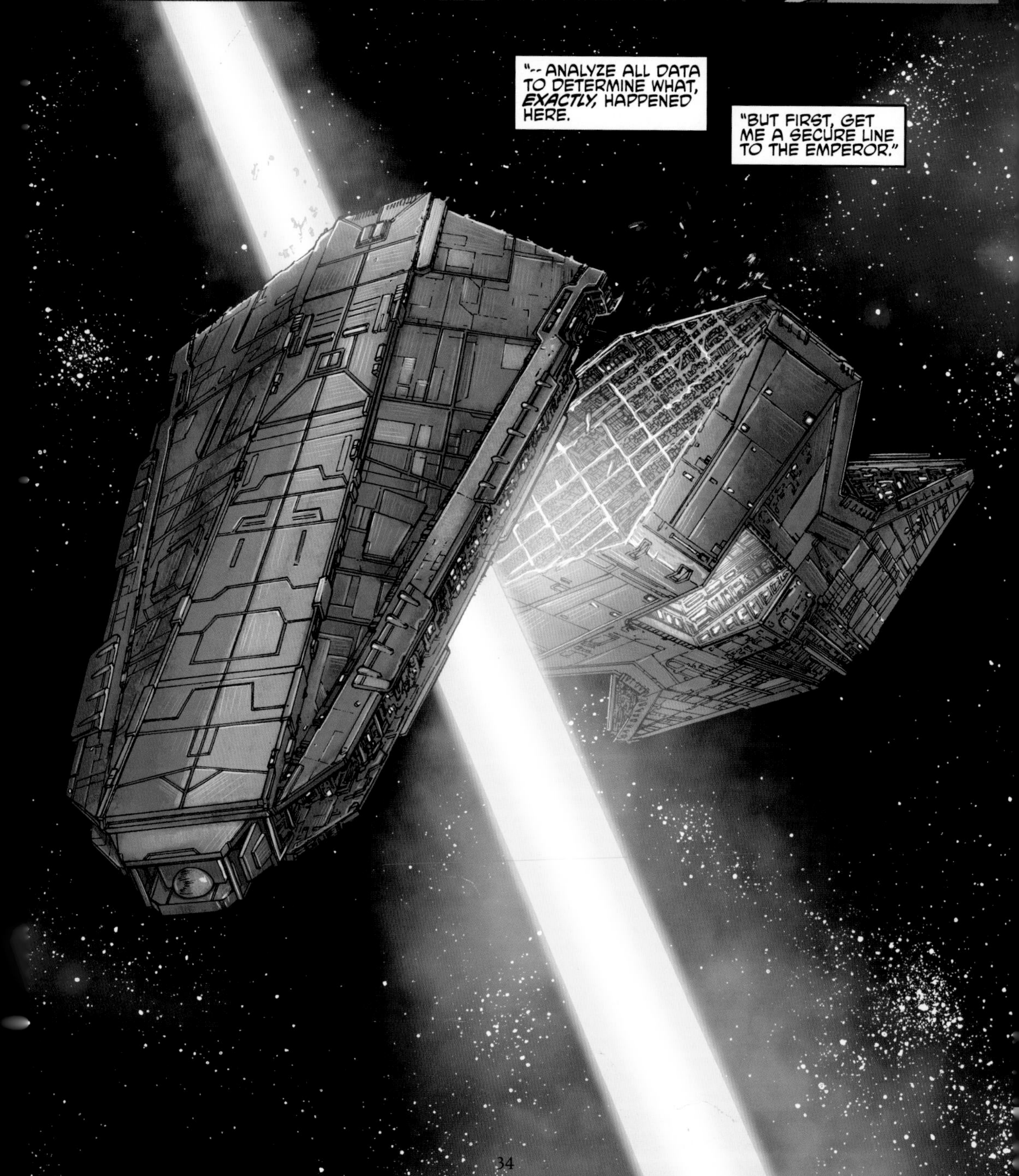
"-- ANALYZE ALL DATA TO DETERMINE WHAT, *EXACTLY,* HAPPENED HERE.
"BUT FIRST, GET ME A SECURE LINE TO THE EMPEROR."

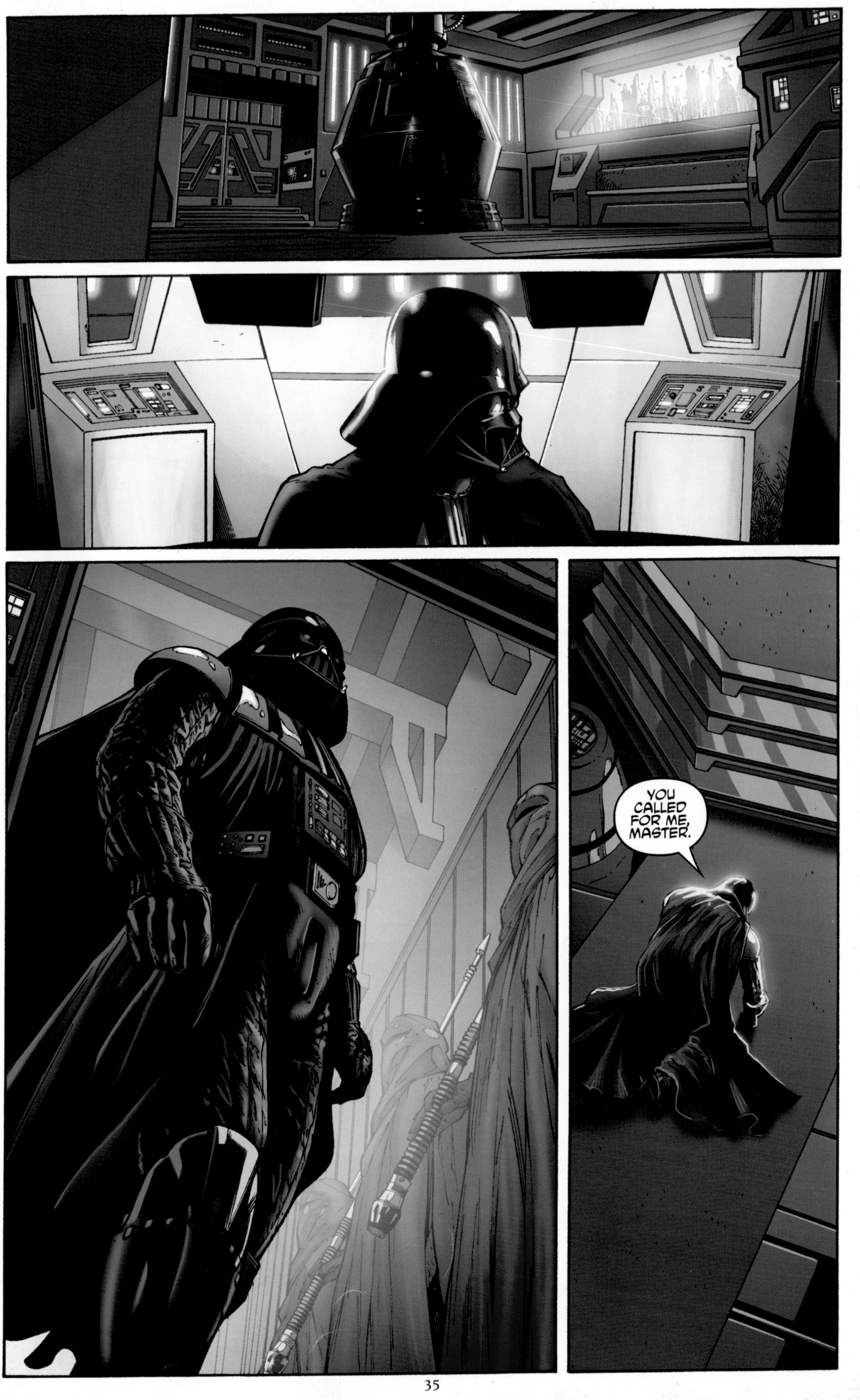
YOU CALLED FOR ME, MASTER.

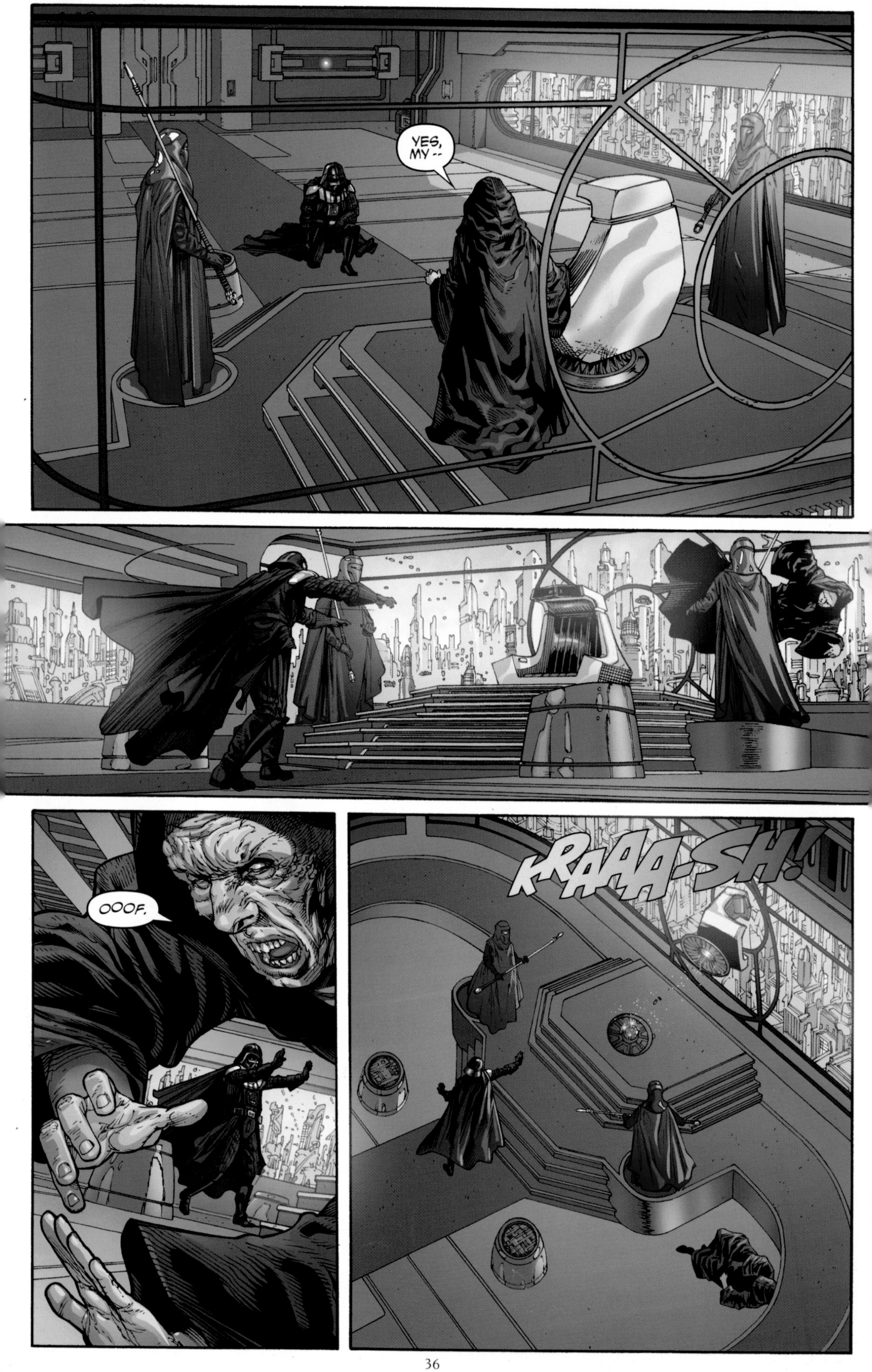
YES, MY --
OOOF.
KRAAA-SH!

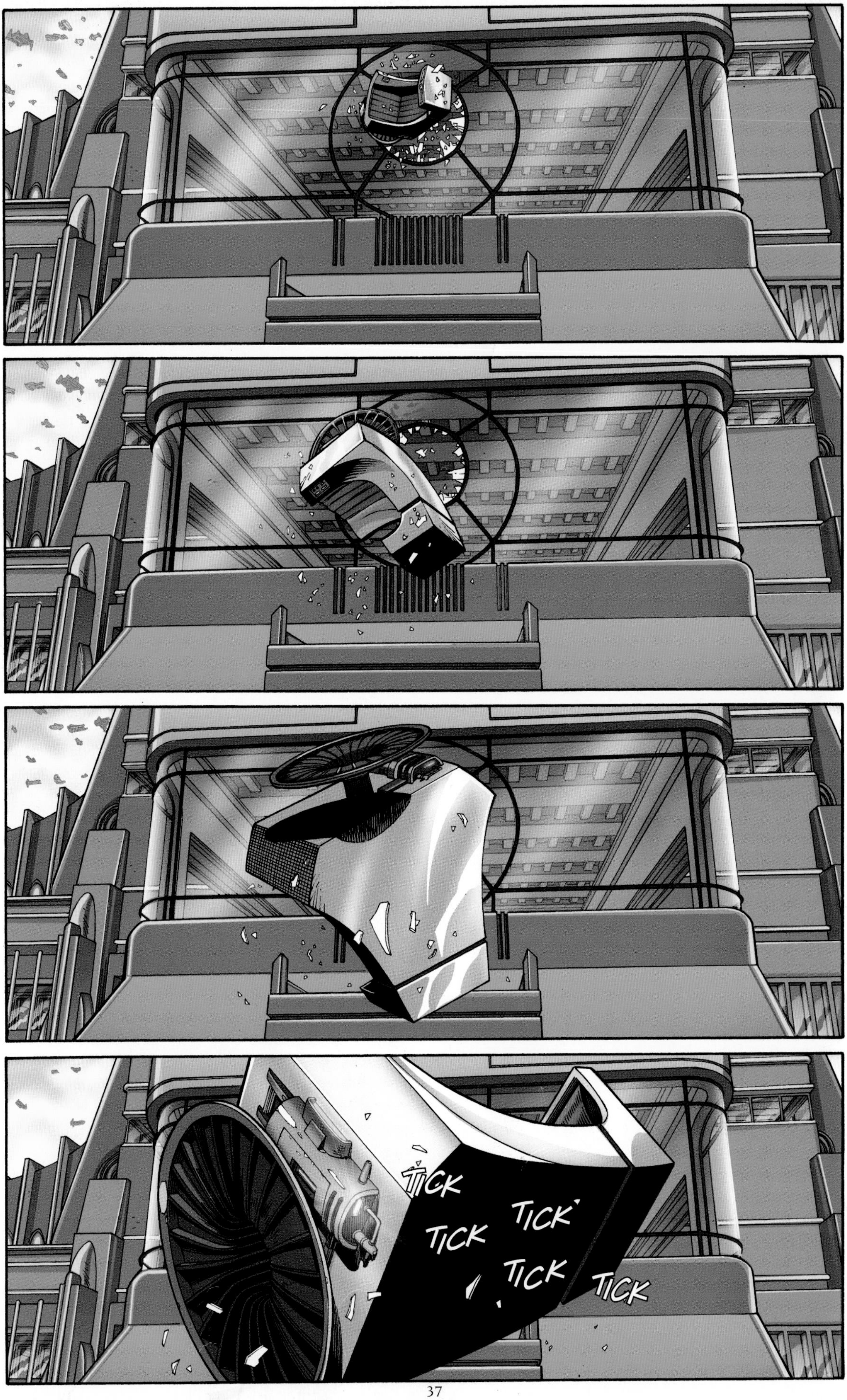
TICK
TICK
TICK
TICK
TICK

YOU HAVE *FAILED* THE EMPEROR --

-- AND DESERVE TO DIE. *SLOWLY.*

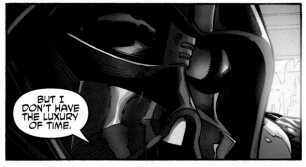

BUT I DON'T HAVE THE LUXURY OF TIME.

NO! NOOOOO...

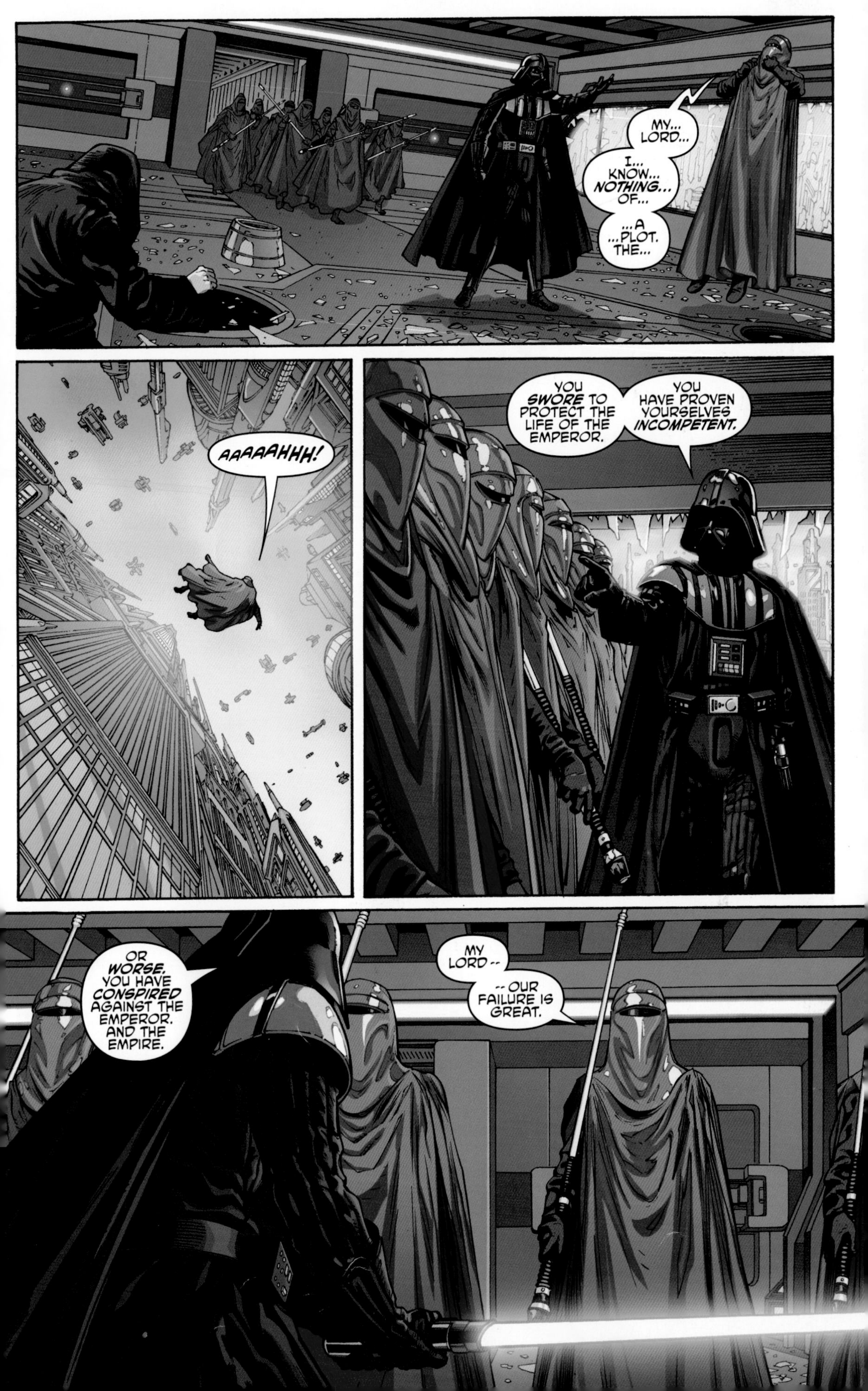
MY... LORD...
I... KNOW... NOTHING... OF...
...A ...PLOT. THE...
AAAAAHHH!
YOU SWORE TO PROTECT THE LIFE OF THE EMPEROR.
YOU HAVE PROVEN YOURSELVES INCOMPETENT.
OR WORSE. YOU HAVE CONSPIRED AGAINST THE EMPEROR. AND THE EMPIRE.
MY LORD --
-- OUR FAILURE IS GREAT.

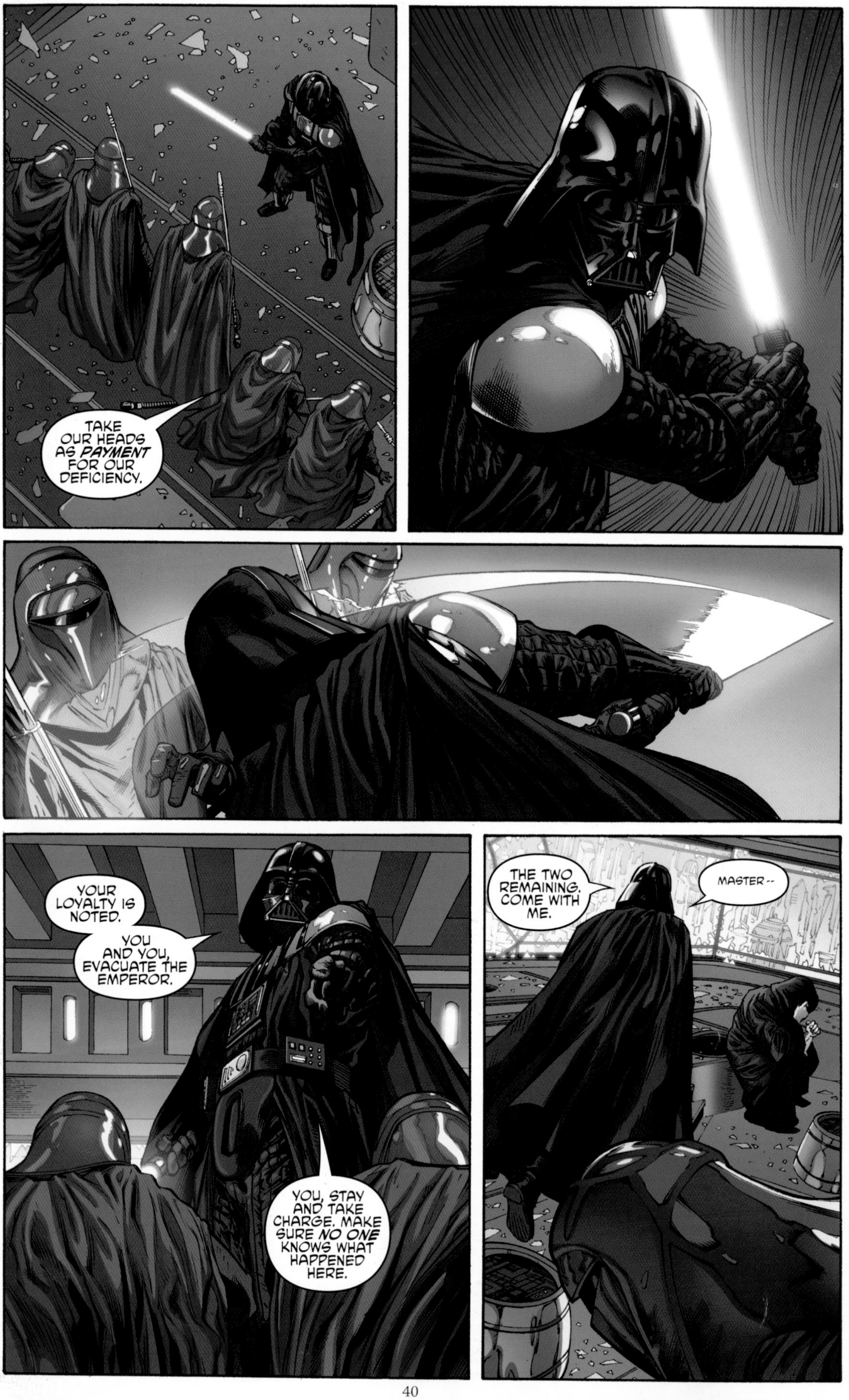
TAKE OUR HEADS AS PAYMENT FOR OUR DEFICIENCY.
YOUR LOYALTY IS NOTED.
YOU AND YOU, EVACUATE THE EMPEROR.
YOU, STAY AND TAKE CHARGE. MAKE SURE NO ONE KNOWS WHAT HAPPENED HERE.
THE TWO REMAINING, COME WITH ME.
MASTER--

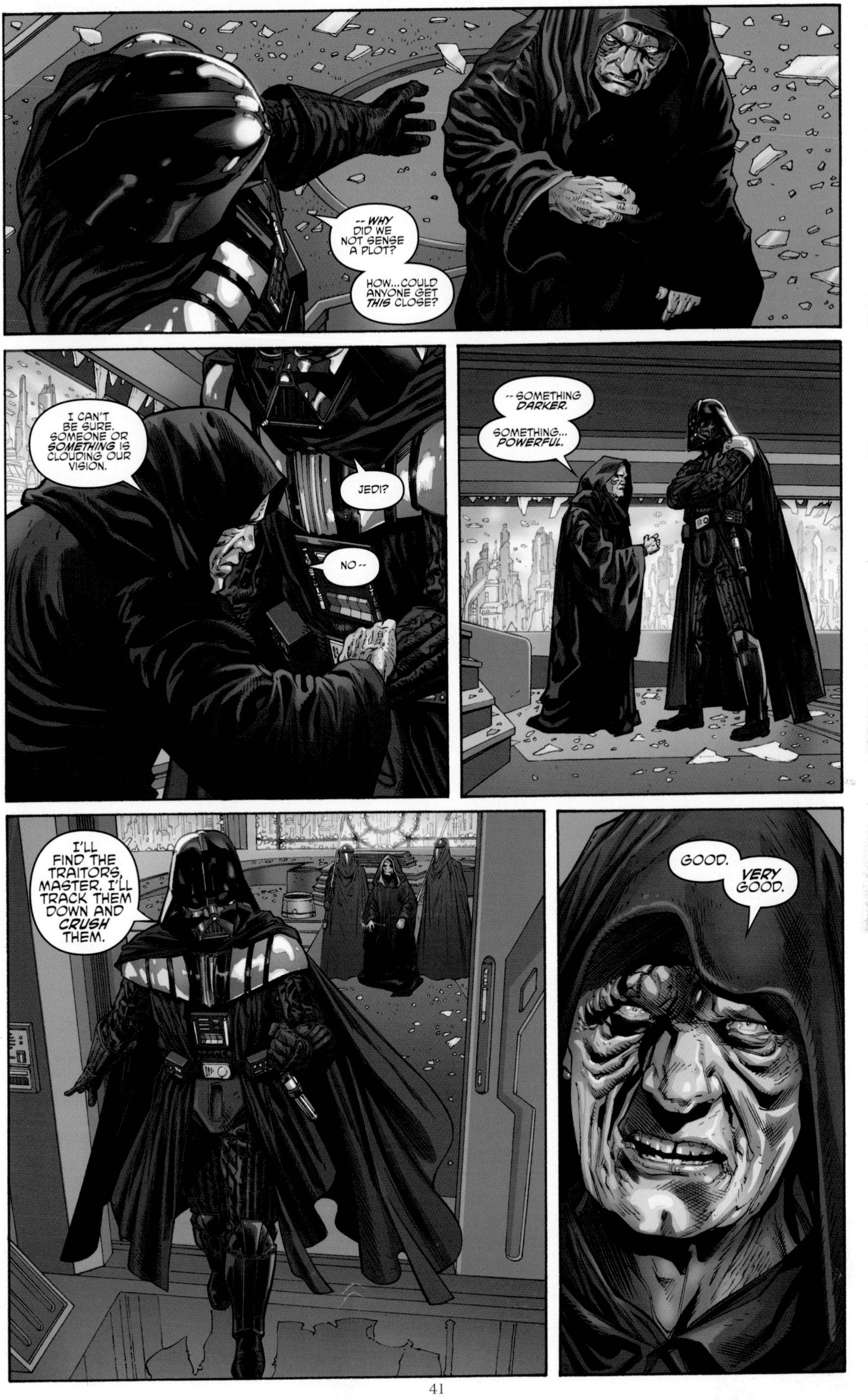
-- WHY DID WE NOT SENSE A PLOT?
HOW...COULD ANYONE GET THIS CLOSE?
I CAN'T BE SURE. SOMEONE OR SOMETHING IS CLOUDING OUR VISION.
JEDI?
NO --
-- SOMETHING DARKER.
SOMETHING... POWERFUL.
I'LL FIND THE TRAITORS, MASTER. I'LL TRACK THEM DOWN AND CRUSH THEM.
GOOD. VERY GOOD.

"BUT BE CAREFUL, LORD VADER.

"YOU ARE DEALING WITH POWERS YOU *DON'T* UNDERSTAND.

"I AWAIT YOUR RETURN --

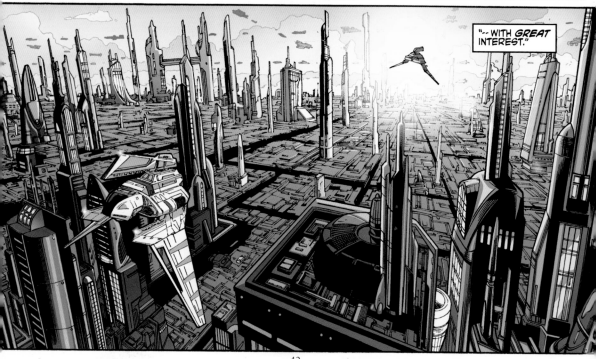

"-- WITH *GREAT* INTEREST."

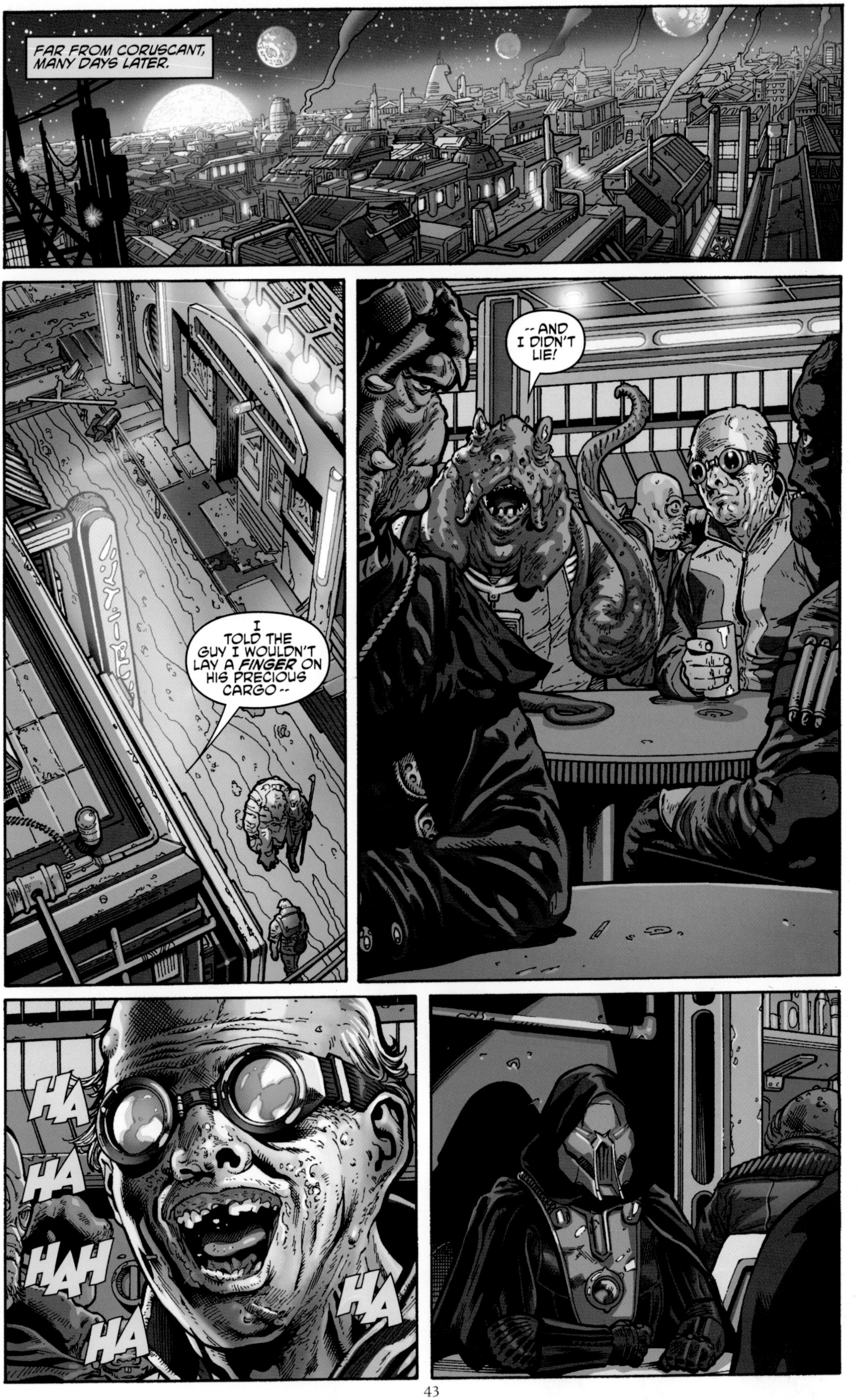
FAR FROM CORUSCANT, MANY DAYS LATER.
I TOLD THE GUY I WOULDN'T LAY A FINGER ON HIS PRECIOUS CARGO --
-- AND I DIDN'T LIE!
HA
HA
HAH
HA
HA

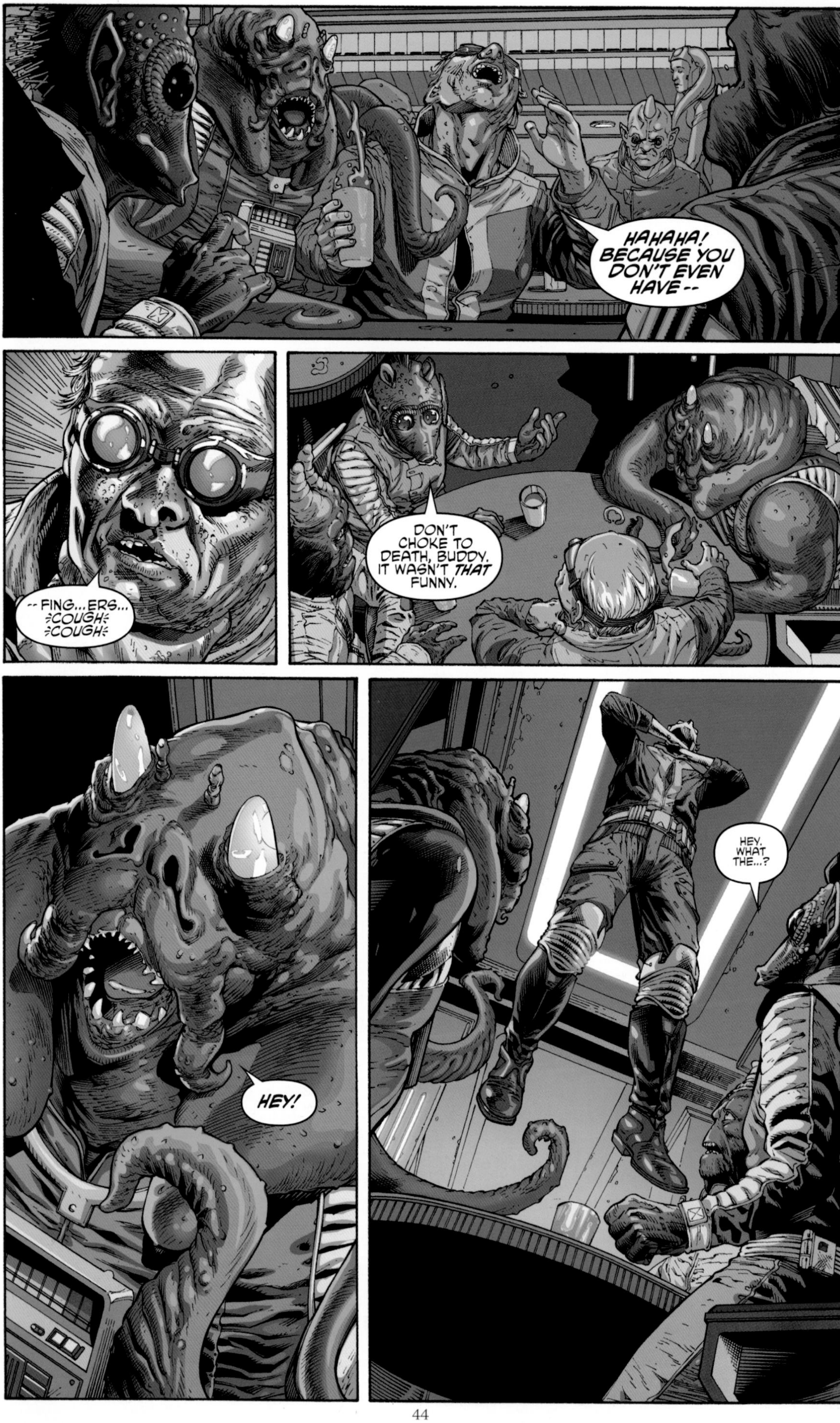
HAHAHA! BECAUSE YOU DON'T EVEN HAVE --
-- FING... ERS... ≷COUGH≷ ≷COUGH≷
DON'T CHOKE TO DEATH, BUDDY. IT WASN'T *THAT* FUNNY.
HEY!
HEY. WHAT THE...?

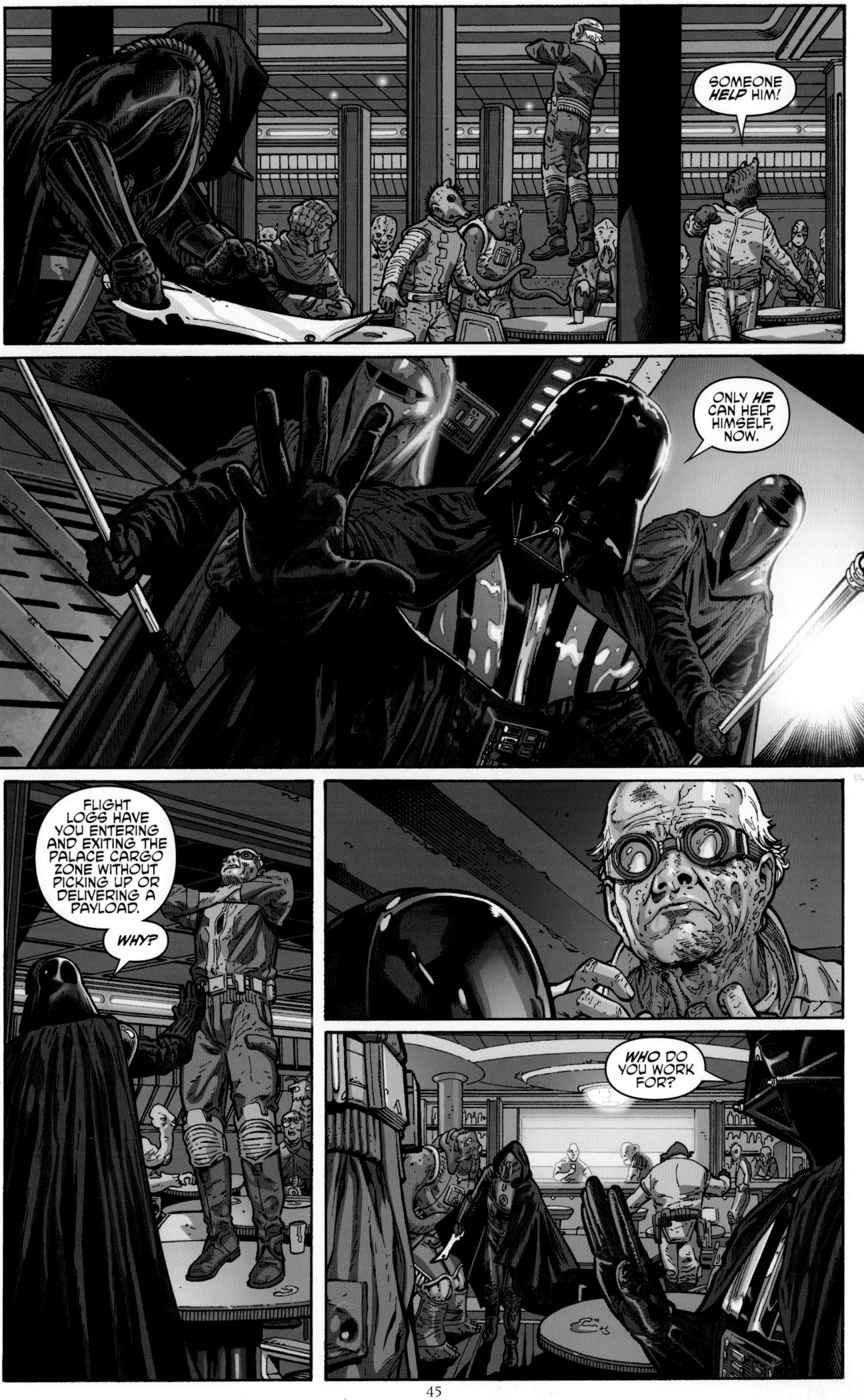
SOMEONE HELP HIM!
ONLY HE CAN HELP HIMSELF, NOW.
FLIGHT LOGS HAVE YOU ENTERING AND EXITING THE PALACE CARGO ZONE WITHOUT PICKING UP OR DELIVERING A PAYLOAD.
WHY?
WHO DO YOU WORK FOR?

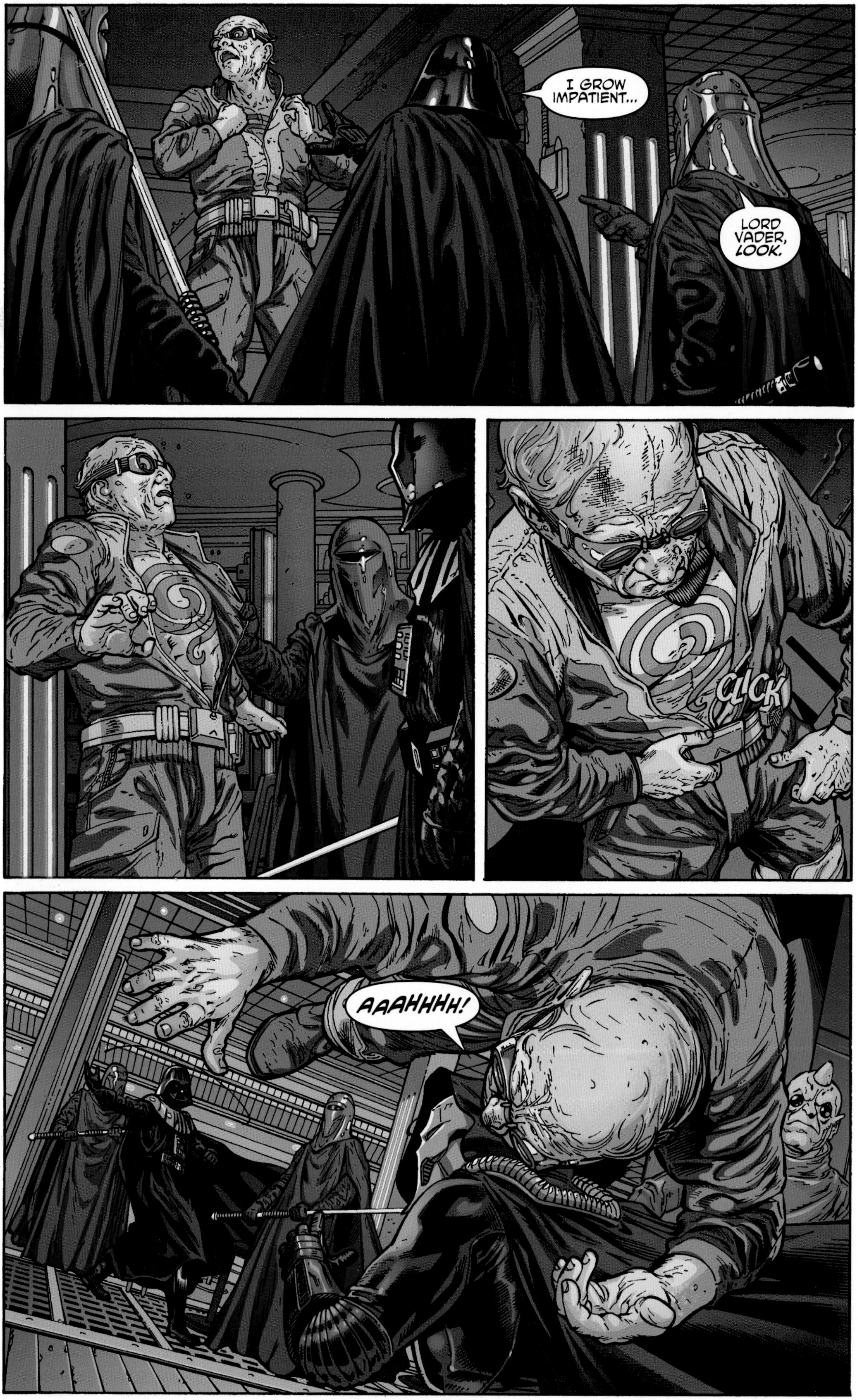
I GROW IMPATIENT...
LORD VADER, LOOK.
CLICK
AAAHHHH!

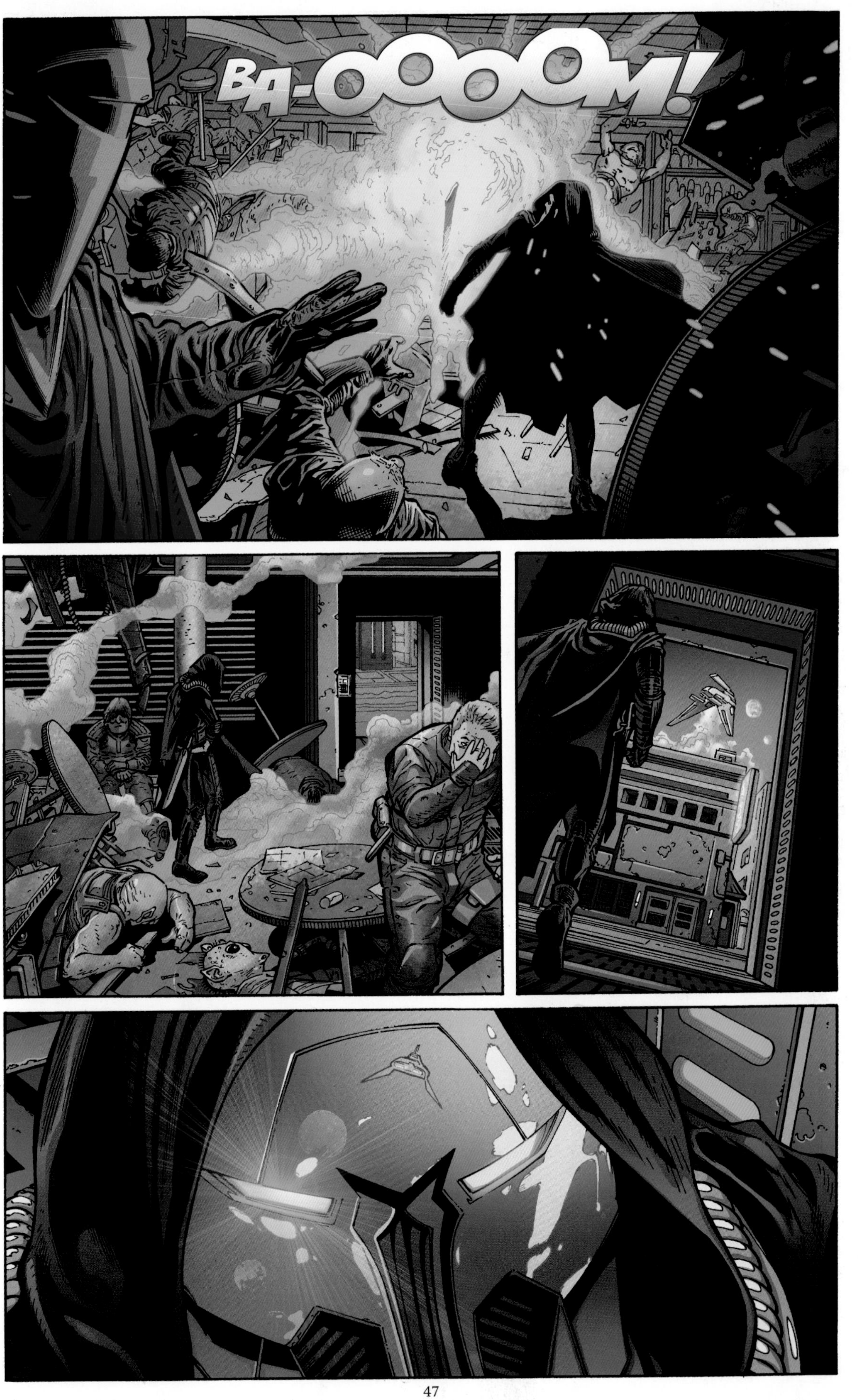
BA-OOOOM!

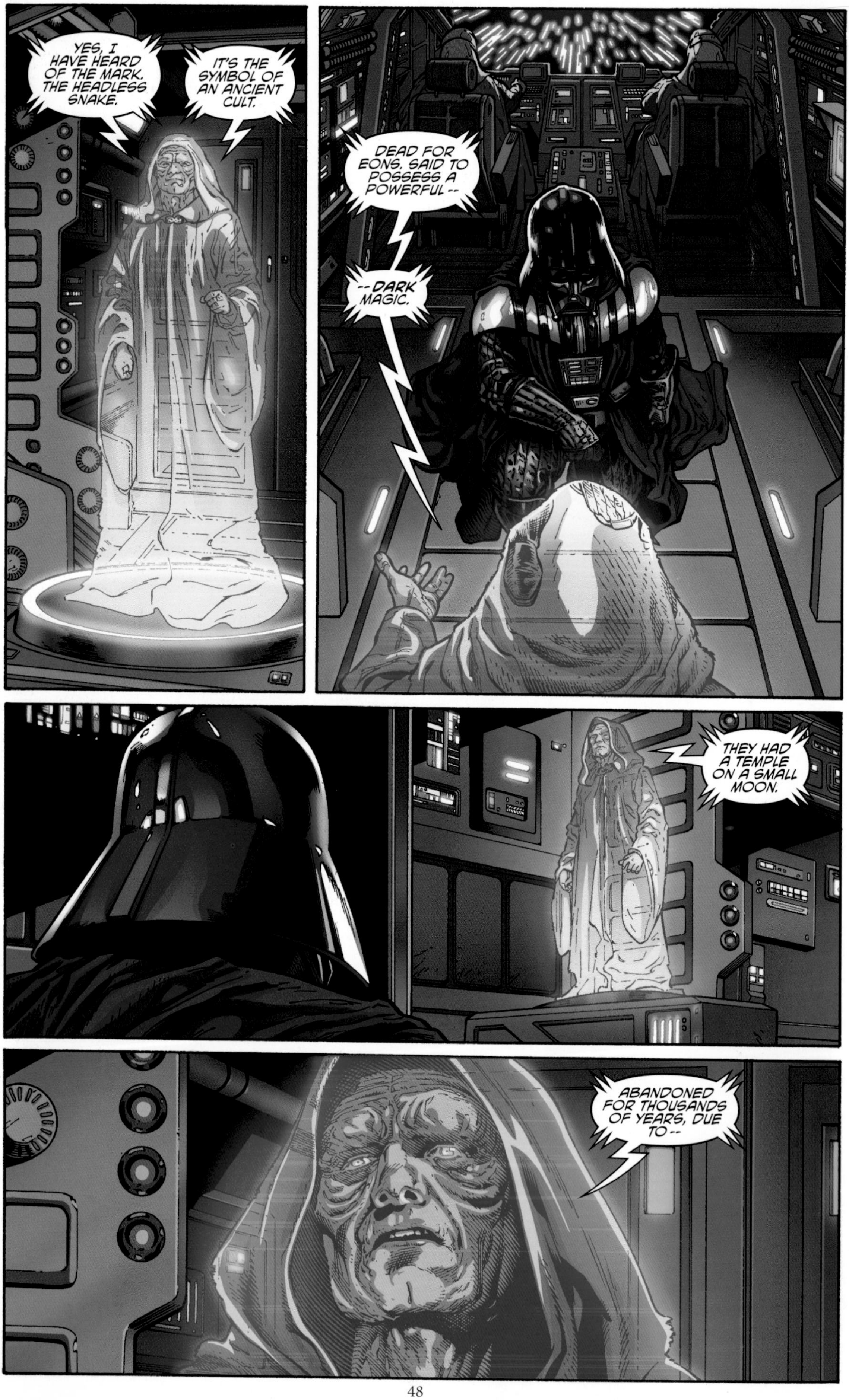
YES, I HAVE HEARD OF THE MARK. THE HEADLESS SNAKE.
IT'S THE SYMBOL OF AN ANCIENT CULT.
DEAD FOR EONS. SAID TO POSSESS A POWERFUL --
--DARK MAGIC.
THEY HAD A TEMPLE ON A SMALL MOON.
ABANDONED FOR THOUSANDS OF YEARS, DUE TO --

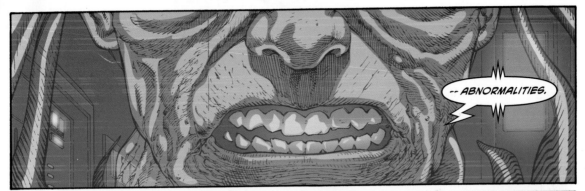

-- ABNORMALITIES.

MASTER, MY SENSES -- -- THEY REMAIN CLOUDED.

AS DO MINE.

I URGE CAUTION, MY APPRENTICE.

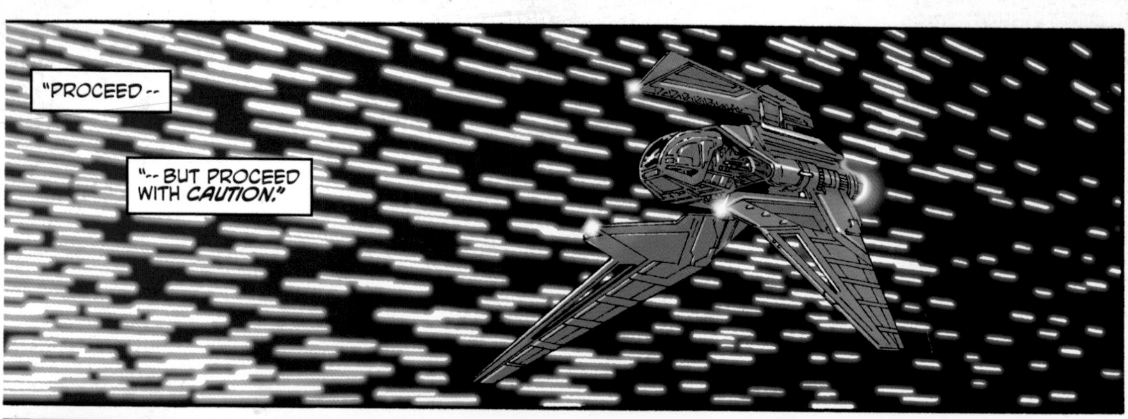
"PROCEED --
"-- BUT PROCEED WITH CAUTION."

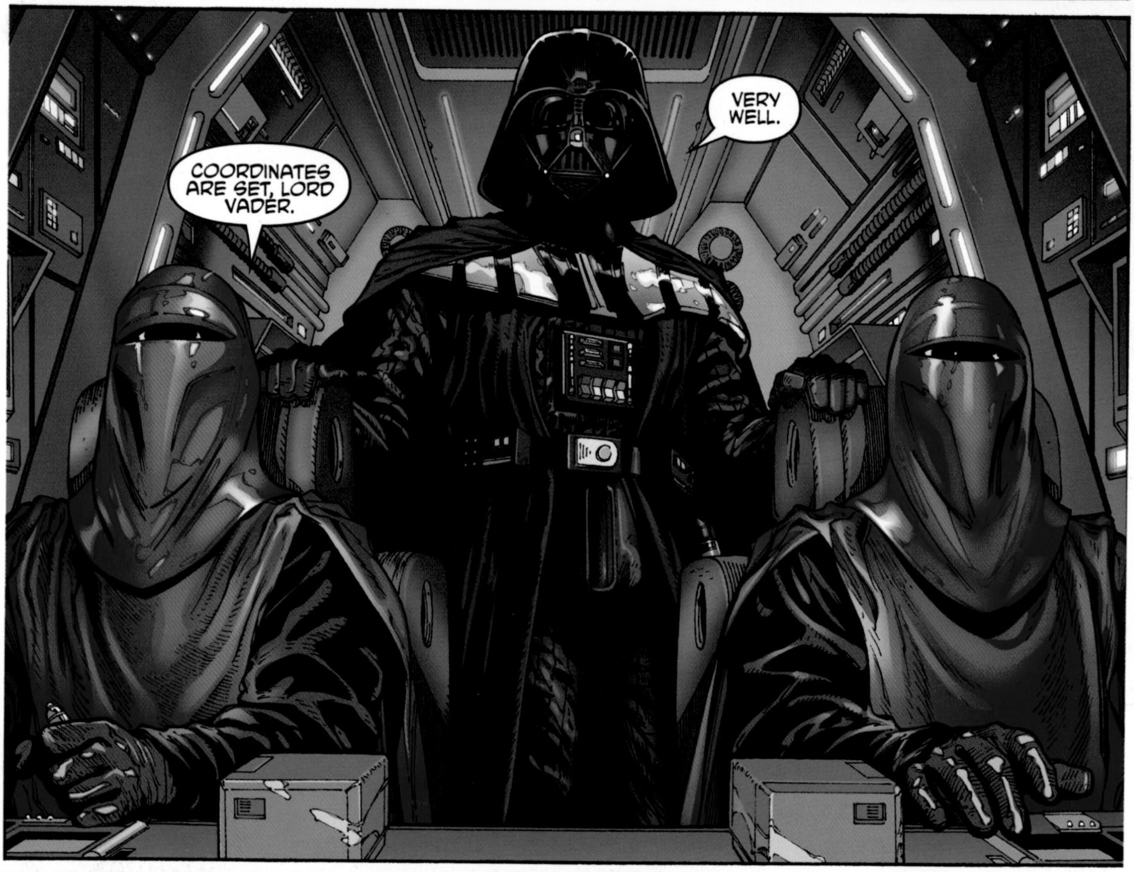
COORDINATES ARE SET, LORD VADER.
VERY WELL.

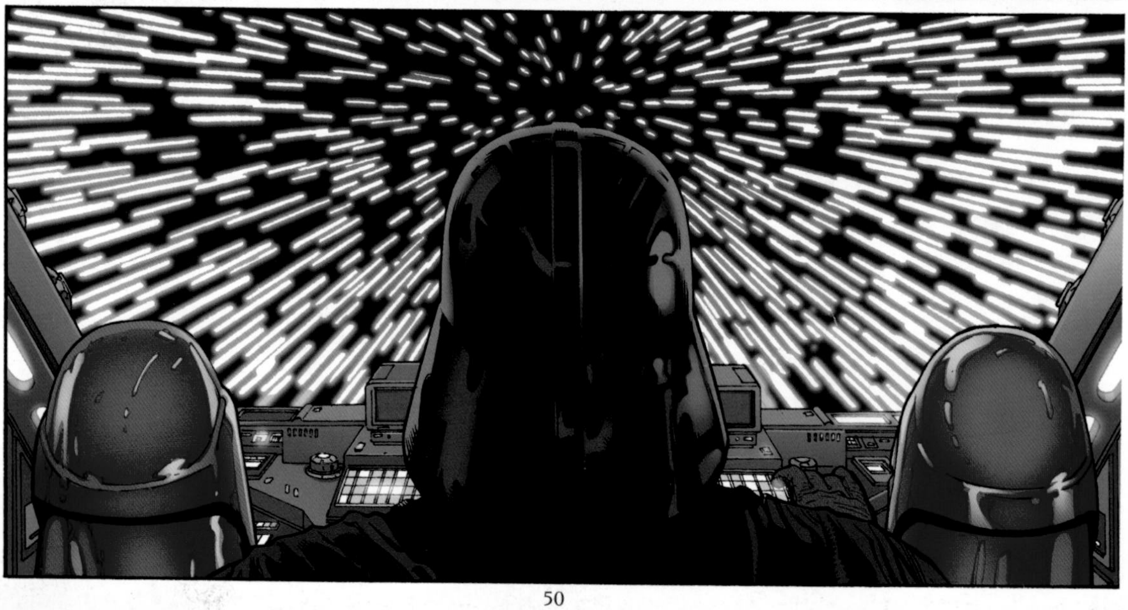

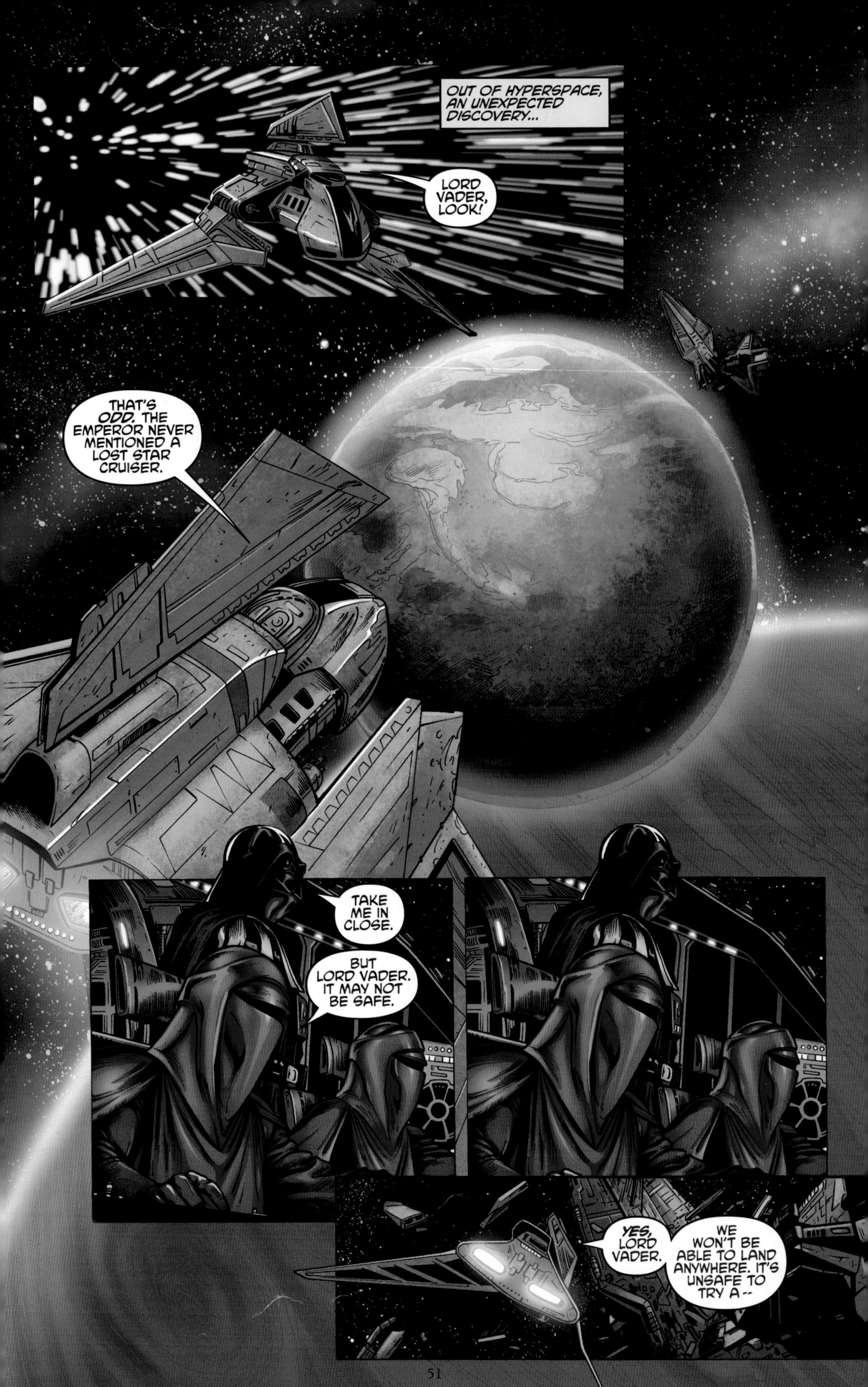
OUT OF HYPERSPACE, AN UNEXPECTED DISCOVERY...
LORD VADER, LOOK!
THAT'S ODD. THE EMPEROR NEVER MENTIONED A LOST STAR CRUISER.
TAKE ME IN CLOSE.
BUT LORD VADER. IT MAY NOT BE SAFE.
YES, LORD VADER.
WE WON'T BE ABLE TO LAND ANYWHERE. IT'S UNSAFE TO TRY A--

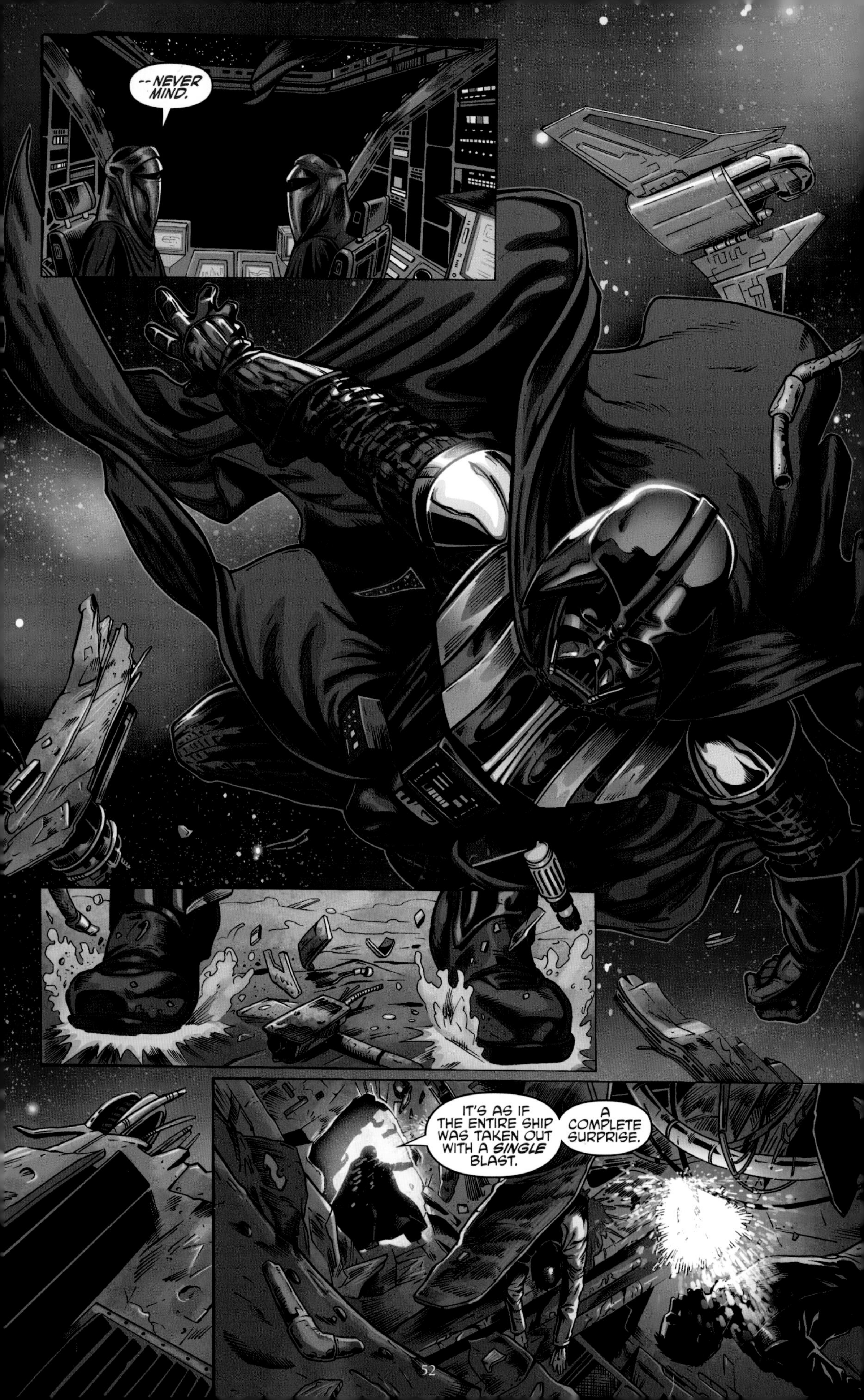
--NEVER MIND.
IT'S AS IF THE ENTIRE SHIP WAS TAKEN OUT WITH A *SINGLE* BLAST.
A COMPLETE SURPRISE.

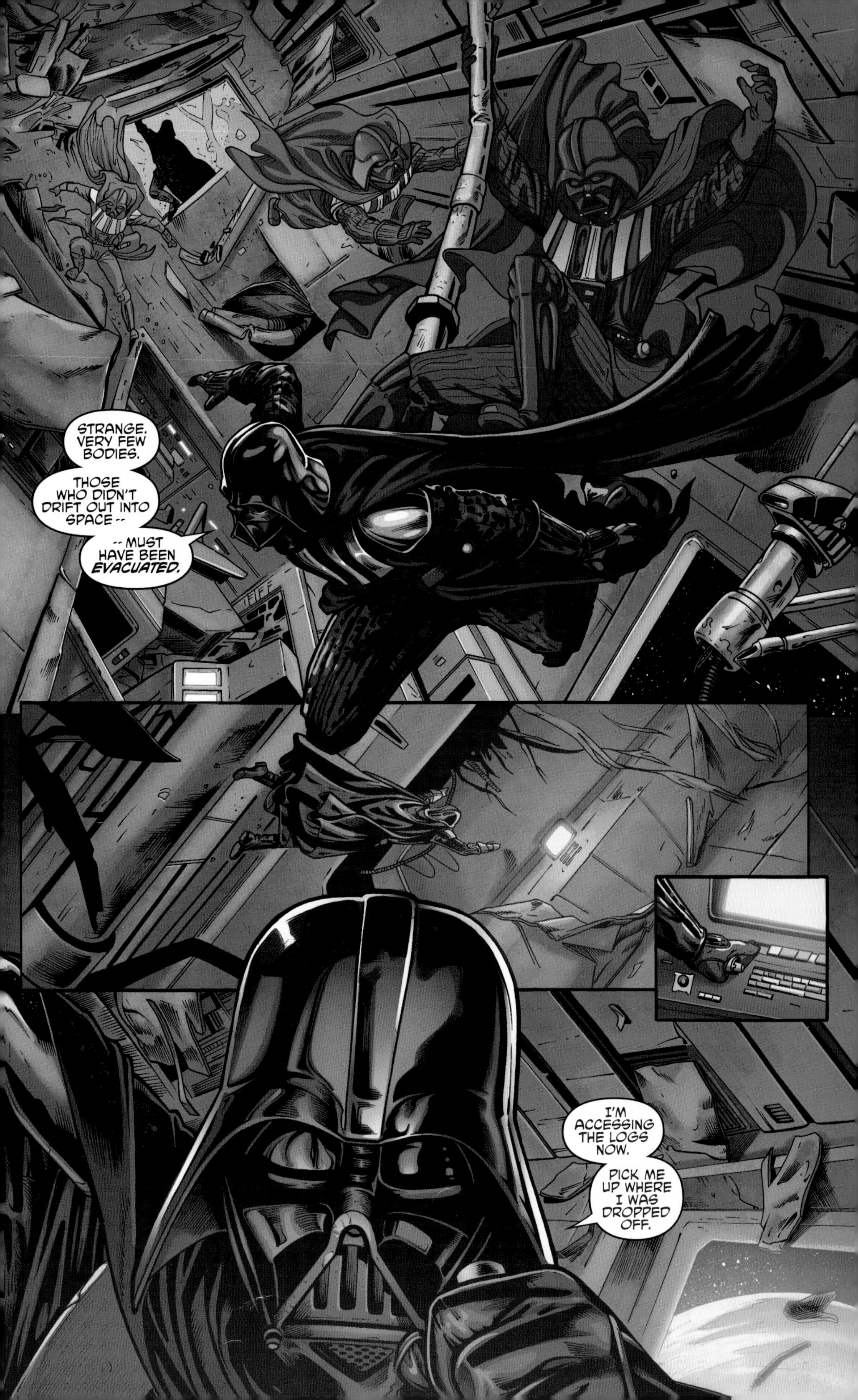
STRANGE. VERY FEW BODIES.
THOSE WHO DIDN'T DRIFT OUT INTO SPACE --
-- MUST HAVE BEEN *EVACUATED.*
I'M ACCESSING THE LOGS NOW.
PICK ME UP WHERE I WAS DROPPED OFF.

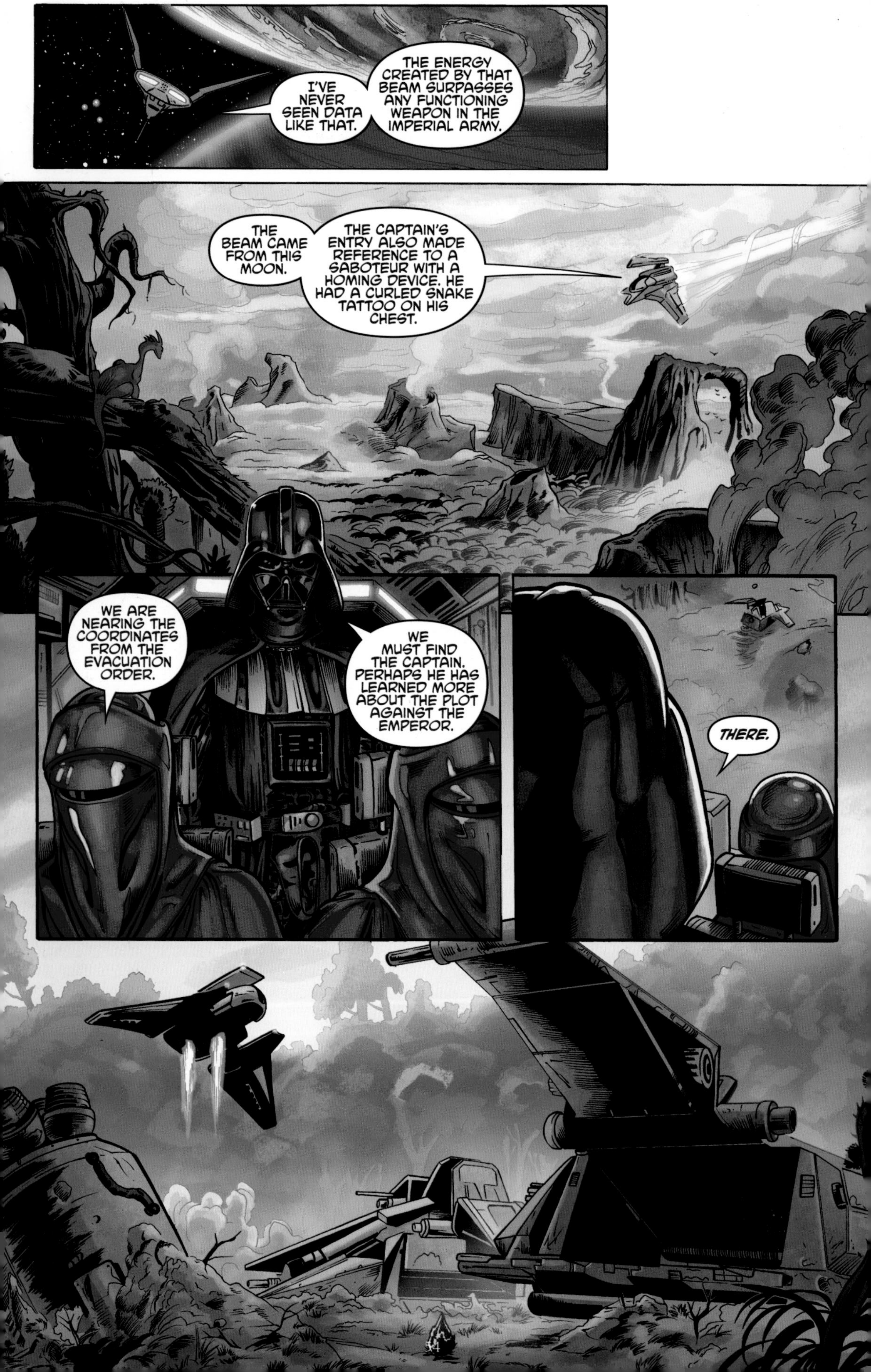
I'VE NEVER SEEN DATA LIKE THAT.
THE ENERGY CREATED BY THAT BEAM SURPASSES ANY FUNCTIONING WEAPON IN THE IMPERIAL ARMY.
THE BEAM CAME FROM THIS MOON.
THE CAPTAIN'S ENTRY ALSO MADE REFERENCE TO A SABOTEUR WITH A HOMING DEVICE. HE HAD A CURLED SNAKE TATTOO ON HIS CHEST.
WE ARE NEARING THE COORDINATES FROM THE EVACUATION ORDER.
WE MUST FIND THE CAPTAIN. PERHAPS HE HAS LEARNED MORE ABOUT THE PLOT AGAINST THE EMPEROR.
THERE.

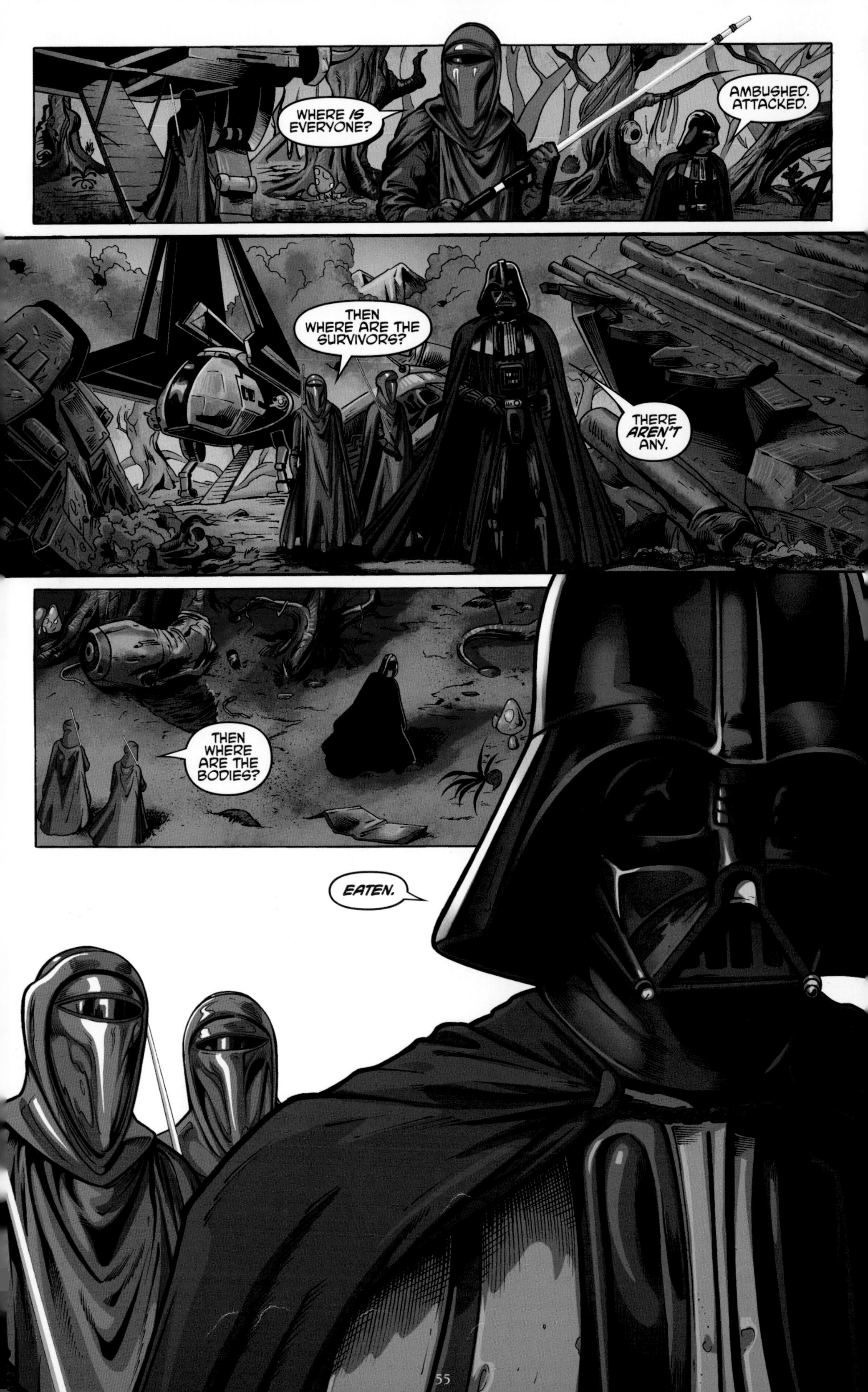
WHERE IS EVERYONE?
AMBUSHED. ATTACKED.
THEN WHERE ARE THE SURVIVORS?
THERE AREN'T ANY.
THEN WHERE ARE THE BODIES?
EATEN.

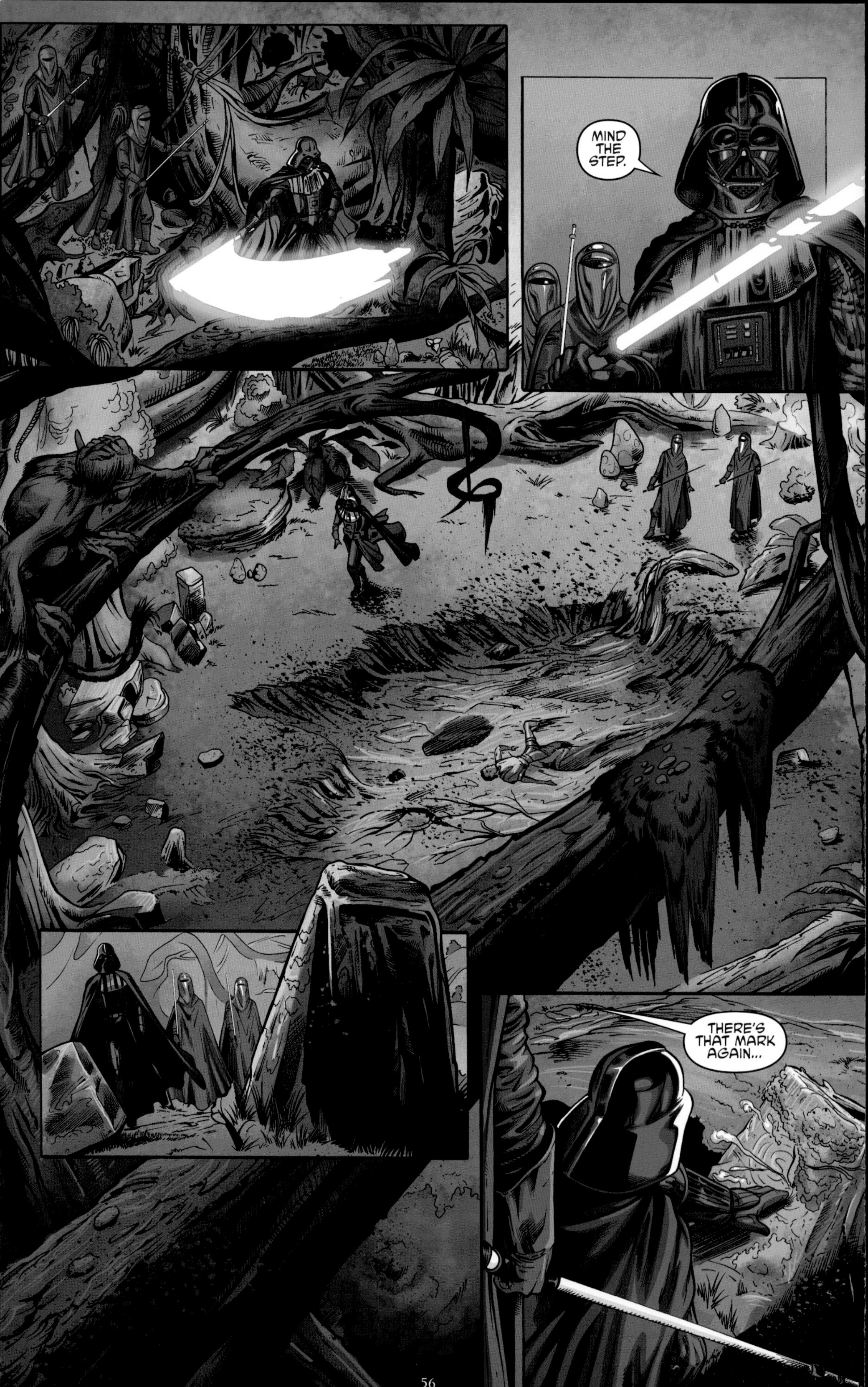

MIND THE STEP.
THERE'S THAT MARK AGAIN...

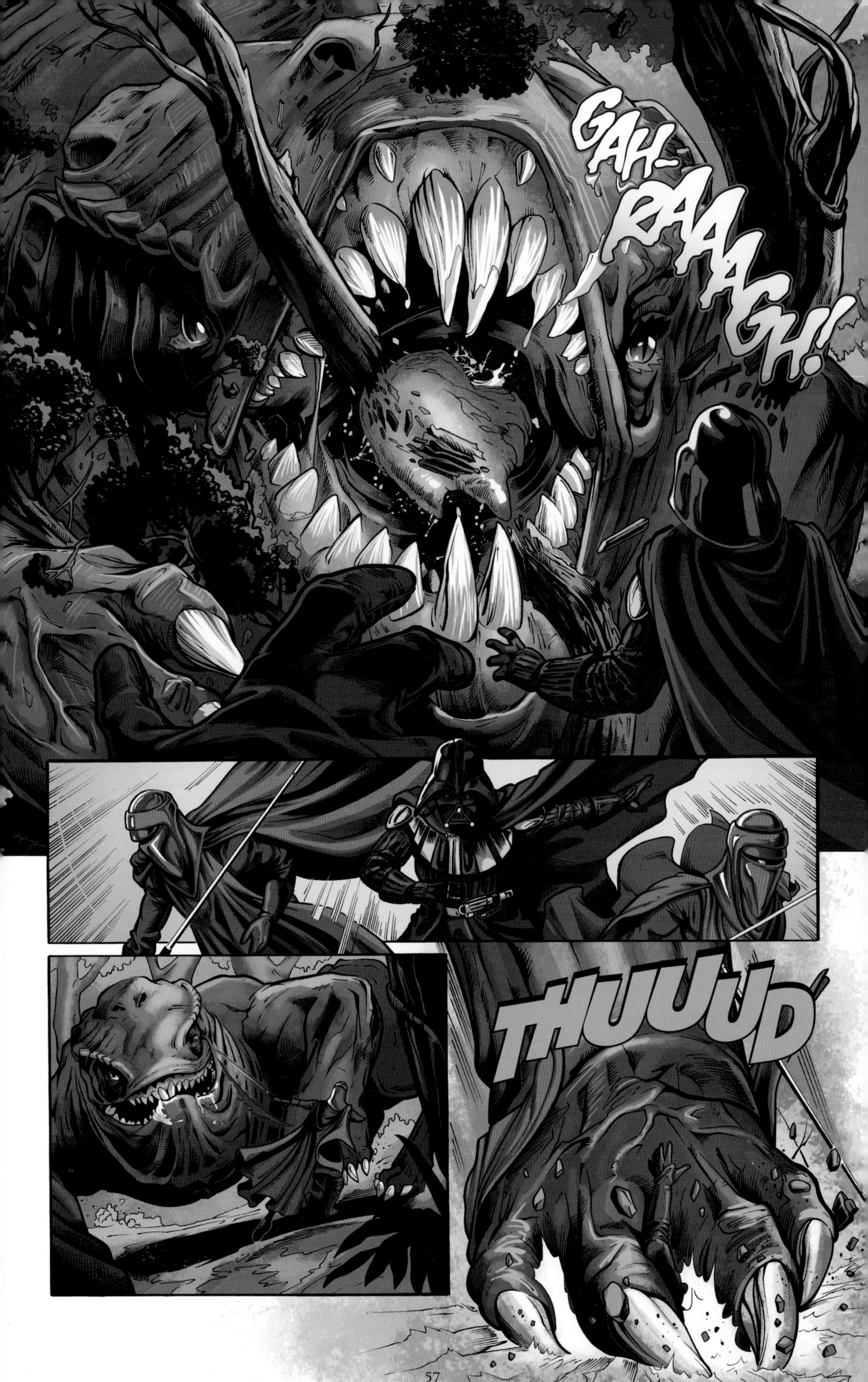
GAH-RAAAGH!!
THUUUD

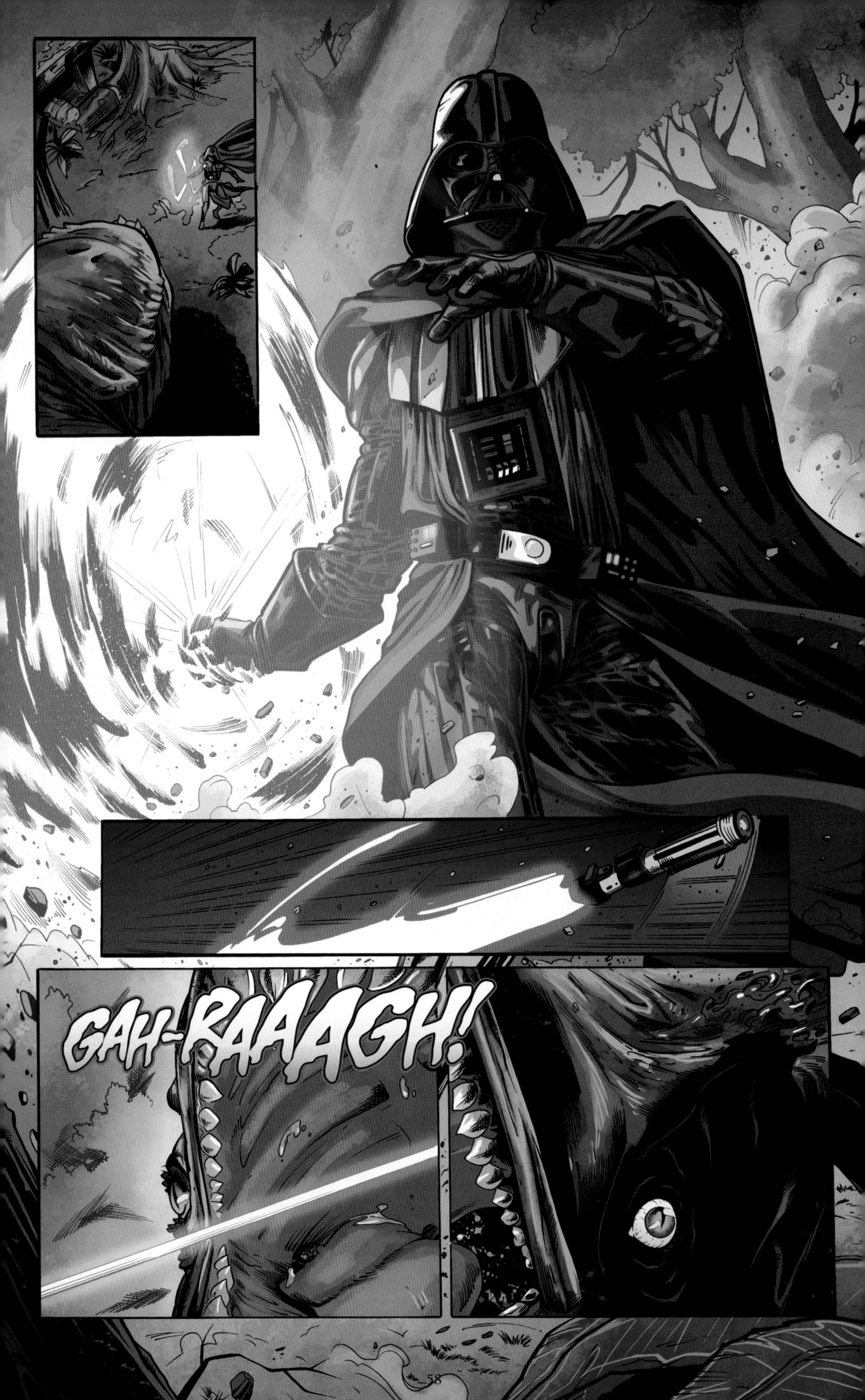
GAH-RAAAGH!

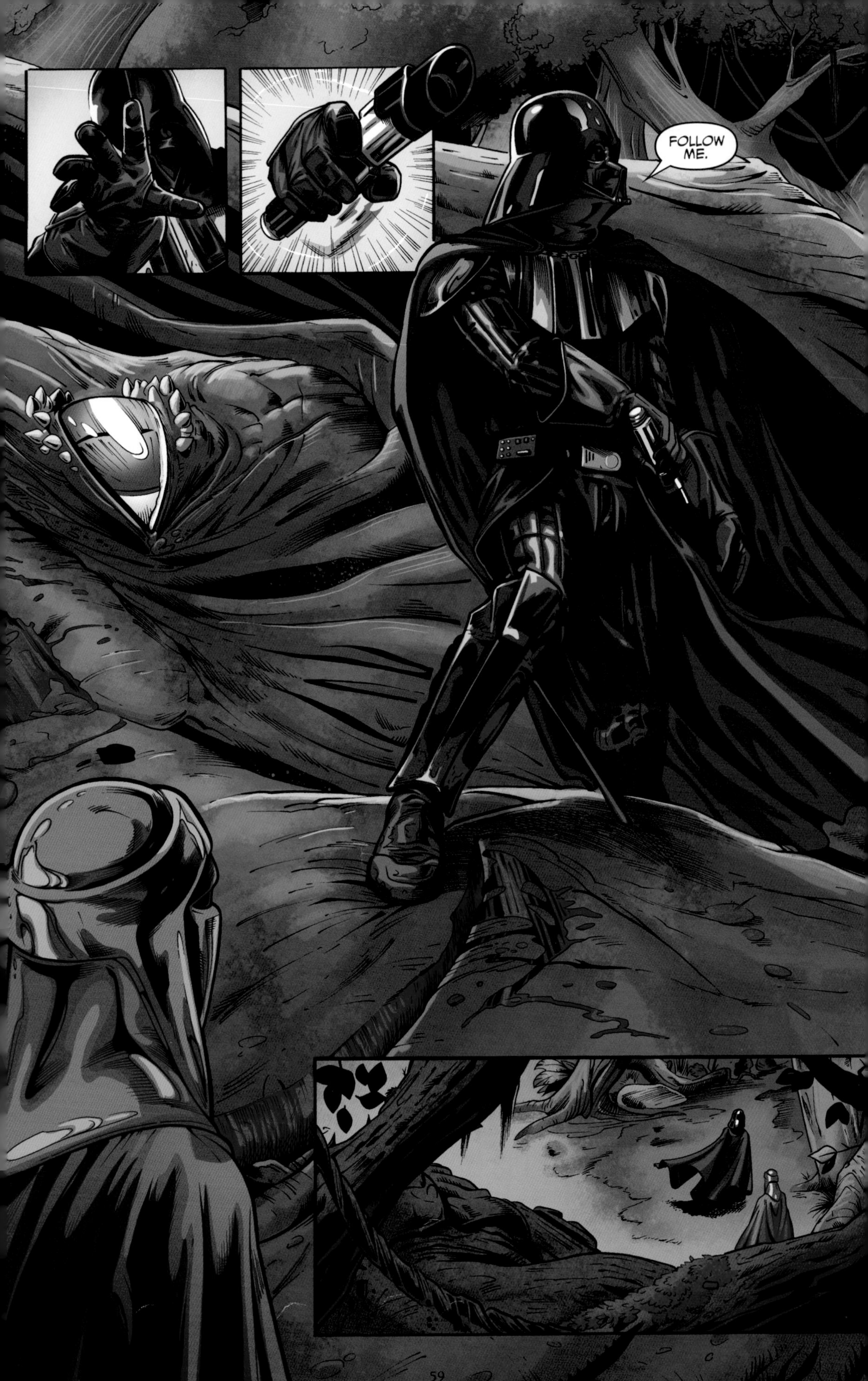
FOLLOW ME.

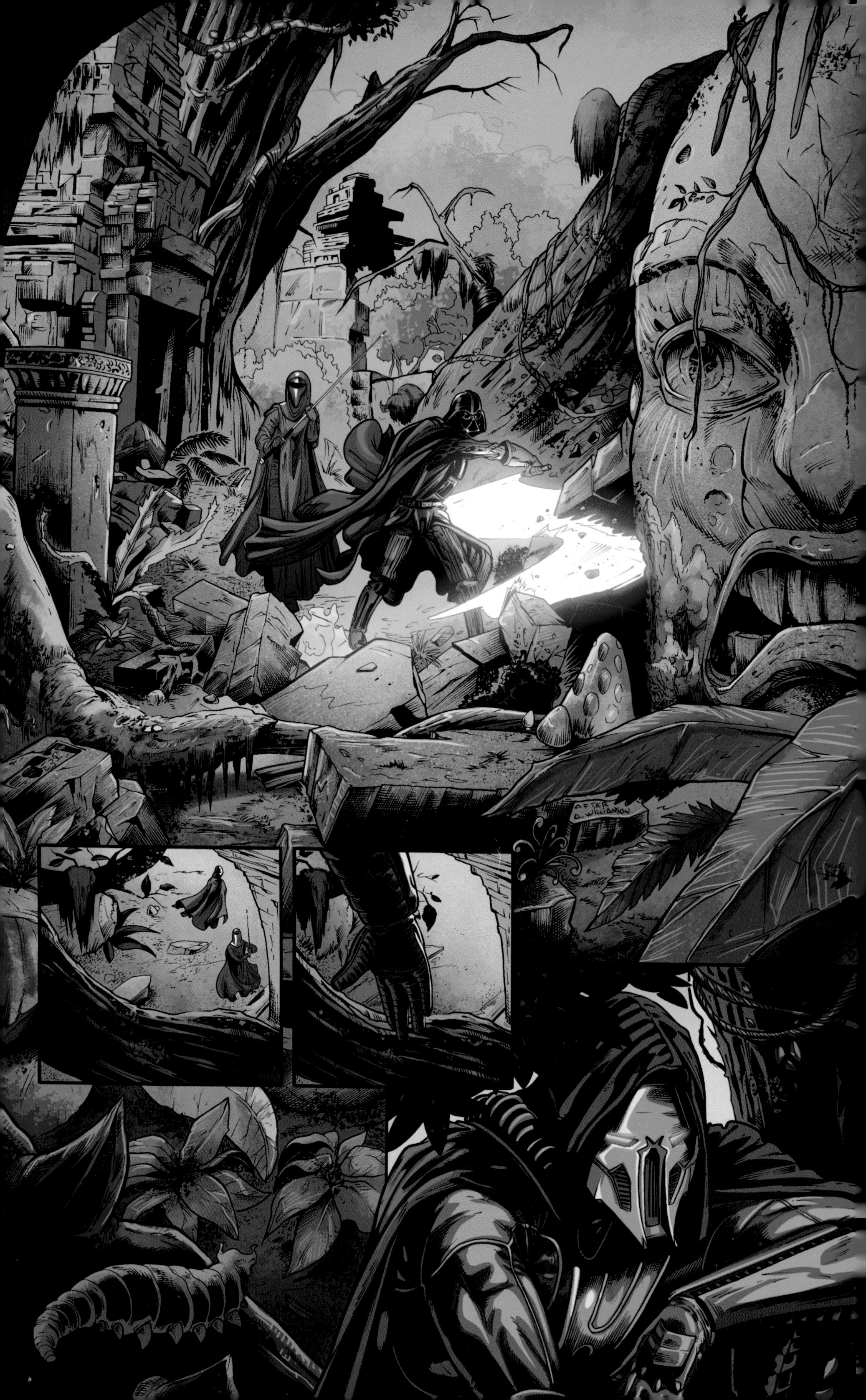
AFTER A. WILLIAMSON

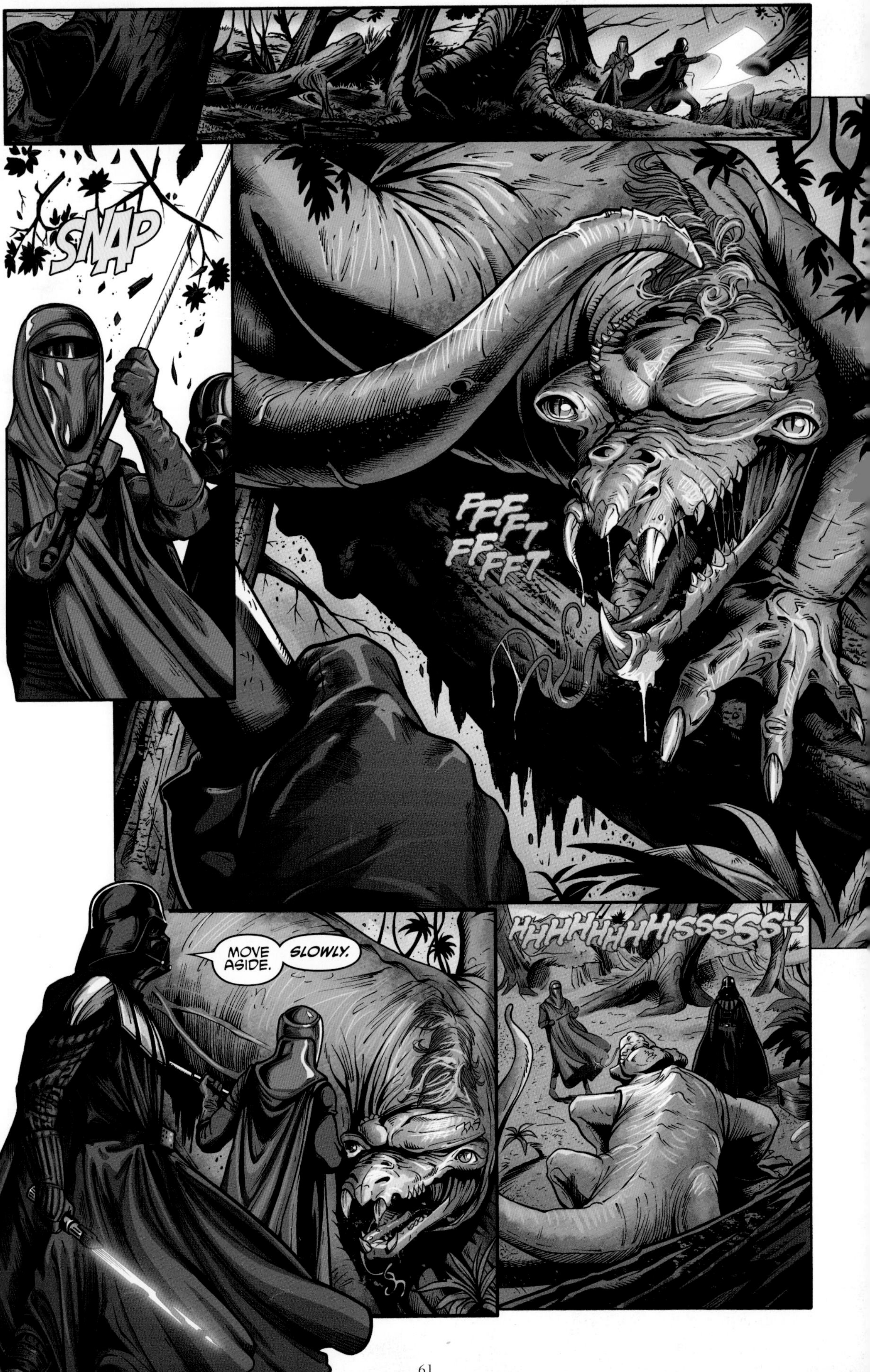
SNAP
FFFFT FFFFT
MOVE ASIDE.
SLOWLY.
HHHHHHHHISSSSS—

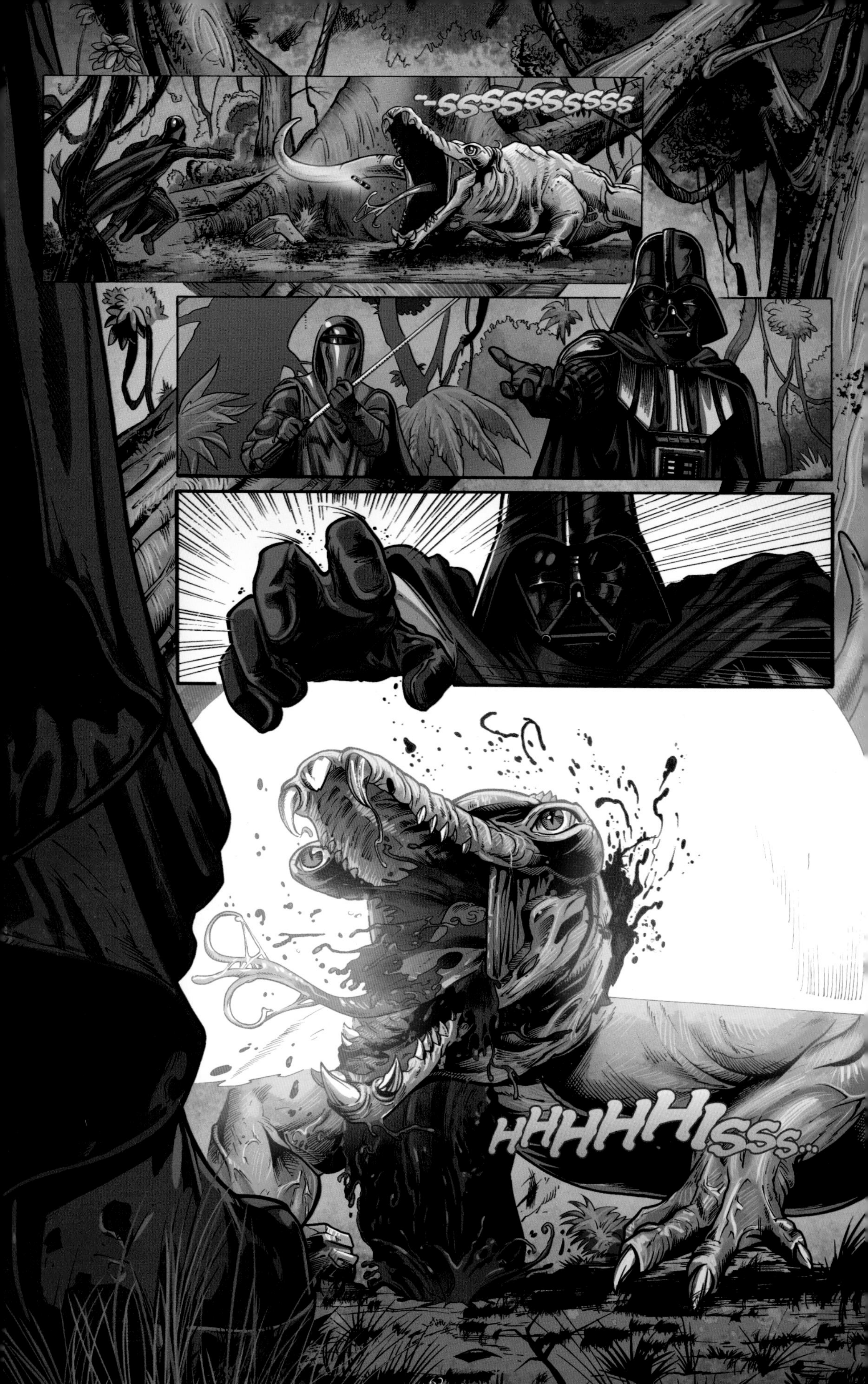

-SSSSSSSSSs
HHHHHISSS...

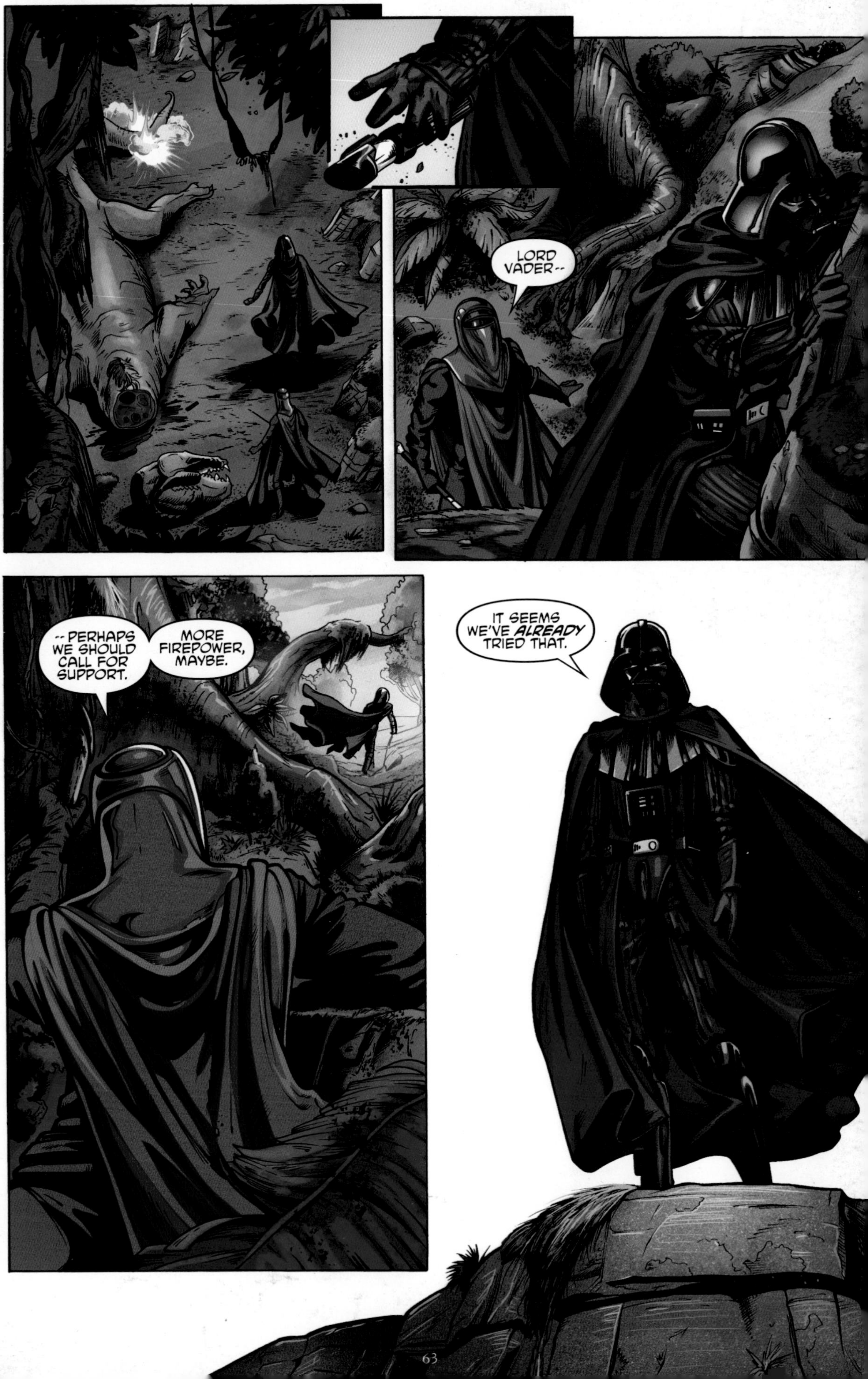
LORD VADER--
--PERHAPS WE SHOULD CALL FOR SUPPORT.
MORE FIREPOWER, MAYBE.
IT SEEMS WE'VE *ALREADY* TRIED THAT.

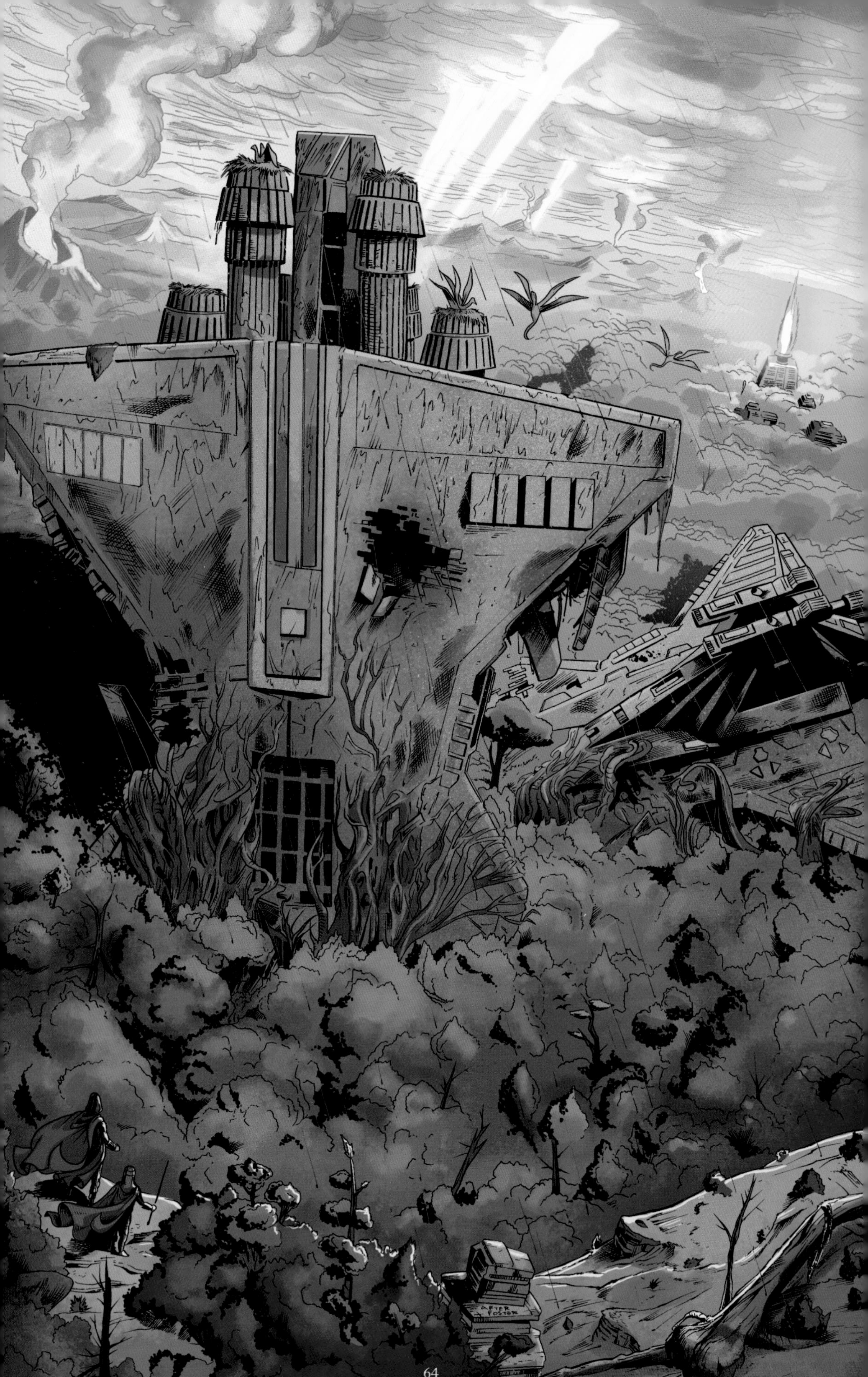
AFTER FOSTER

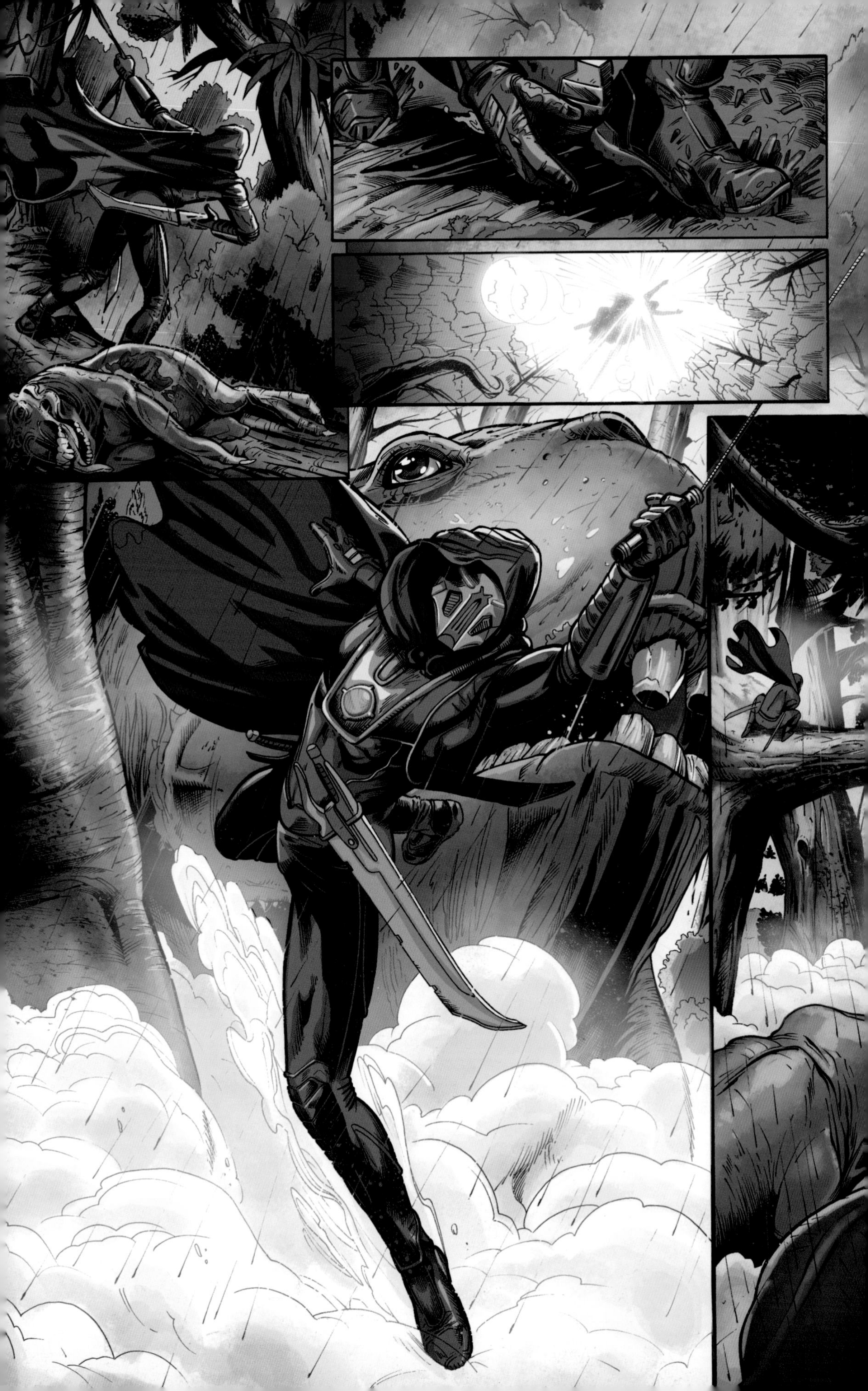

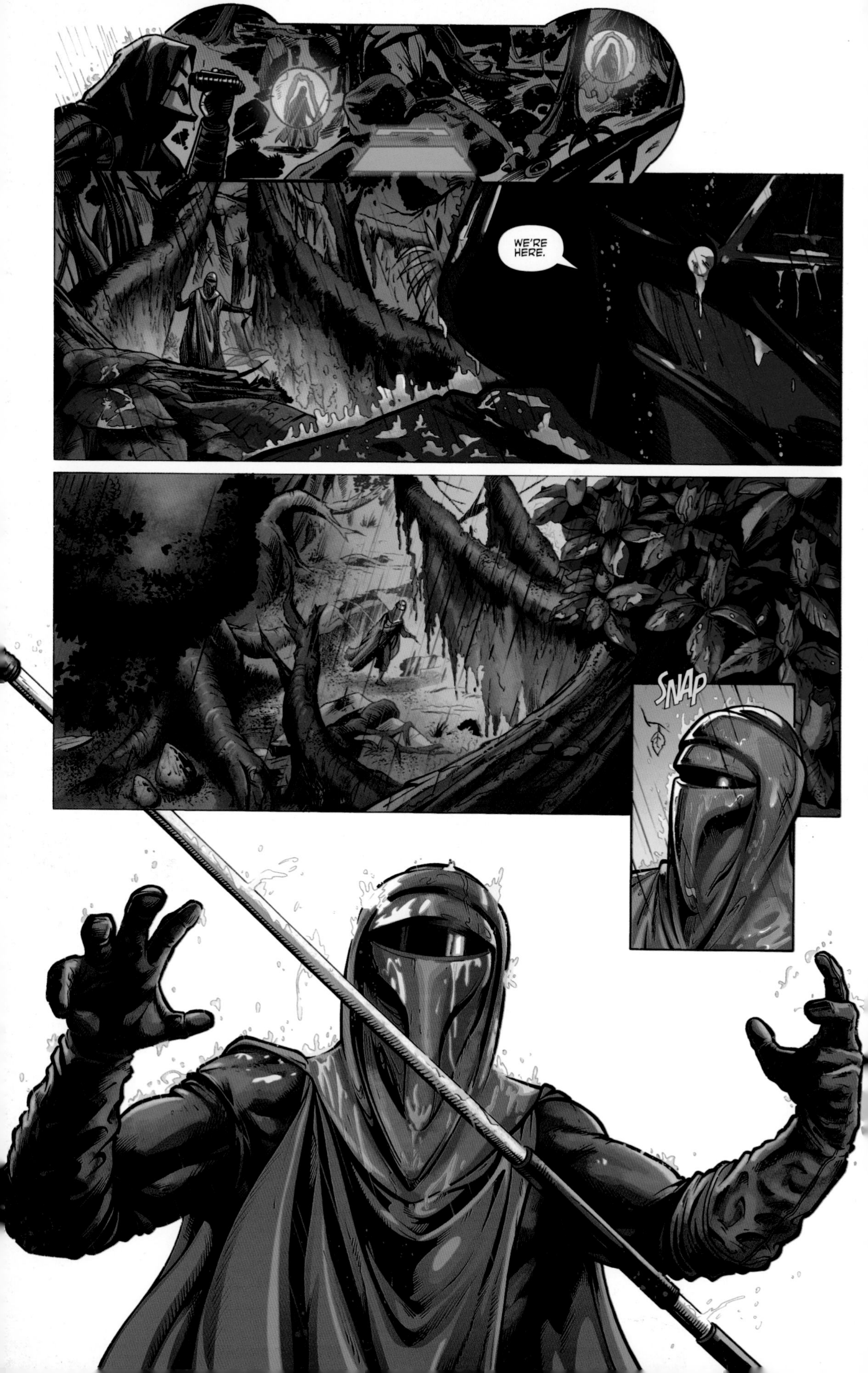
WE'RE HERE.
SNAP

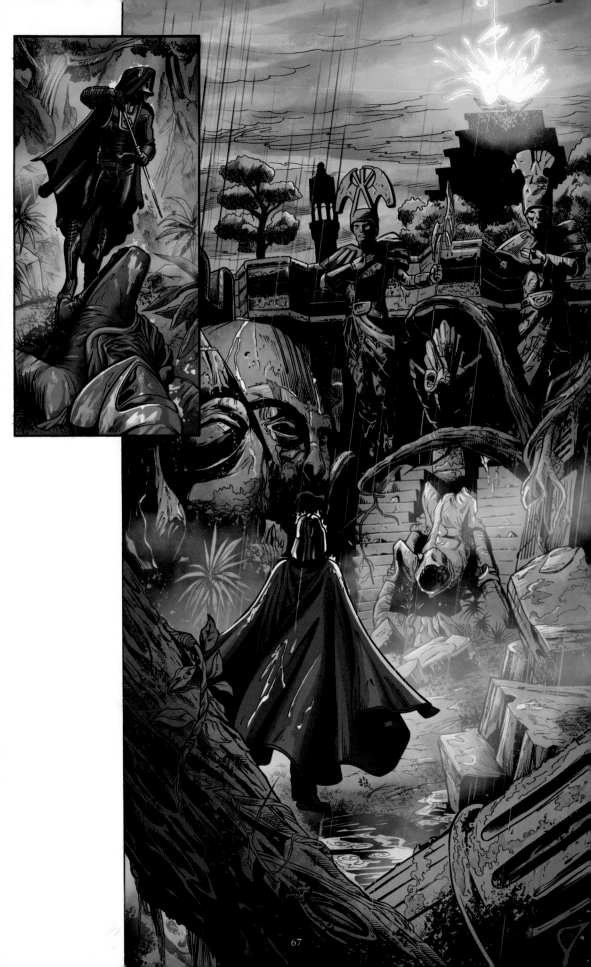

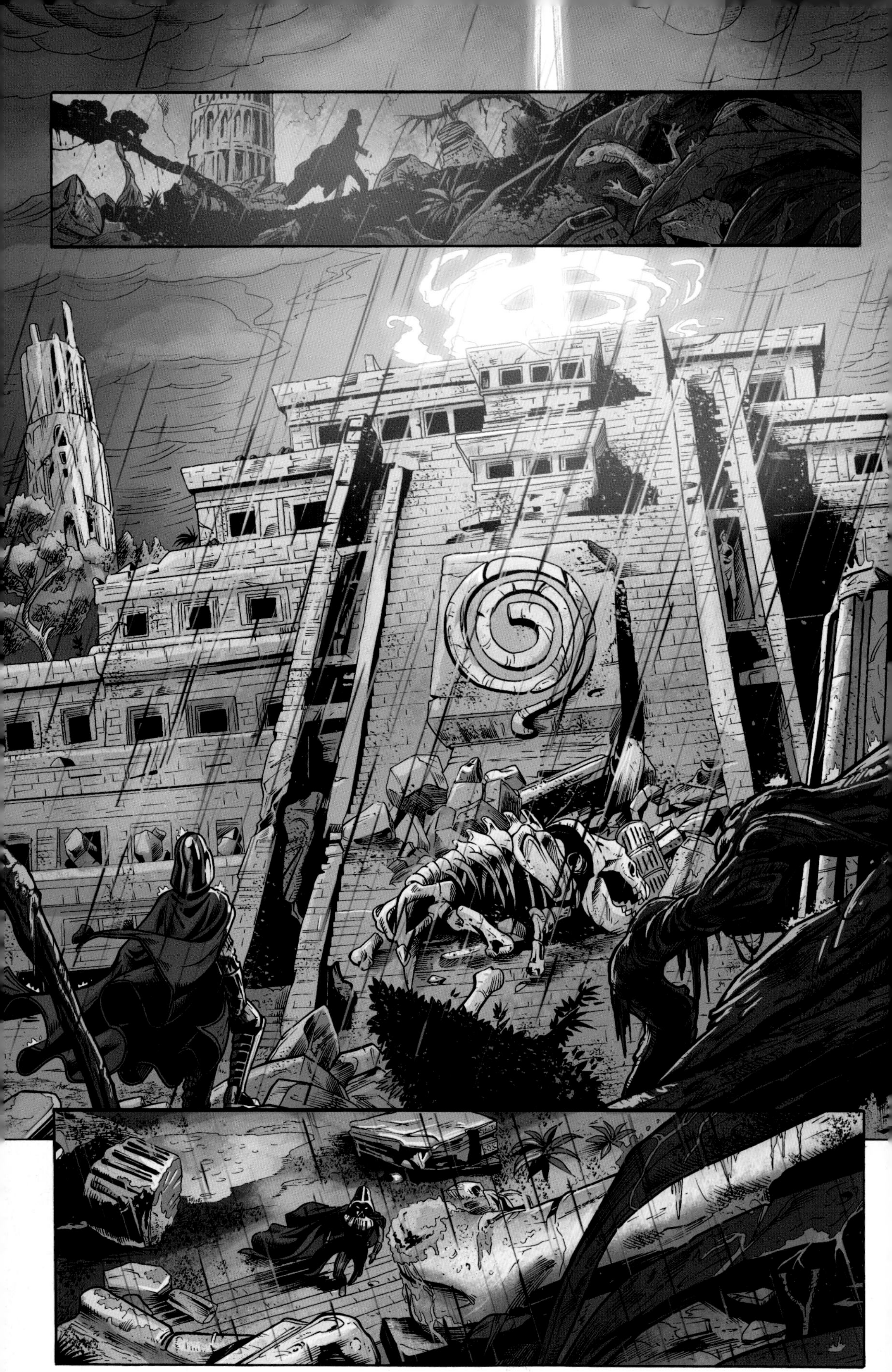

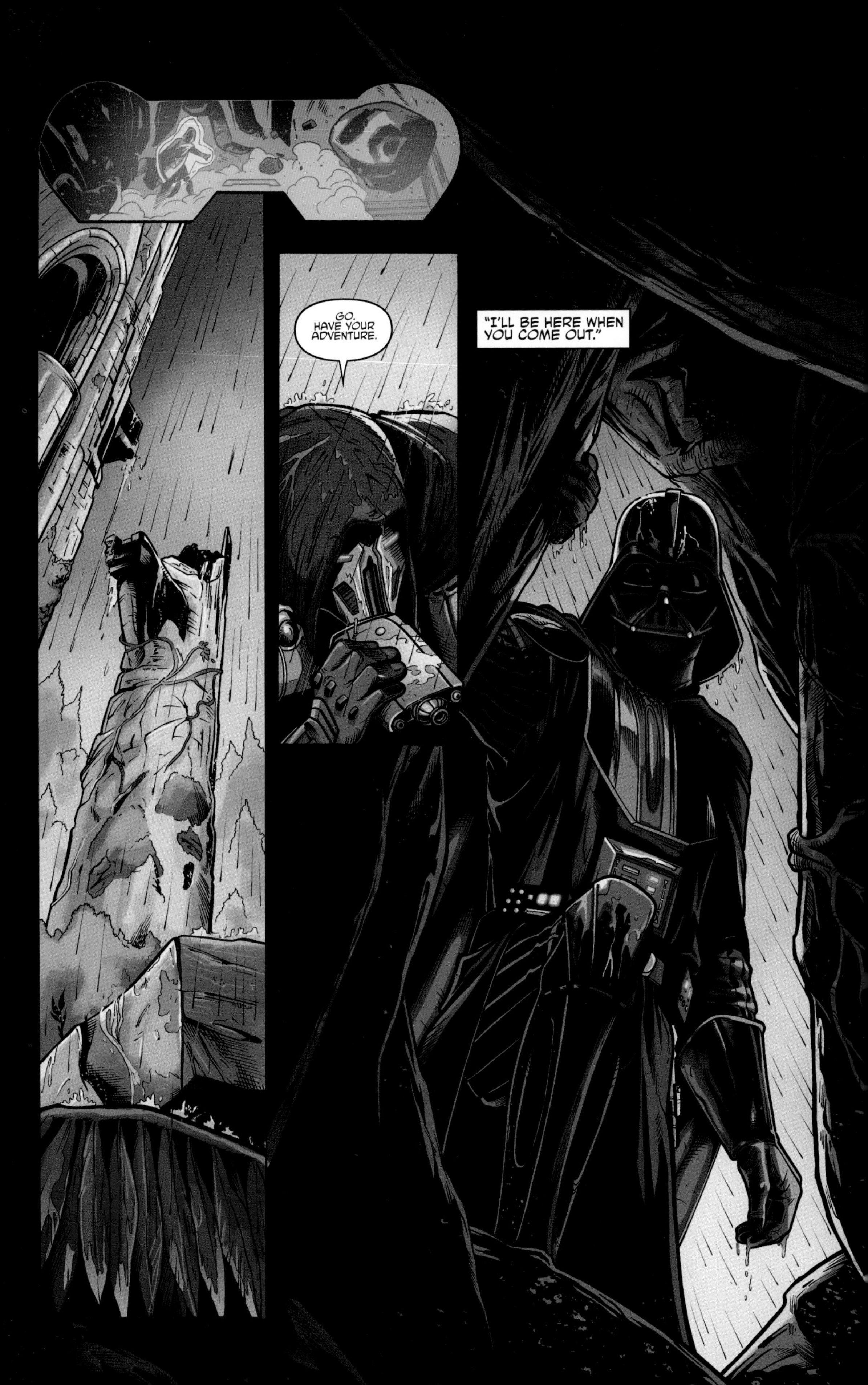
GO. HAVE YOUR ADVENTURE.
"I'LL BE HERE WHEN YOU COME OUT."

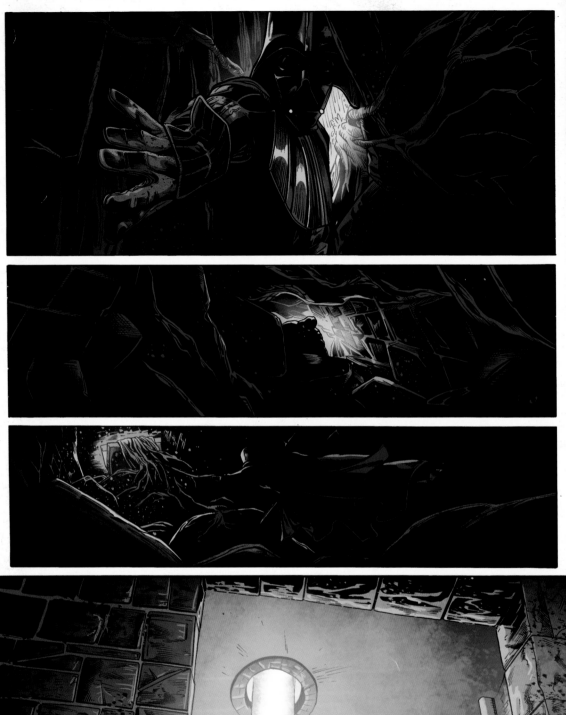

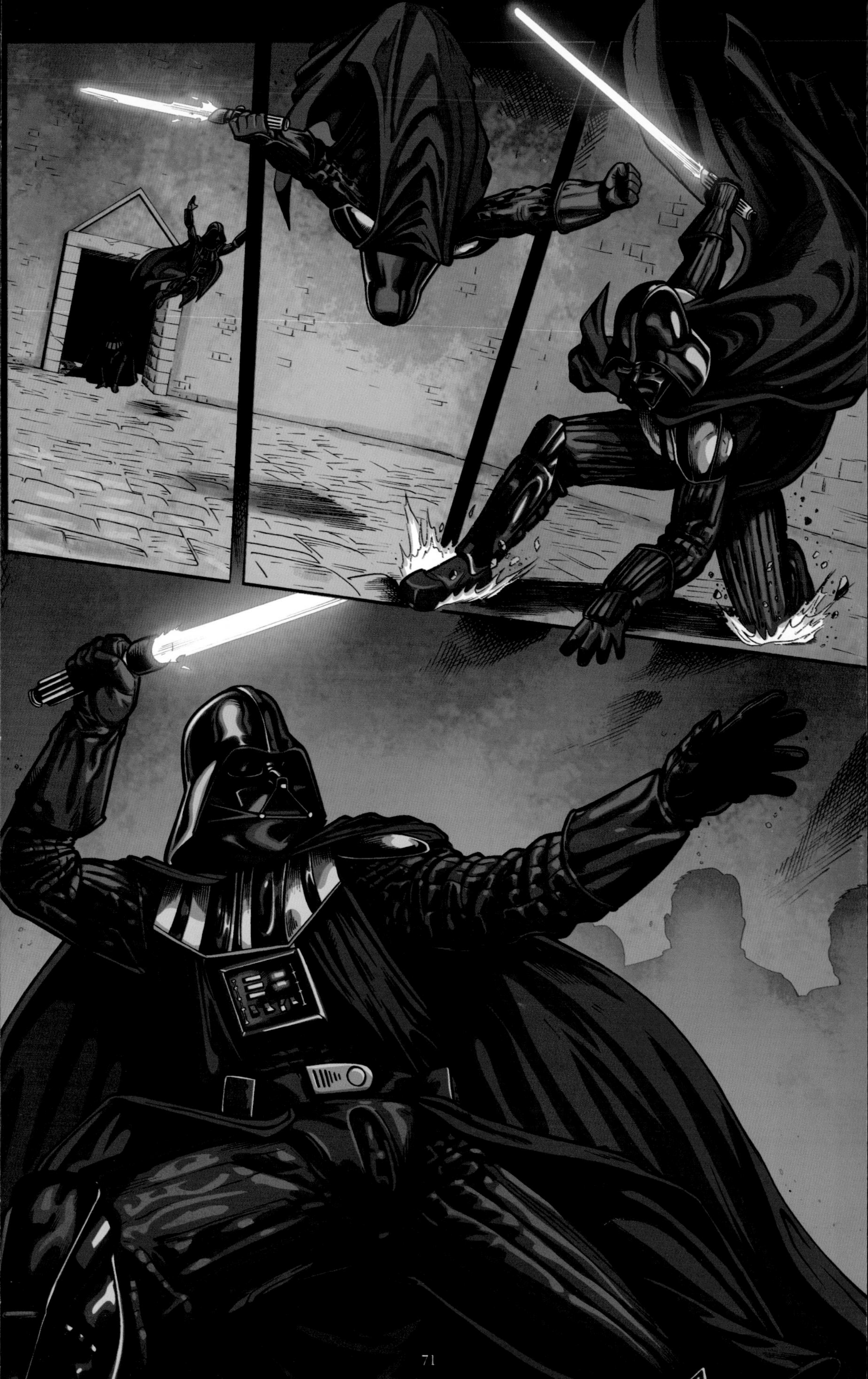

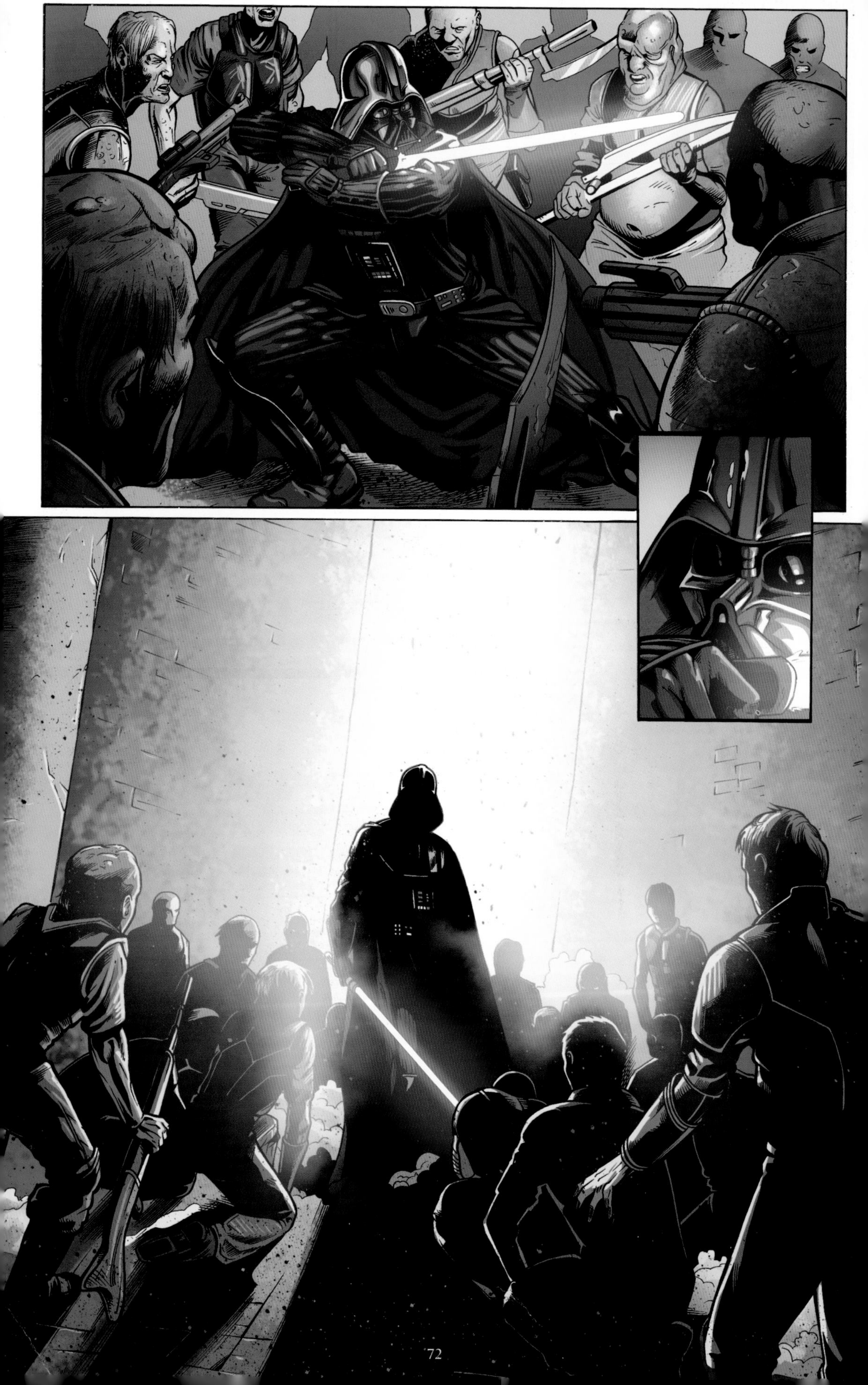

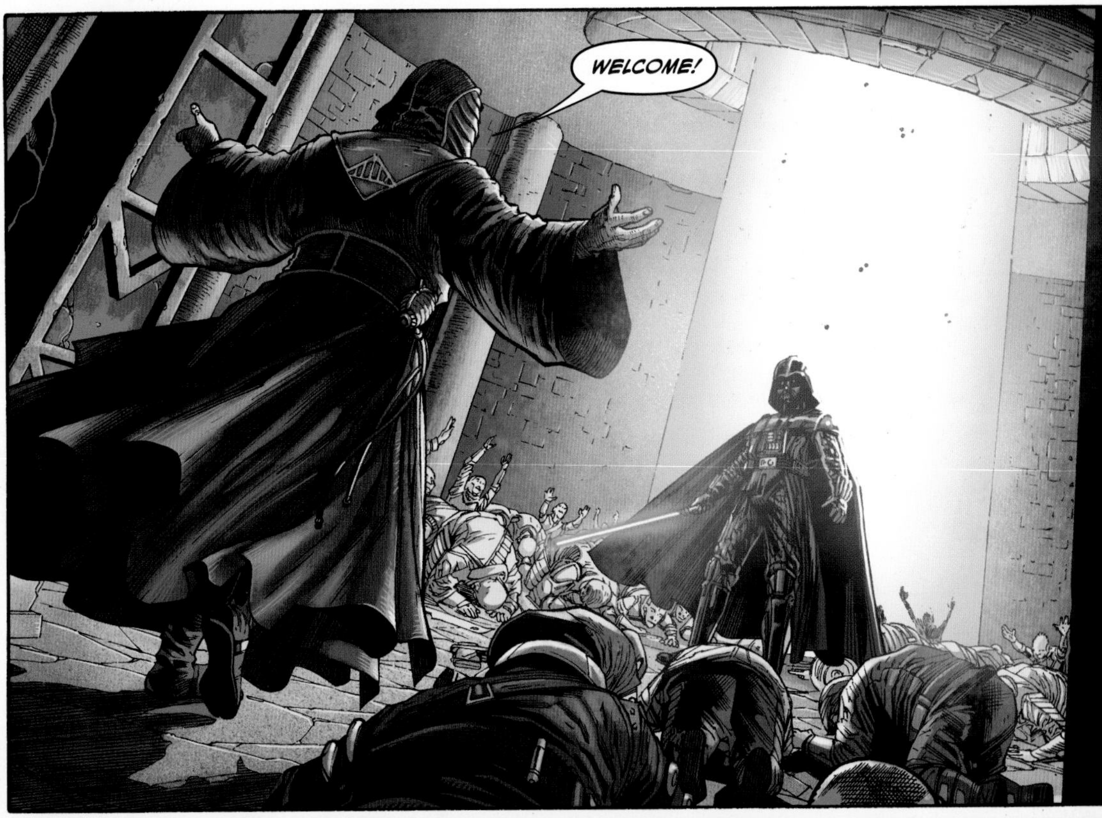
WELCOME!

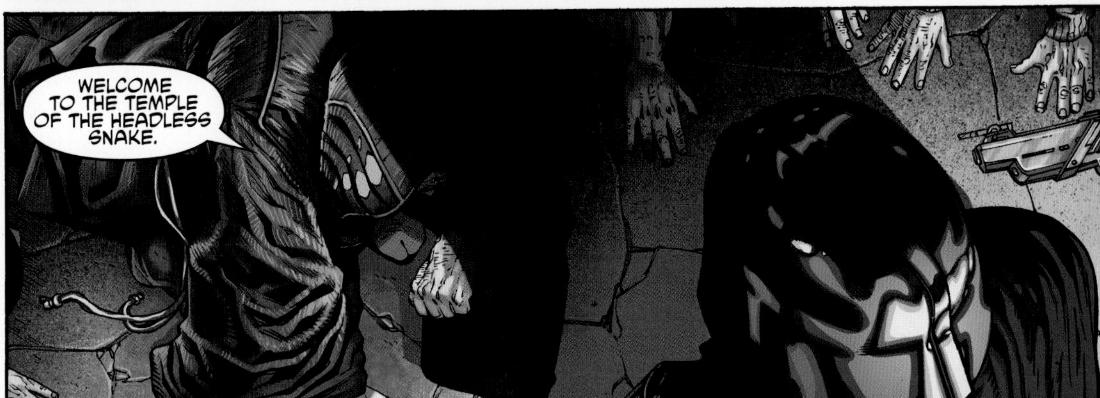
WELCOME TO THE TEMPLE OF THE HEADLESS SNAKE.

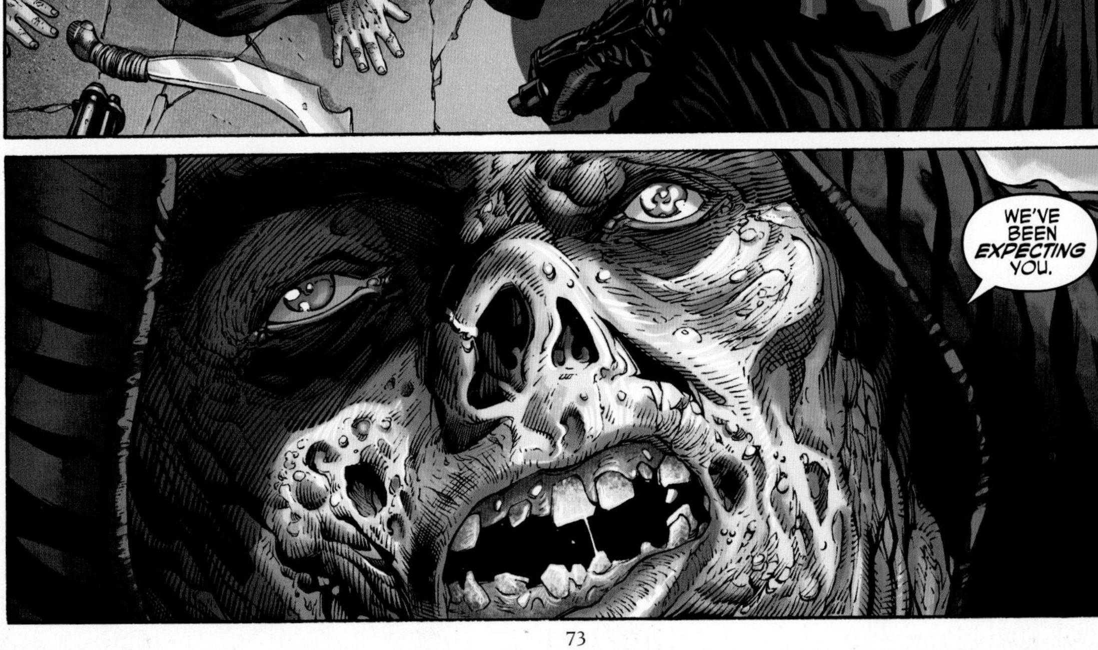
WE'VE BEEN *EXPECTING* YOU.

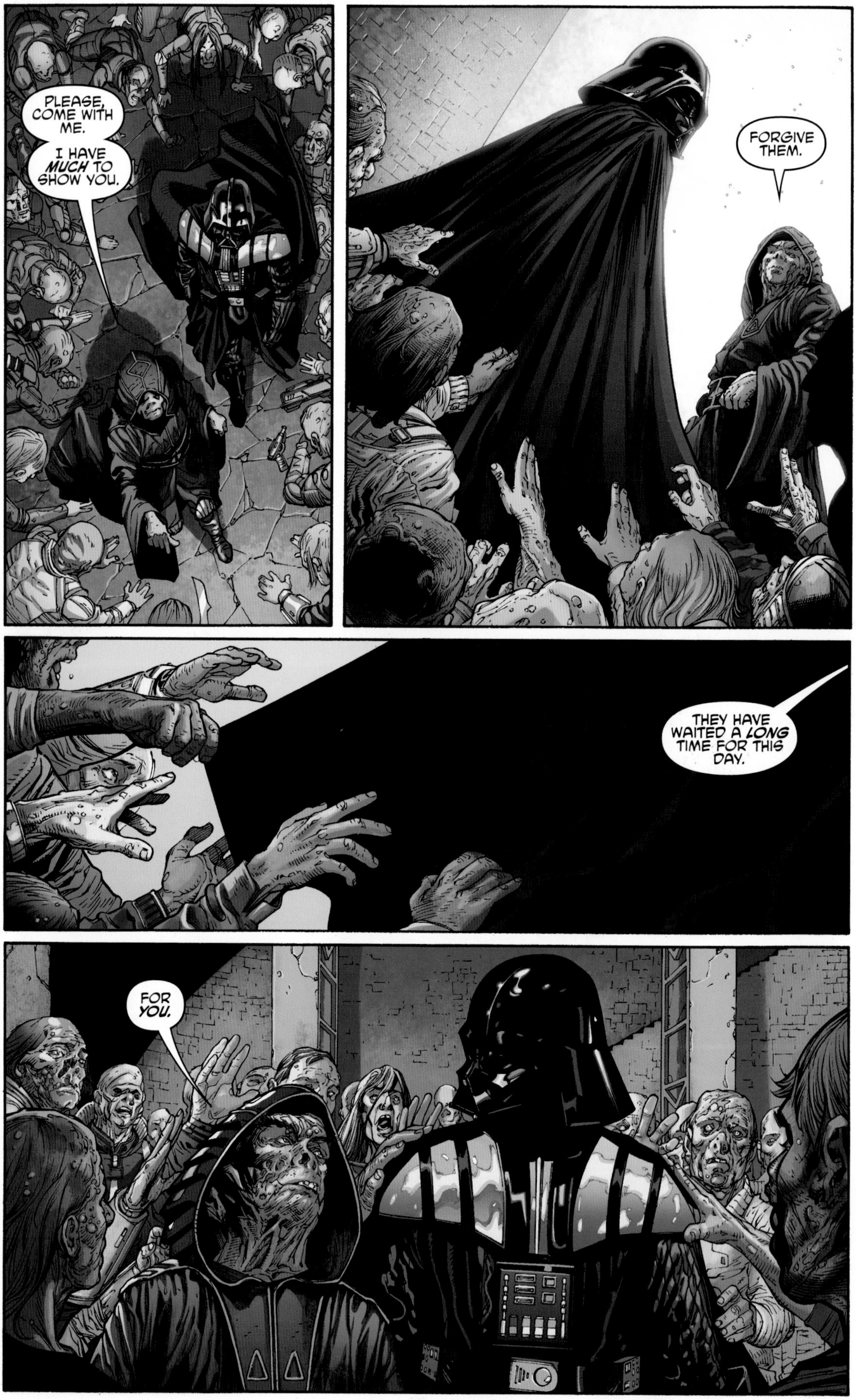
PLEASE, COME WITH ME.
I HAVE MUCH TO SHOW YOU.
FORGIVE THEM.
THEY HAVE WAITED A LONG TIME FOR THIS DAY.
FOR YOU.

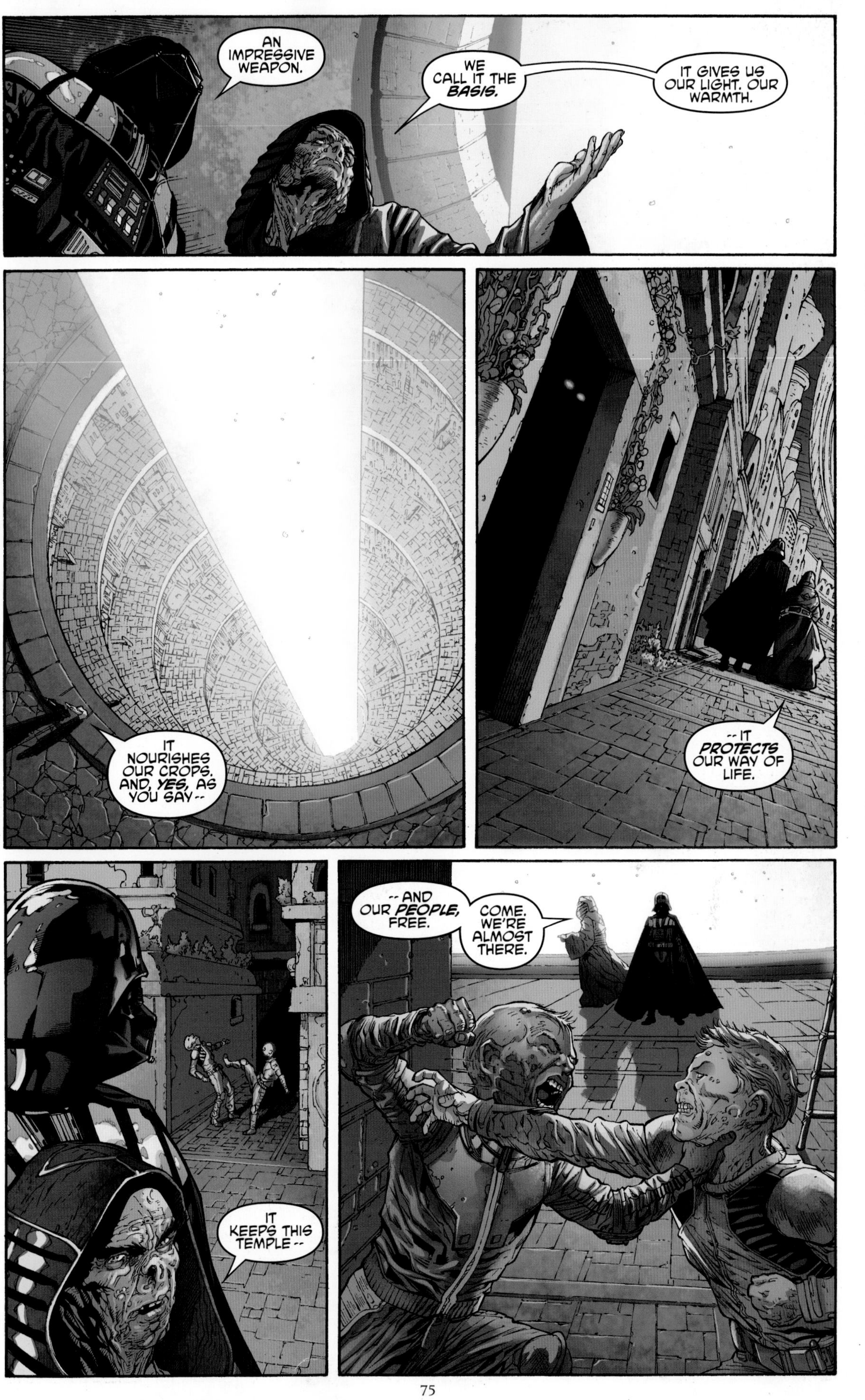
AN IMPRESSIVE WEAPON.
WE CALL IT THE *BASIS.*
IT GIVES US OUR LIGHT. OUR WARMTH.
IT NOURISHES OUR CROPS. AND, *YES,* AS YOU SAY--
--IT *PROTECTS* OUR WAY OF LIFE.
IT KEEPS THIS TEMPLE--
--AND OUR *PEOPLE,* FREE.
COME. WE'RE ALMOST THERE.

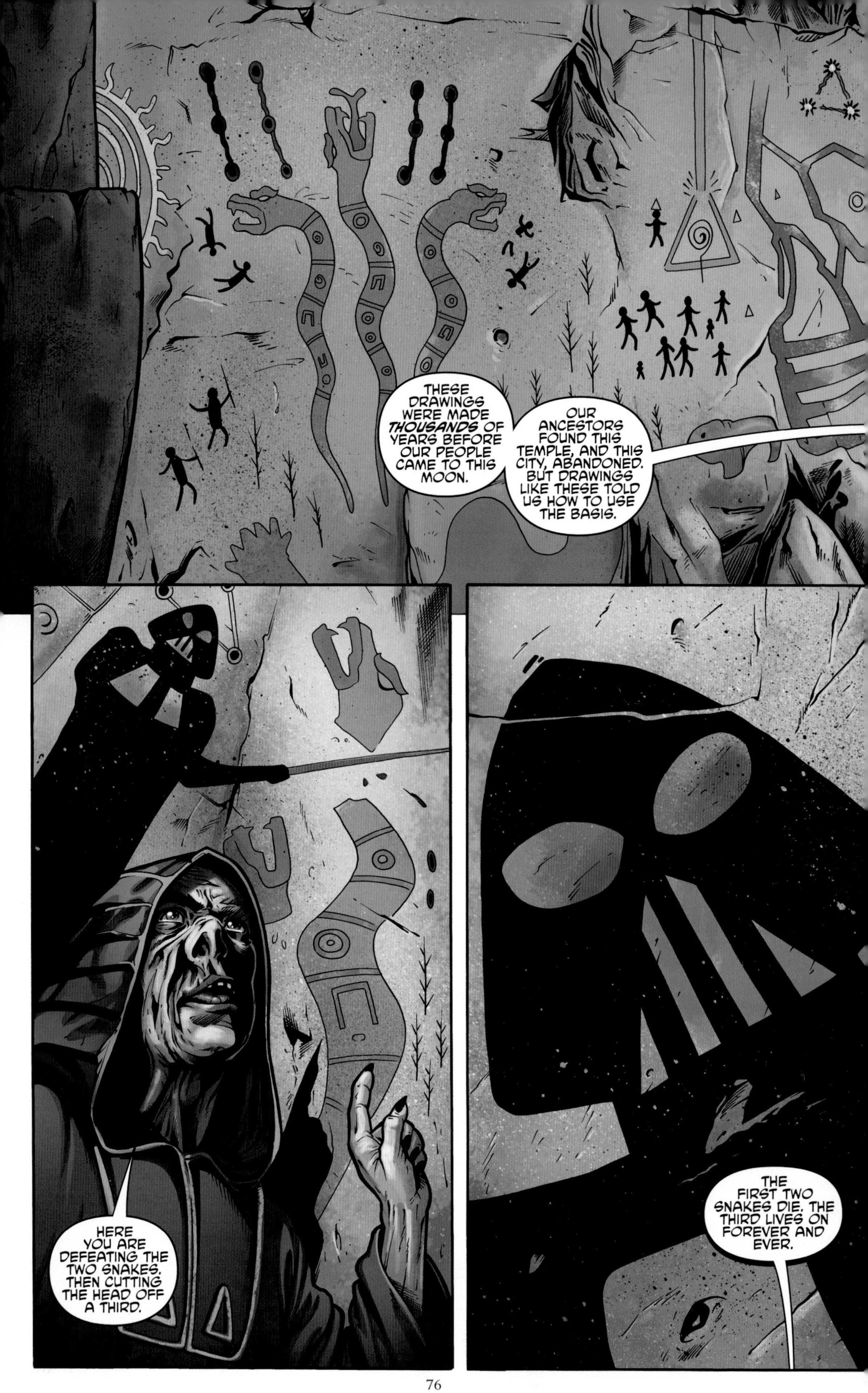
THESE DRAWINGS WERE MADE THOUSANDS OF YEARS BEFORE OUR PEOPLE CAME TO THIS MOON.
OUR ANCESTORS FOUND THIS TEMPLE, AND THIS CITY, ABANDONED. BUT DRAWINGS LIKE THESE TOLD US HOW TO USE THE BASIS.
HERE YOU ARE DEFEATING THE TWO SNAKES. THEN CUTTING THE HEAD OFF A THIRD.
THE FIRST TWO SNAKES DIE. THE THIRD LIVES ON FOREVER AND EVER.

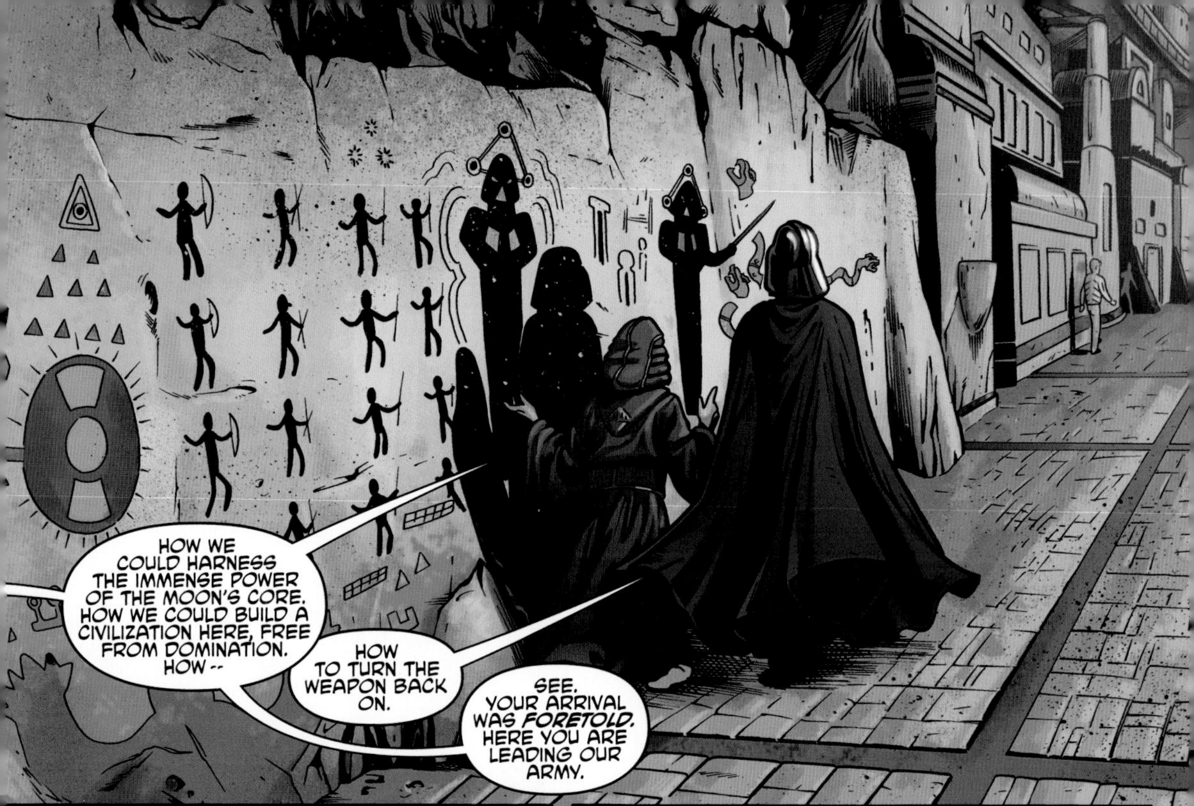
HOW WE COULD HARNESS THE IMMENSE POWER OF THE MOON'S CORE. HOW WE COULD BUILD A CIVILIZATION HERE, FREE FROM DOMINATION. HOW --
HOW TO TURN THE WEAPON BACK ON.
SEE. YOUR ARRIVAL WAS *FORETOLD.* HERE YOU ARE LEADING OUR ARMY.

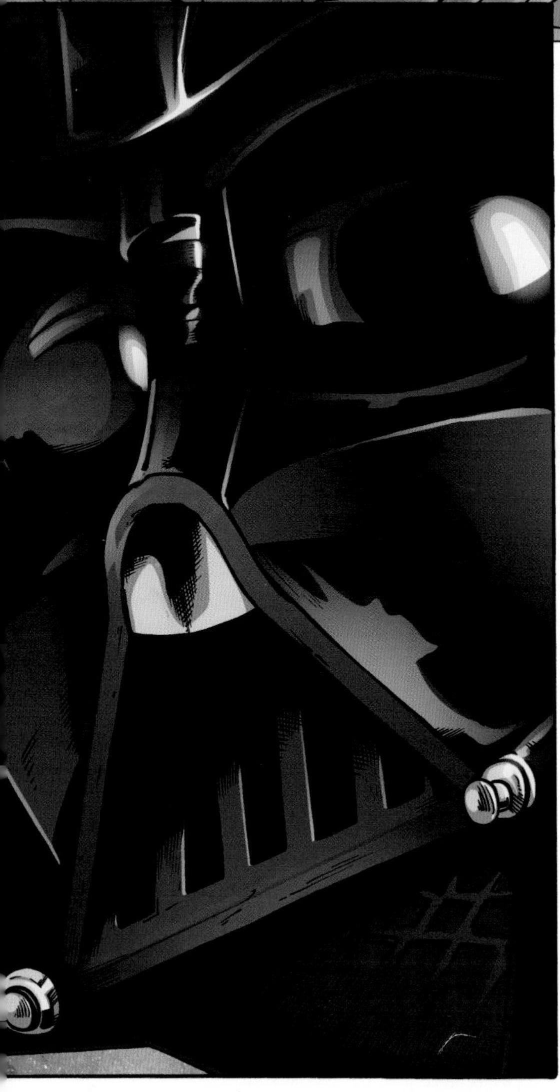

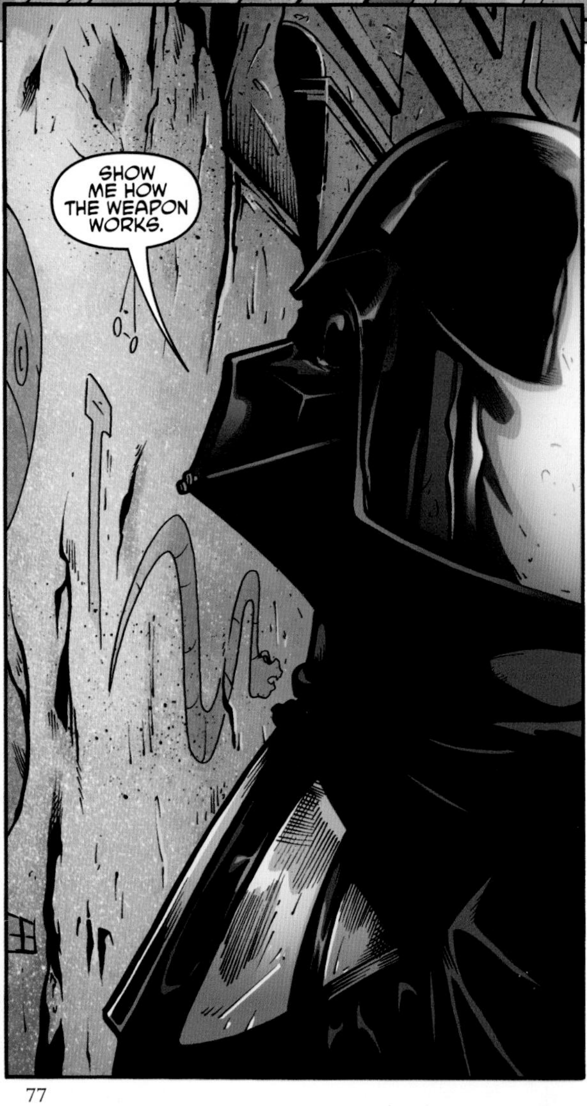
SHOW ME HOW THE WEAPON WORKS.

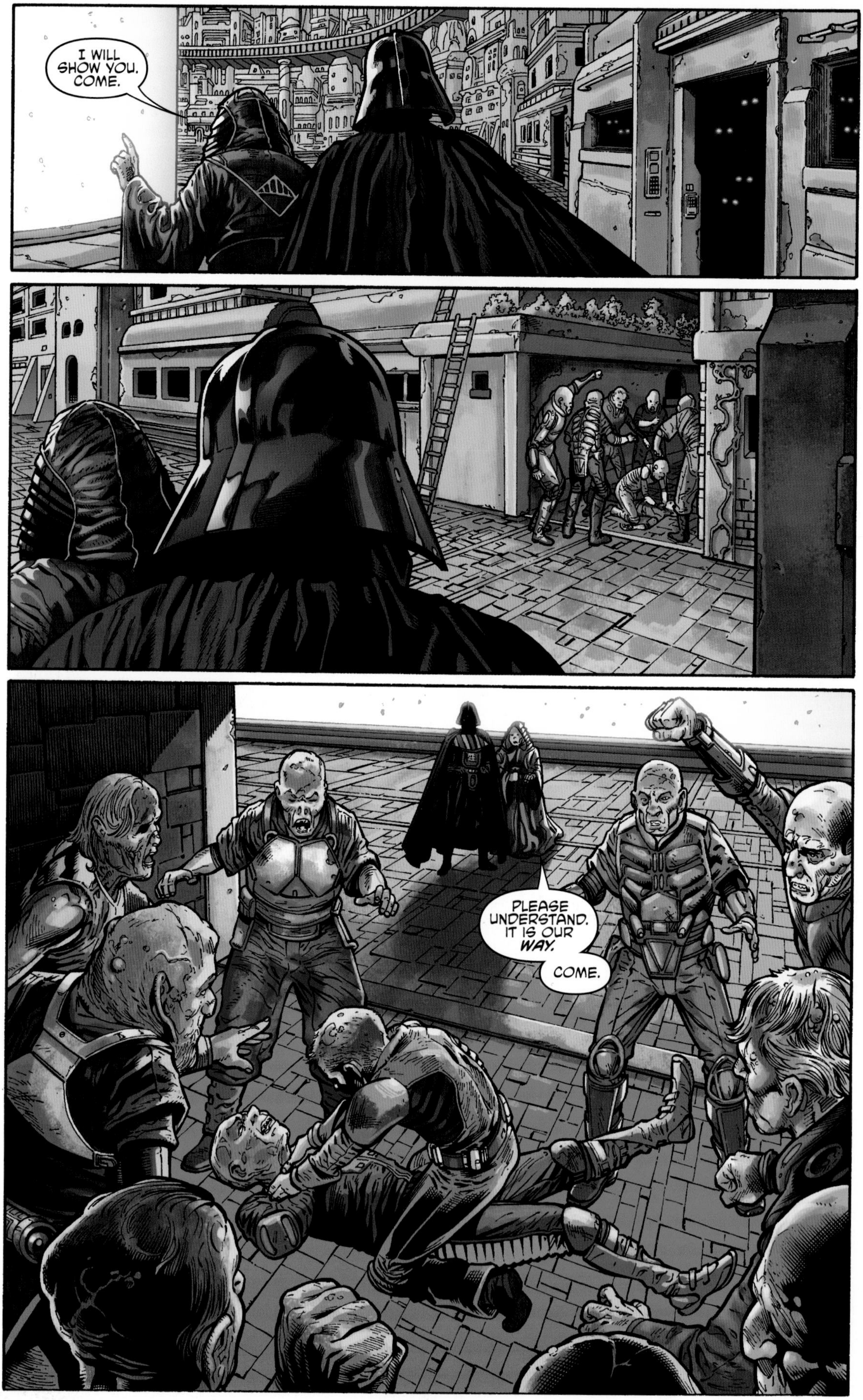
I WILL SHOW YOU. COME.
PLEASE UNDERSTAND. IT IS OUR *WAY.*
COME.

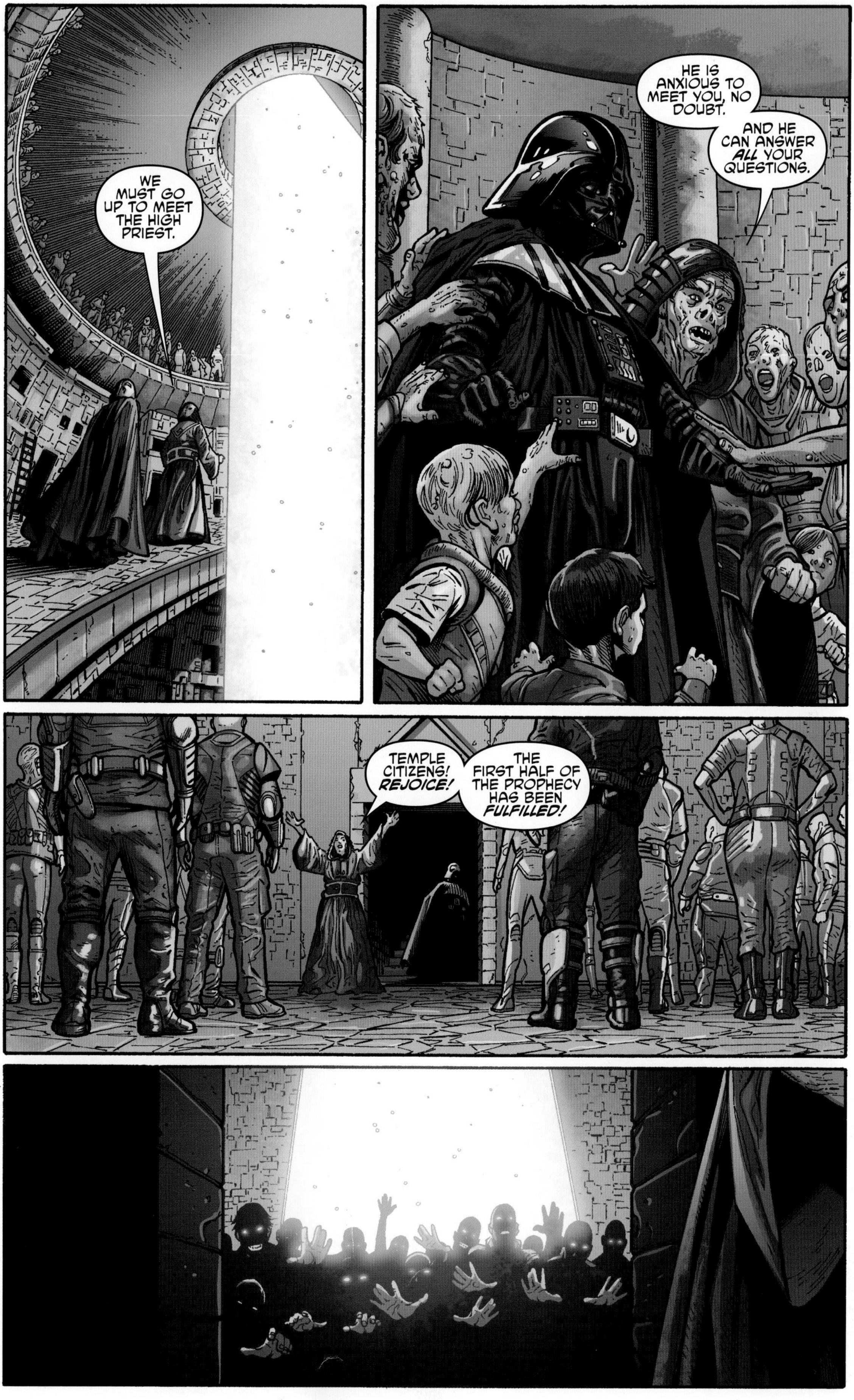
WE MUST GO UP TO MEET THE HIGH PRIEST.
HE IS ANXIOUS TO MEET YOU, NO DOUBT.
AND HE CAN ANSWER ALL YOUR QUESTIONS.
TEMPLE CITIZENS! REJOICE!
THE FIRST HALF OF THE PROPHECY HAS BEEN FULFILLED!

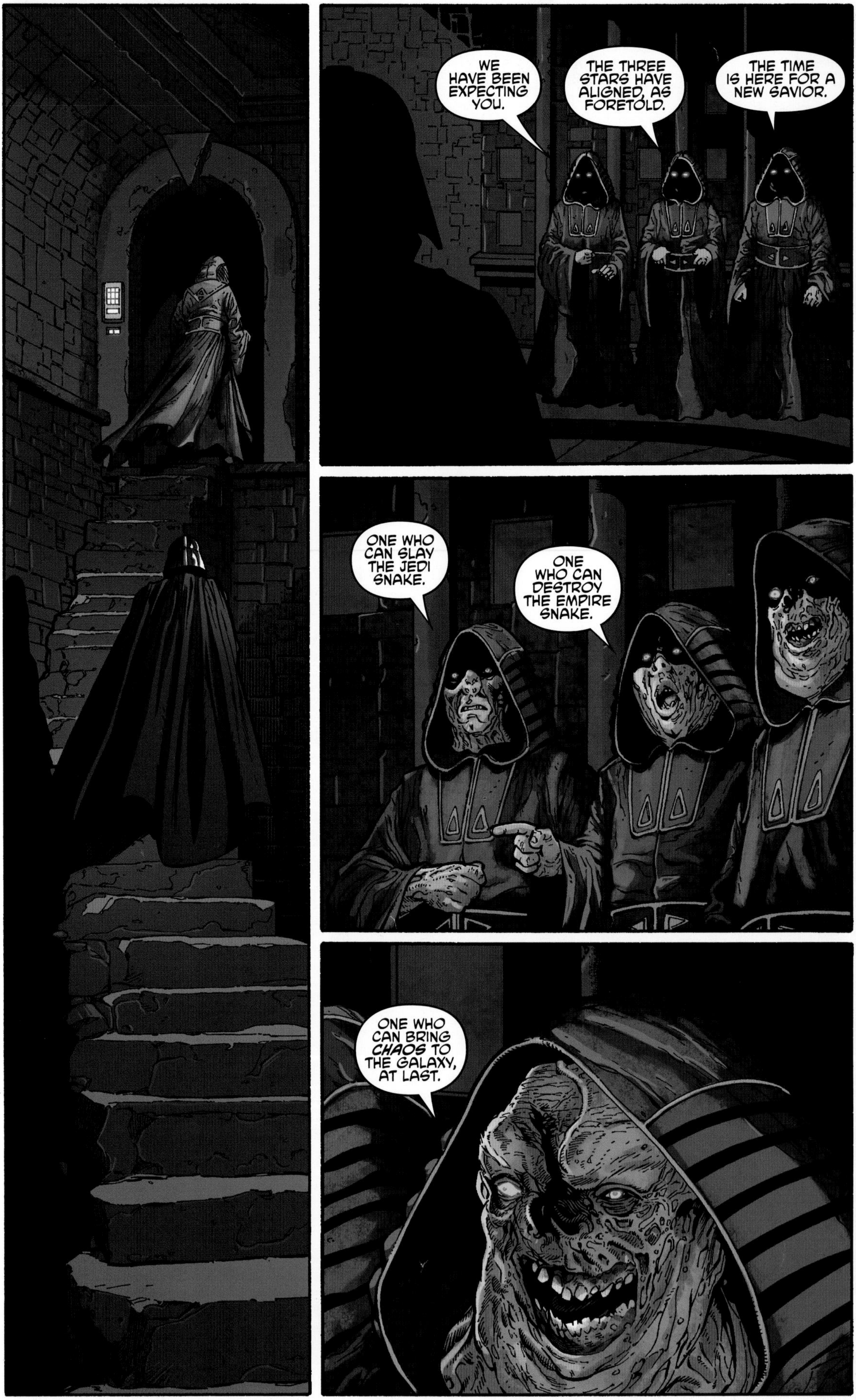
WE HAVE BEEN EXPECTING YOU.
THE THREE STARS HAVE ALIGNED, AS FORETOLD.
THE TIME IS HERE FOR A NEW SAVIOR.
ONE WHO CAN SLAY THE JEDI SNAKE.
ONE WHO CAN DESTROY THE EMPIRE SNAKE.
ONE WHO CAN BRING *CHAOS* TO THE GALAXY, AT LAST.

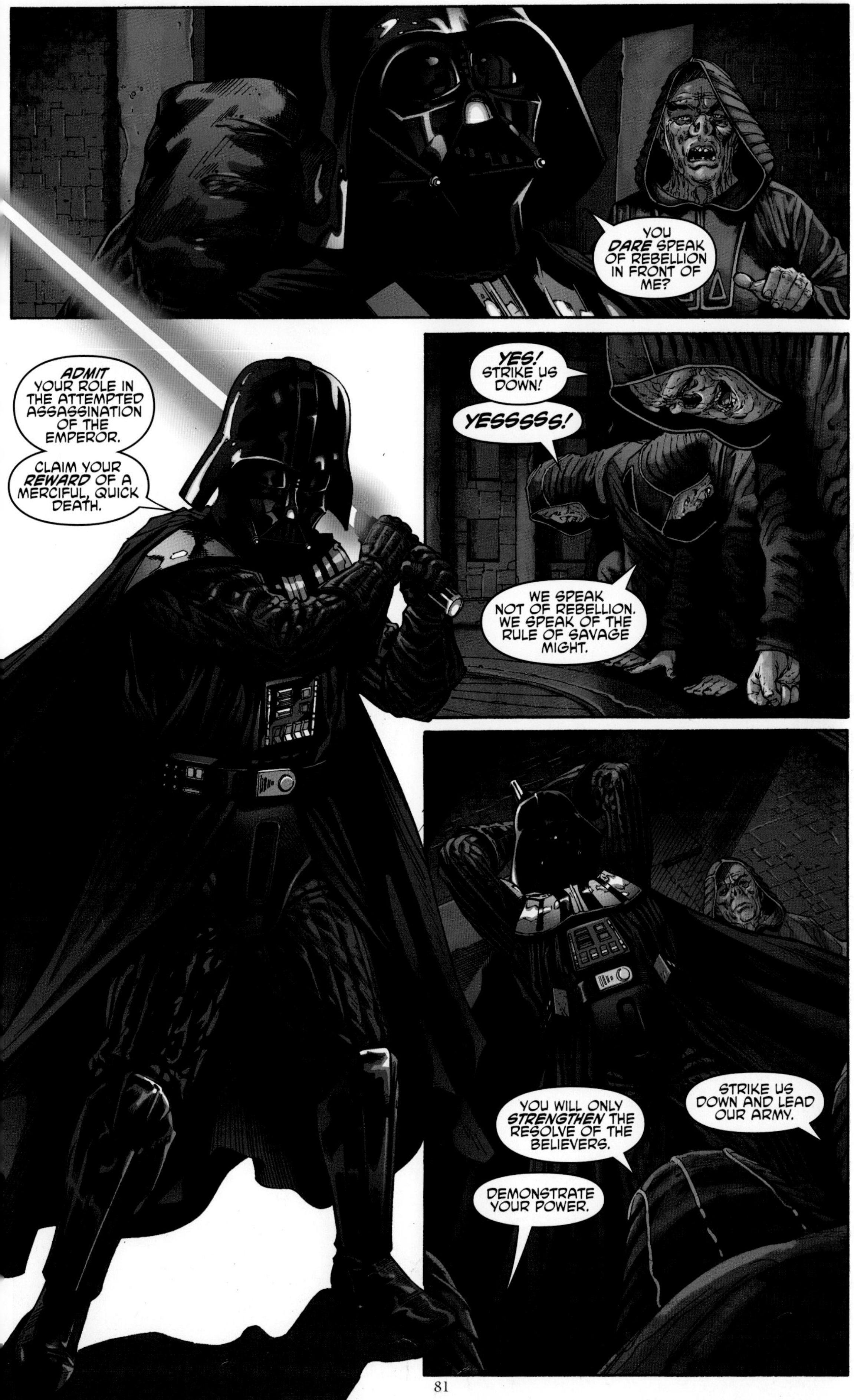
YOU DARE SPEAK OF REBELLION IN FRONT OF ME?
ADMIT YOUR ROLE IN THE ATTEMPTED ASSASSINATION OF THE EMPEROR.
CLAIM YOUR REWARD OF A MERCIFUL, QUICK DEATH.
YES! STRIKE US DOWN!
YESSSSS!
WE SPEAK NOT OF REBELLION. WE SPEAK OF THE RULE OF SAVAGE MIGHT.
STRIKE US DOWN AND LEAD OUR ARMY.
YOU WILL ONLY STRENGTHEN THE RESOLVE OF THE BELIEVERS.
DEMONSTRATE YOUR POWER.

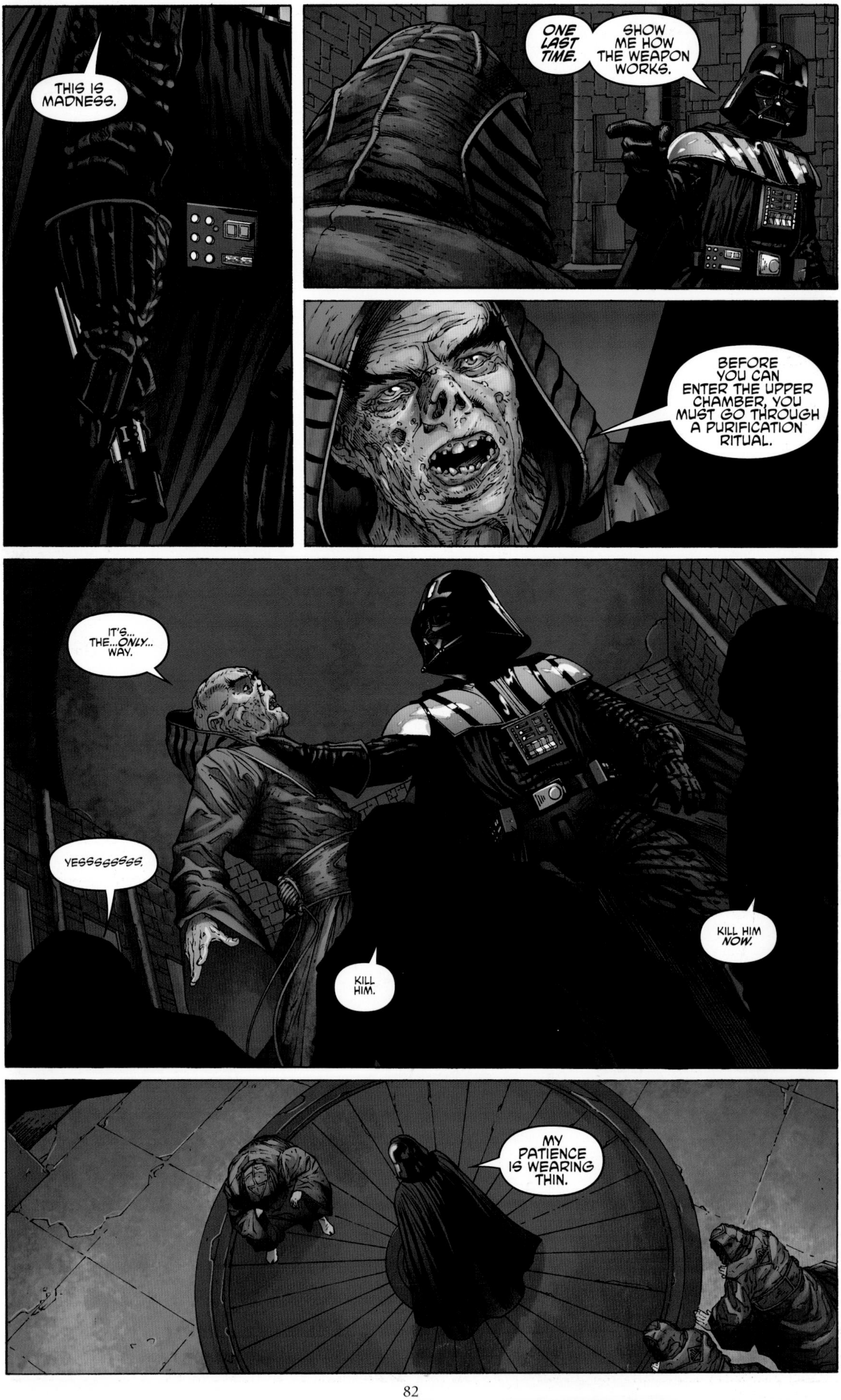
THIS IS MADNESS.
ONE LAST TIME.
SHOW ME HOW THE WEAPON WORKS.
BEFORE YOU CAN ENTER THE UPPER CHAMBER, YOU MUST GO THROUGH A PURIFICATION RITUAL.
IT'S... THE...ONLY... WAY.
YESSSSSSSS.
KILL HIM.
KILL HIM NOW.
MY PATIENCE IS WEARING THIN.

JUST LOOK -- *COUGH*

--THAT'S ALL YOU NEED TO DO.

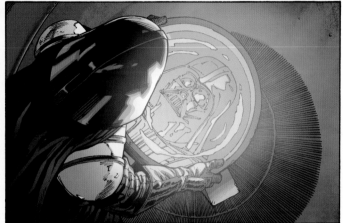

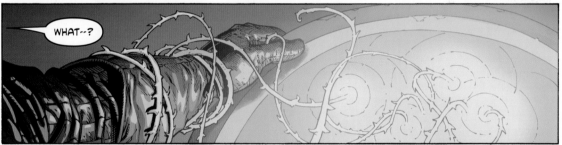

WHAT--?

CAN'T... BREATHE...

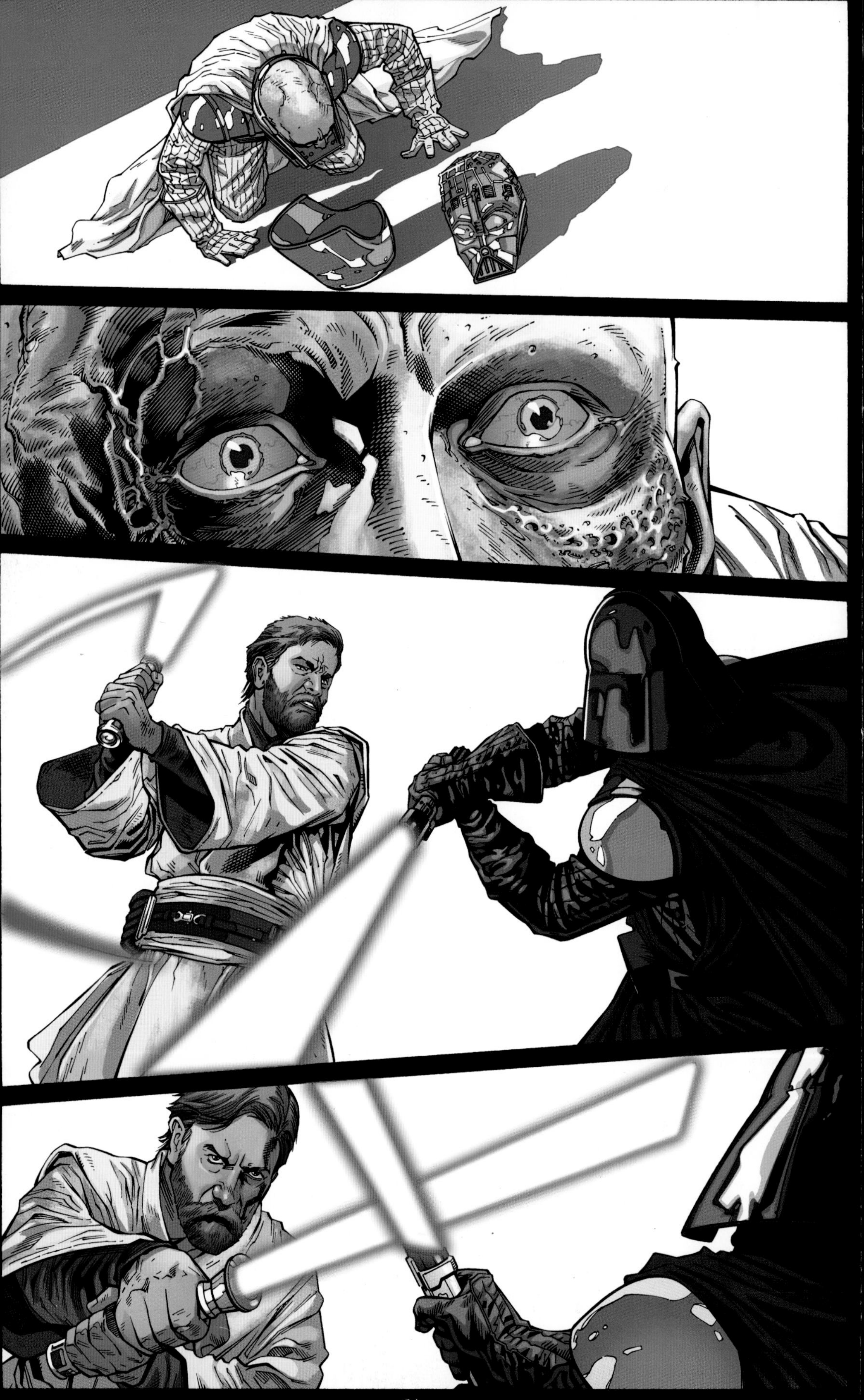

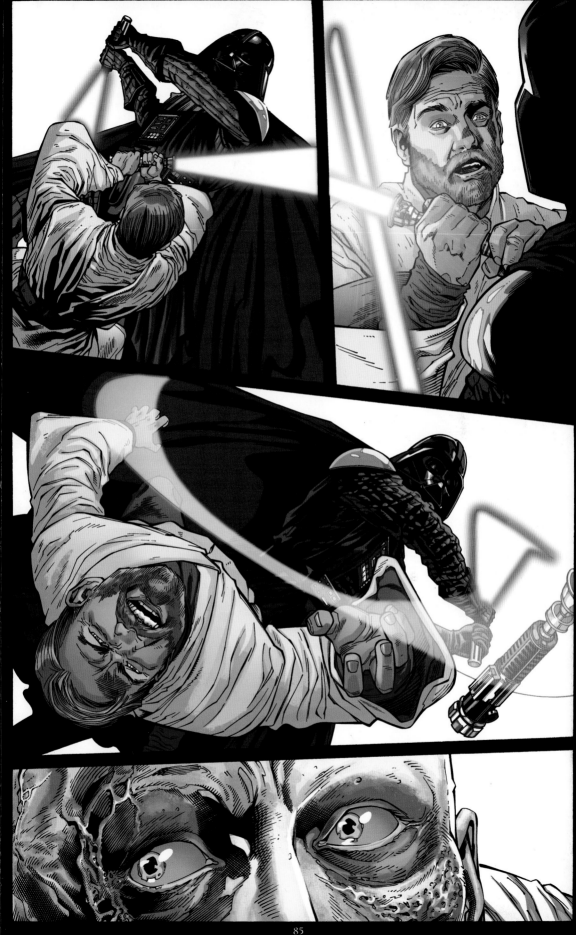

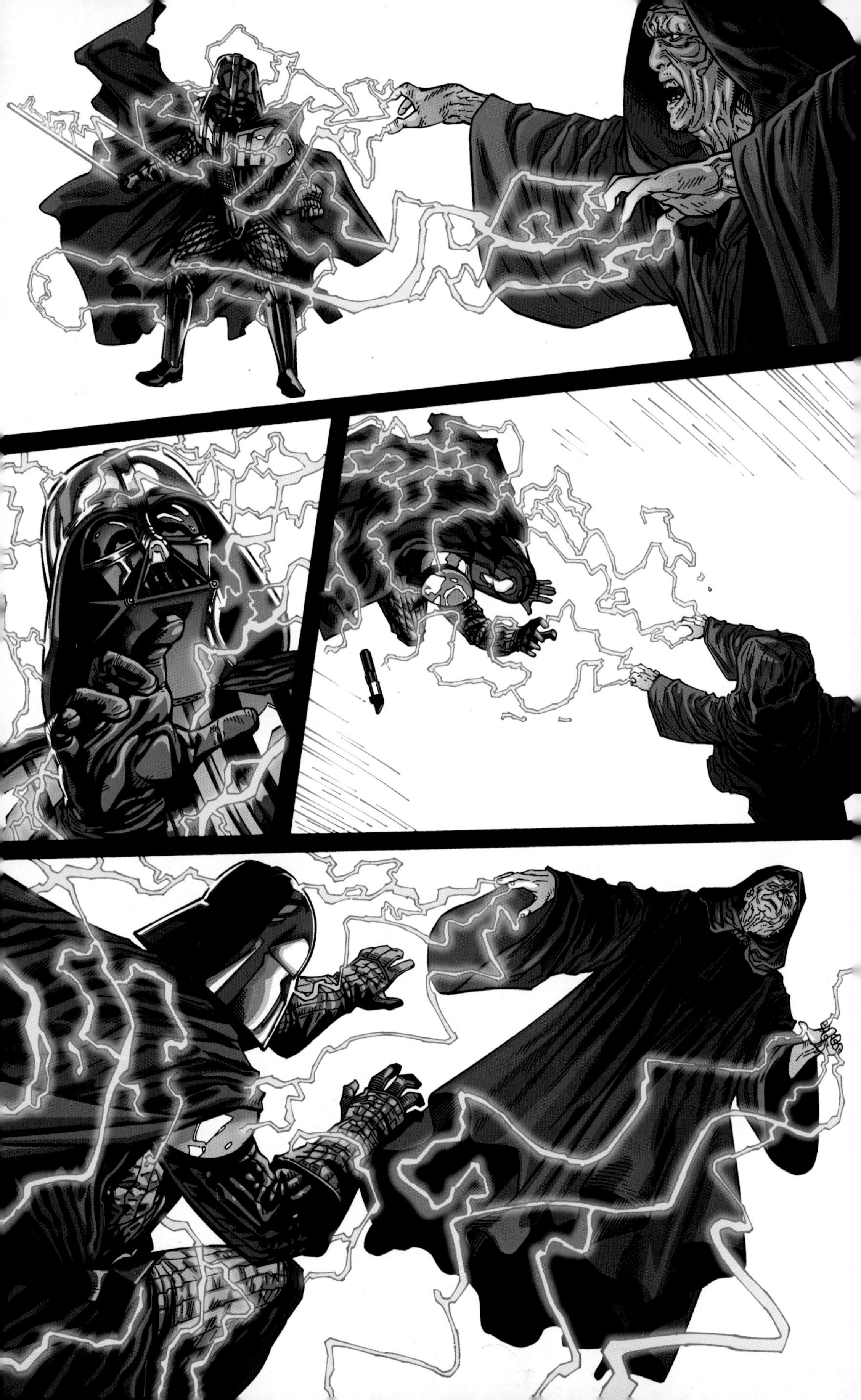

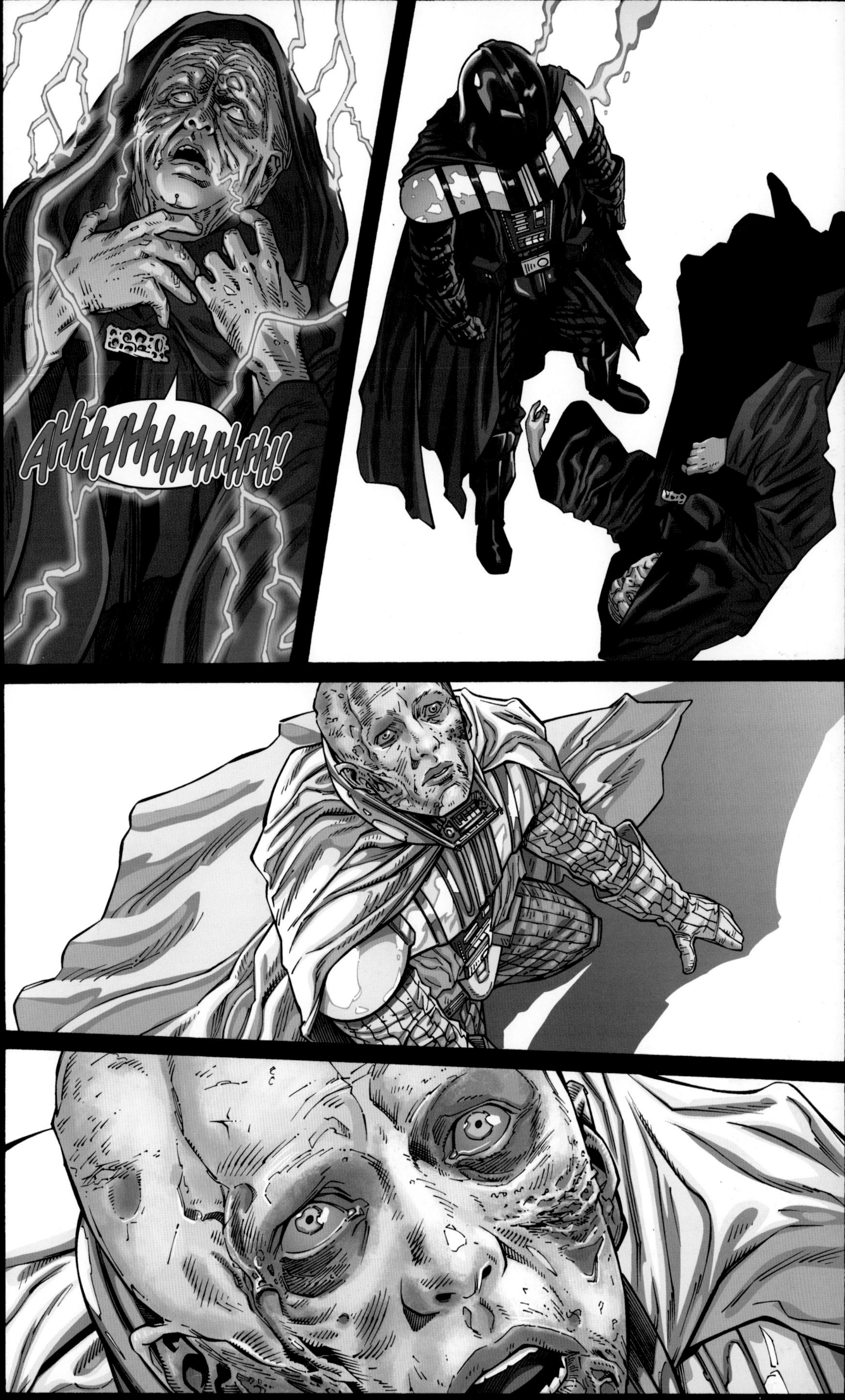
AHHHHHHHHHHHHH!

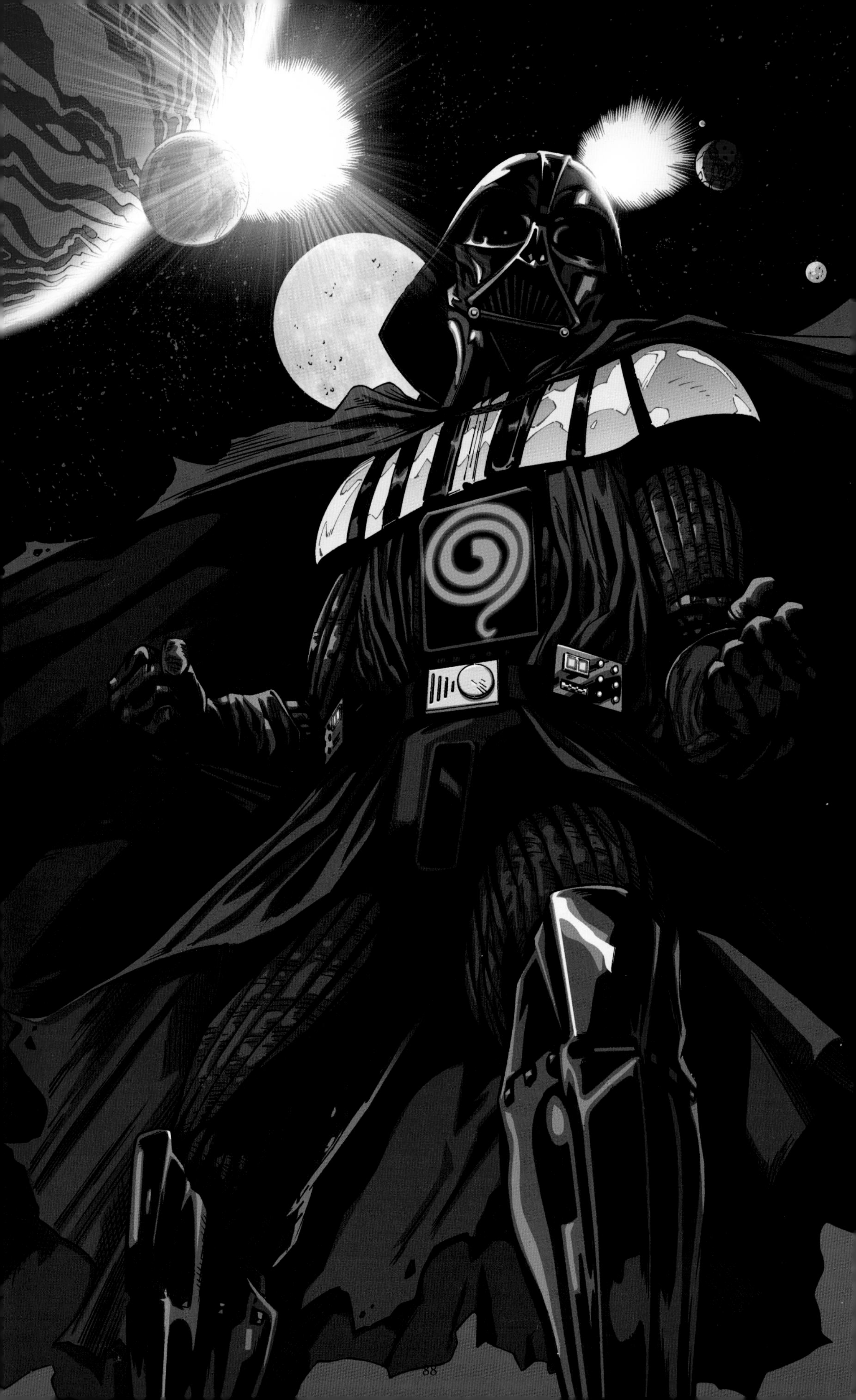

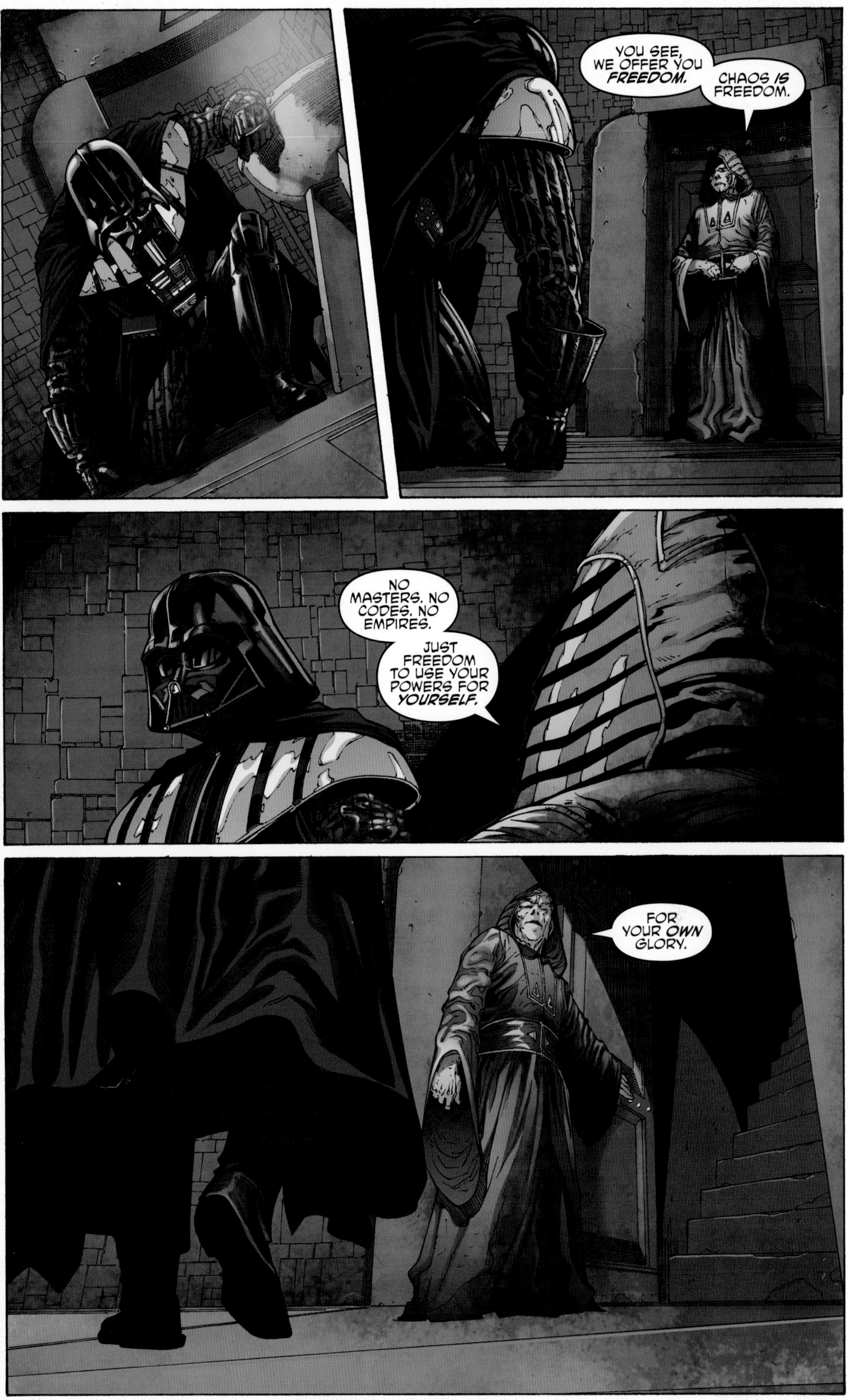
YOU SEE, WE OFFER YOU *FREEDOM.*
CHAOS *IS* FREEDOM.
NO MASTERS. NO CODES. NO EMPIRES.
JUST FREEDOM TO USE YOUR POWERS FOR *YOURSELF.*
FOR YOUR *OWN* GLORY.

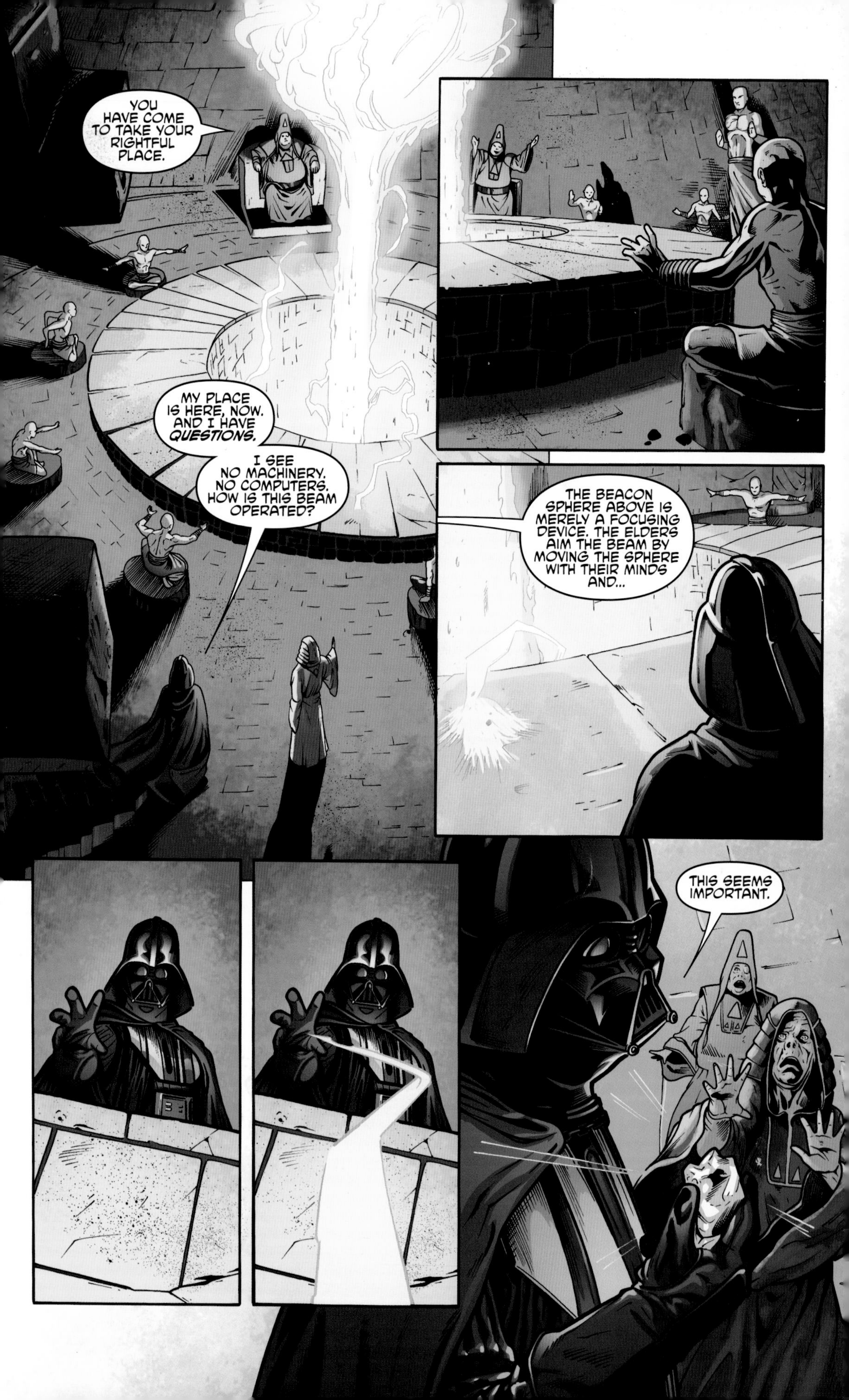
YOU HAVE COME TO TAKE YOUR RIGHTFUL PLACE.
MY PLACE IS HERE, NOW. AND I HAVE *QUESTIONS.*
I SEE NO MACHINERY. NO COMPUTERS. HOW IS THIS BEAM OPERATED?
THE BEACON SPHERE ABOVE IS MERELY A FOCUSING DEVICE. THE ELDERS AIM THE BEAM BY MOVING THE SPHERE WITH THEIR MINDS AND...
THIS SEEMS IMPORTANT.

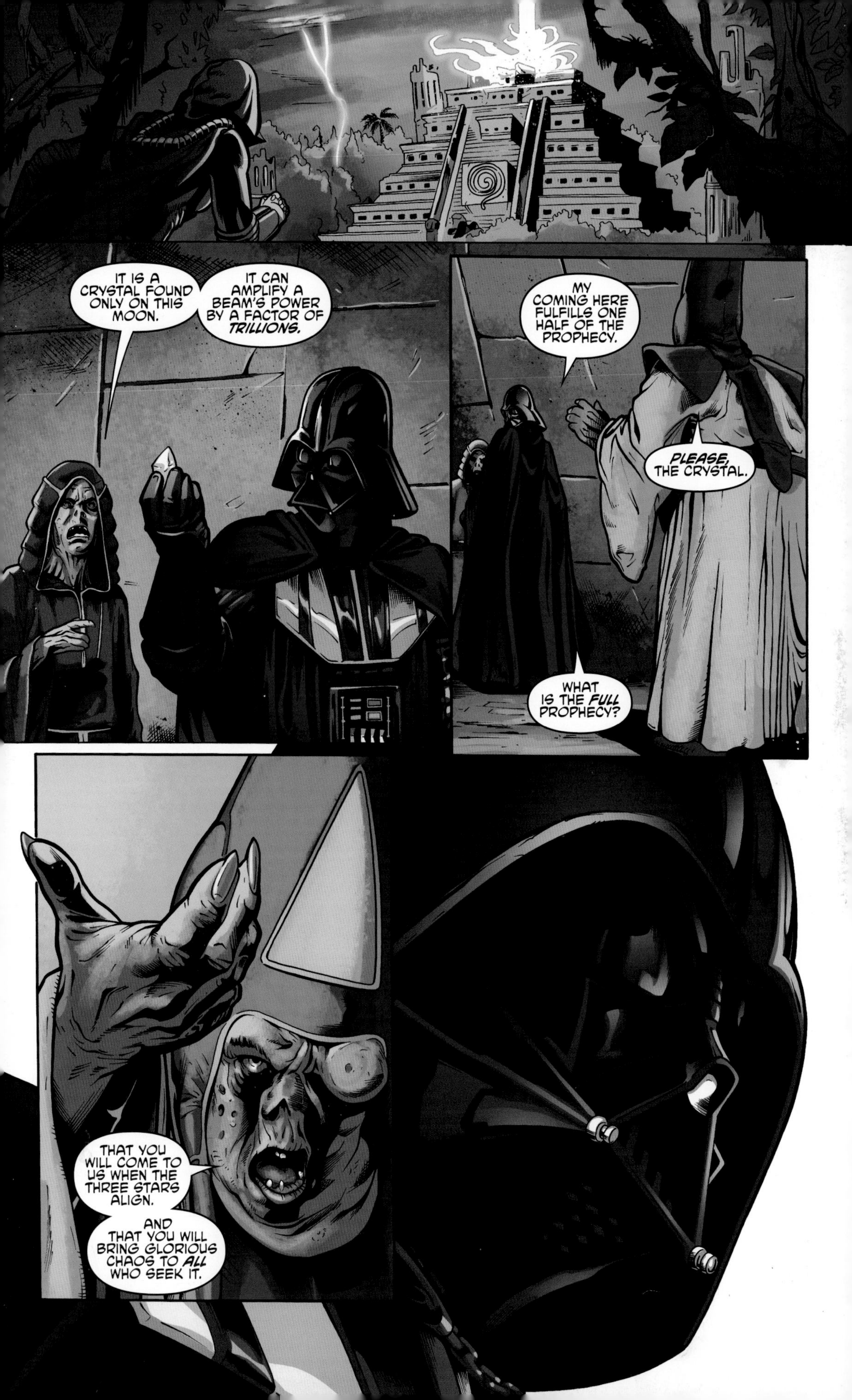
IT IS A CRYSTAL FOUND ONLY ON THIS MOON.
IT CAN AMPLIFY A BEAM'S POWER BY A FACTOR OF *TRILLIONS.*
MY COMING HERE FULFILLS ONE HALF OF THE PROPHECY.
PLEASE, THE CRYSTAL.
WHAT IS THE *FULL* PROPHECY?
THAT YOU WILL COME TO US WHEN THE THREE STARS ALIGN.
AND THAT YOU WILL BRING GLORIOUS CHAOS TO *ALL* WHO SEEK IT.

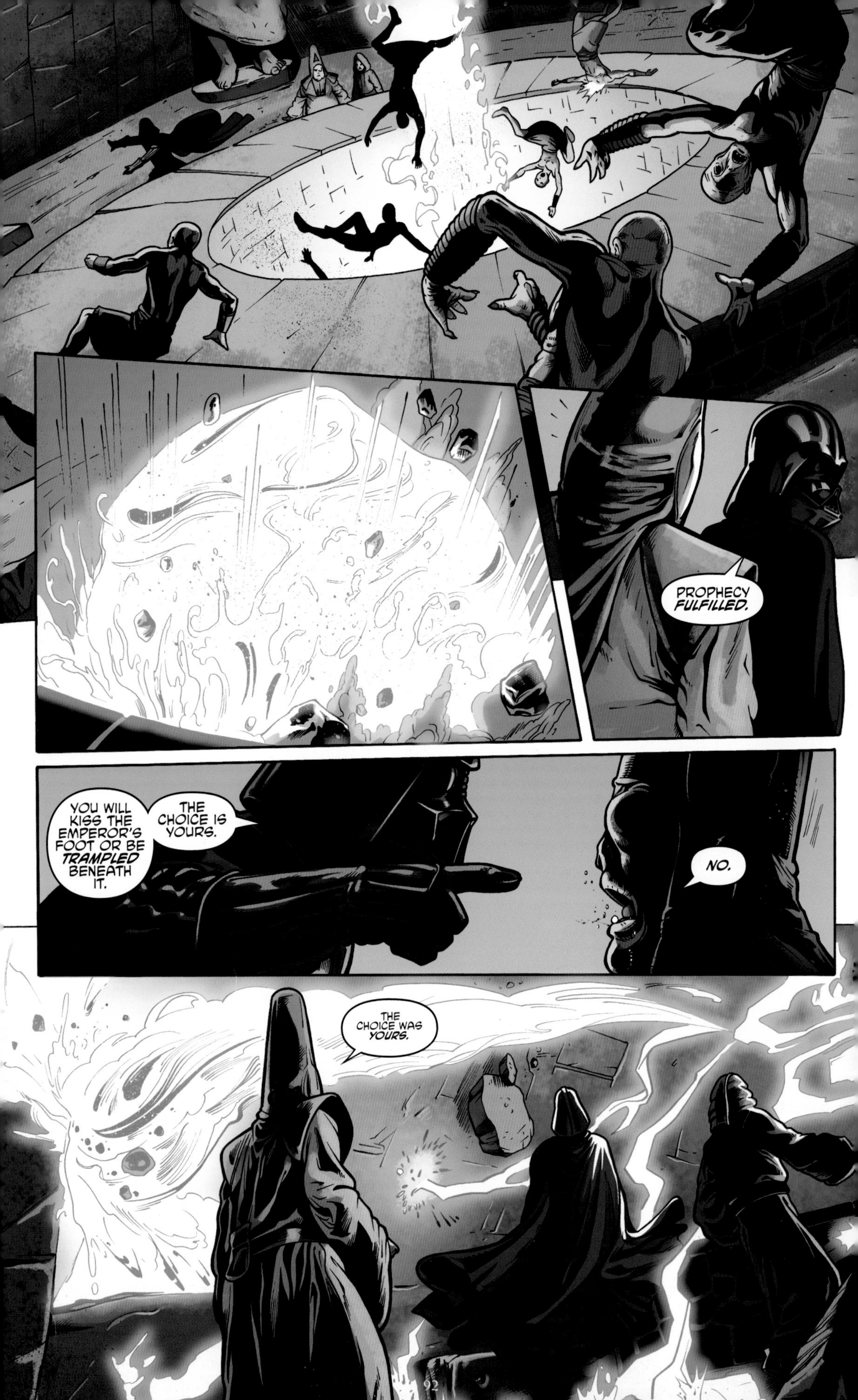
PROPHECY
FULFILLED.
YOU WILL KISS THE EMPEROR'S FOOT OR BE TRAMPLED BENEATH IT.
THE CHOICE IS YOURS.
NO.
THE CHOICE WAS YOURS.

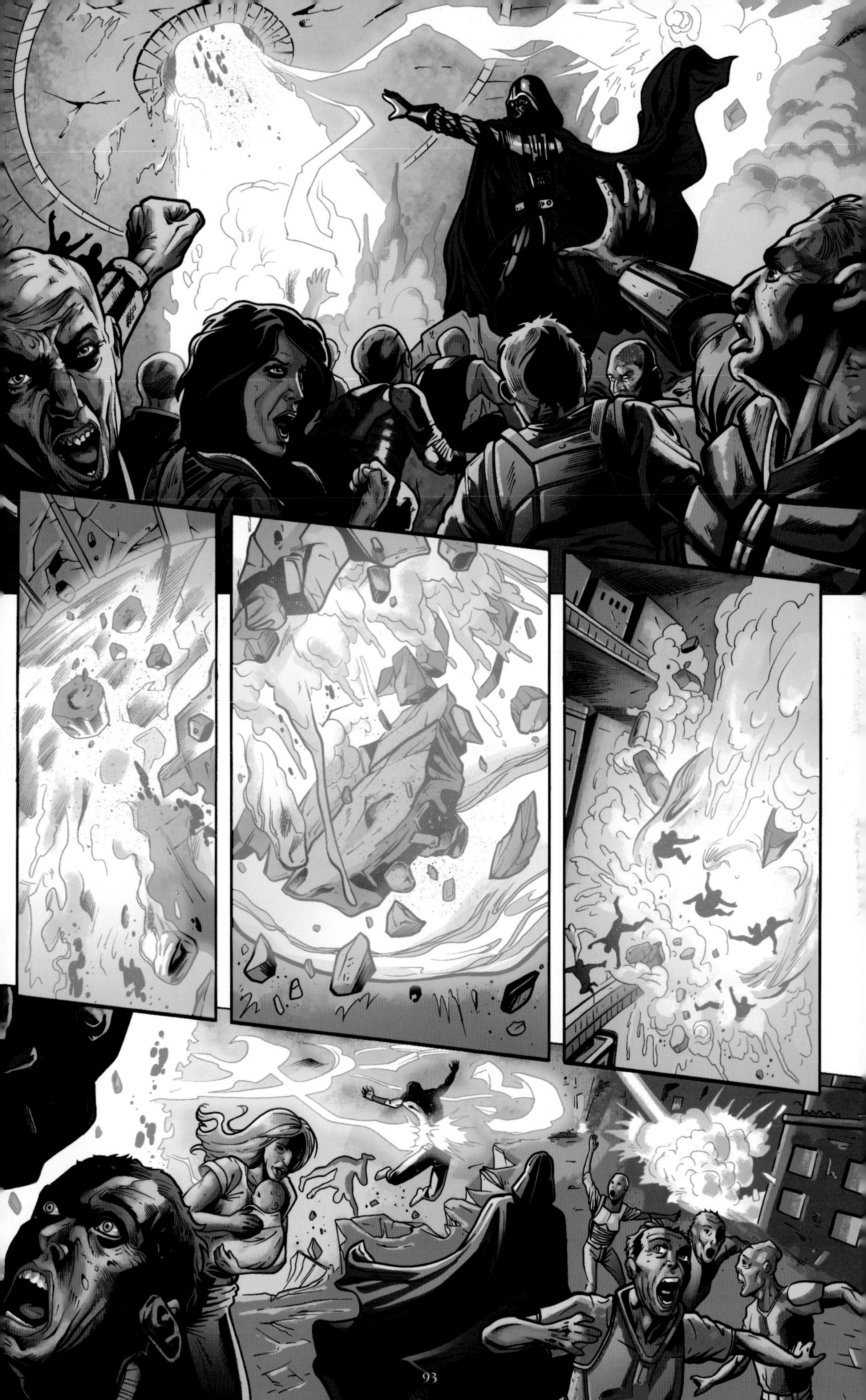

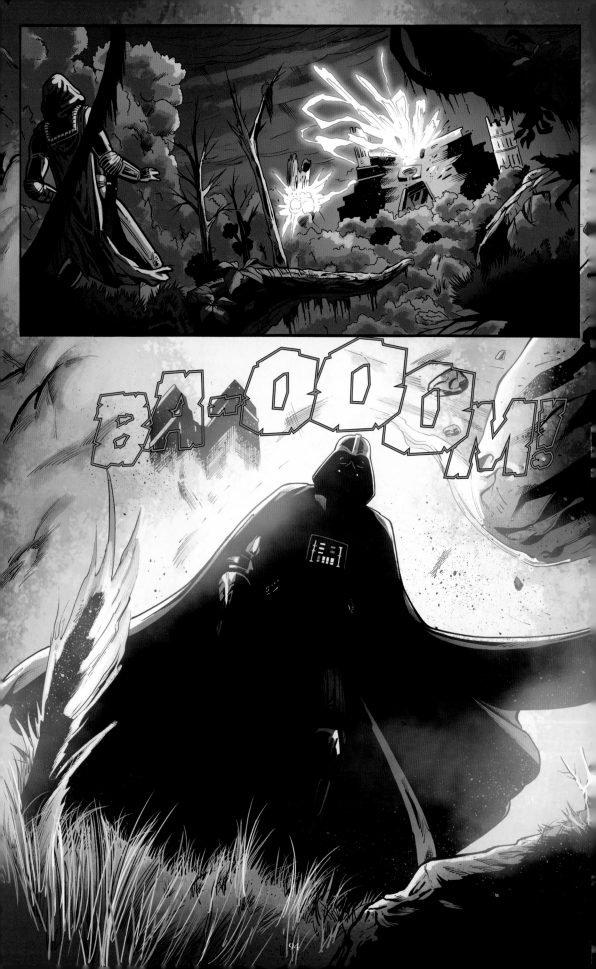

BA-OOOOM!

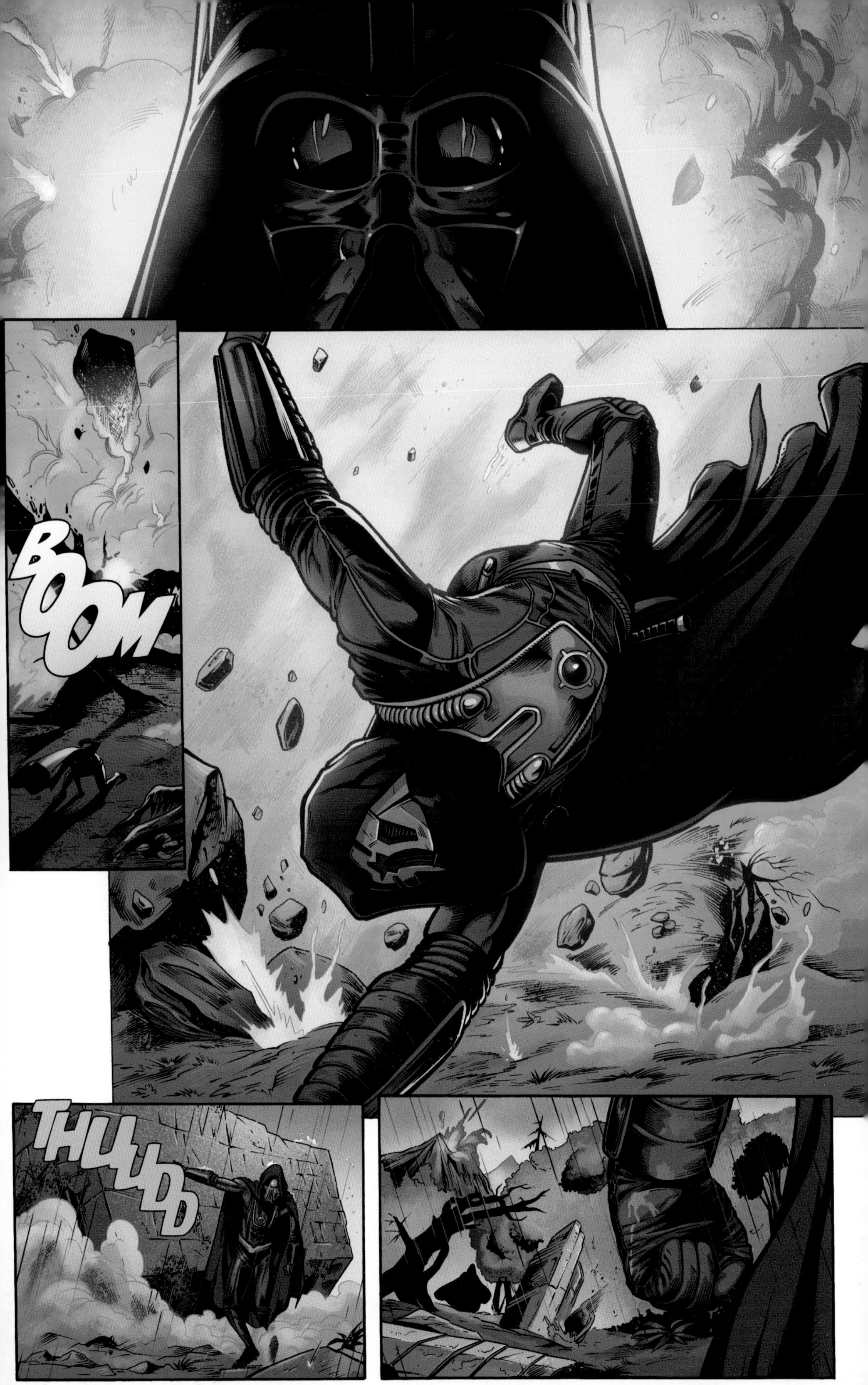
BOOM
THUDD

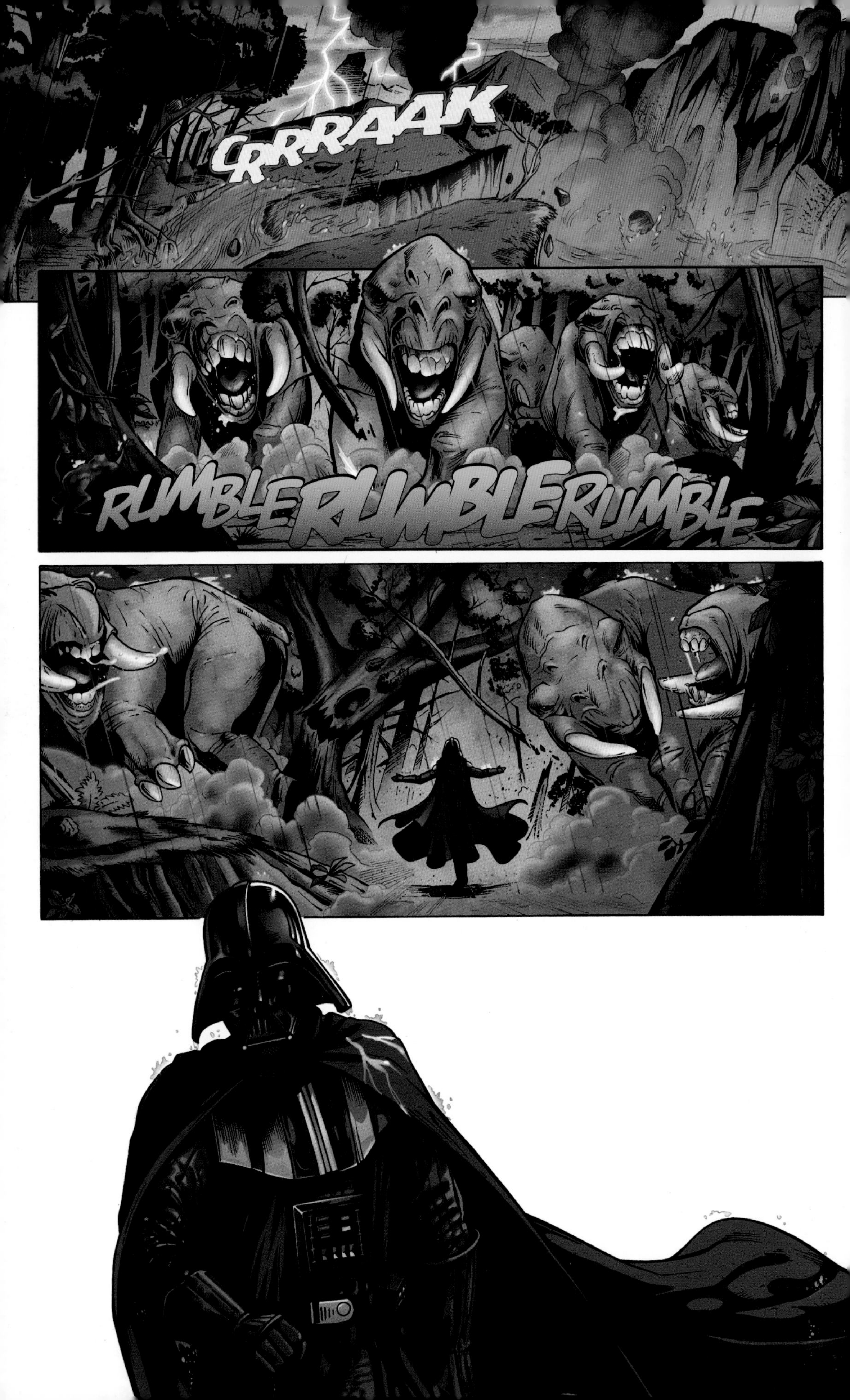
CRRRAAK
RUMBLE RUMBLE RUMBLE

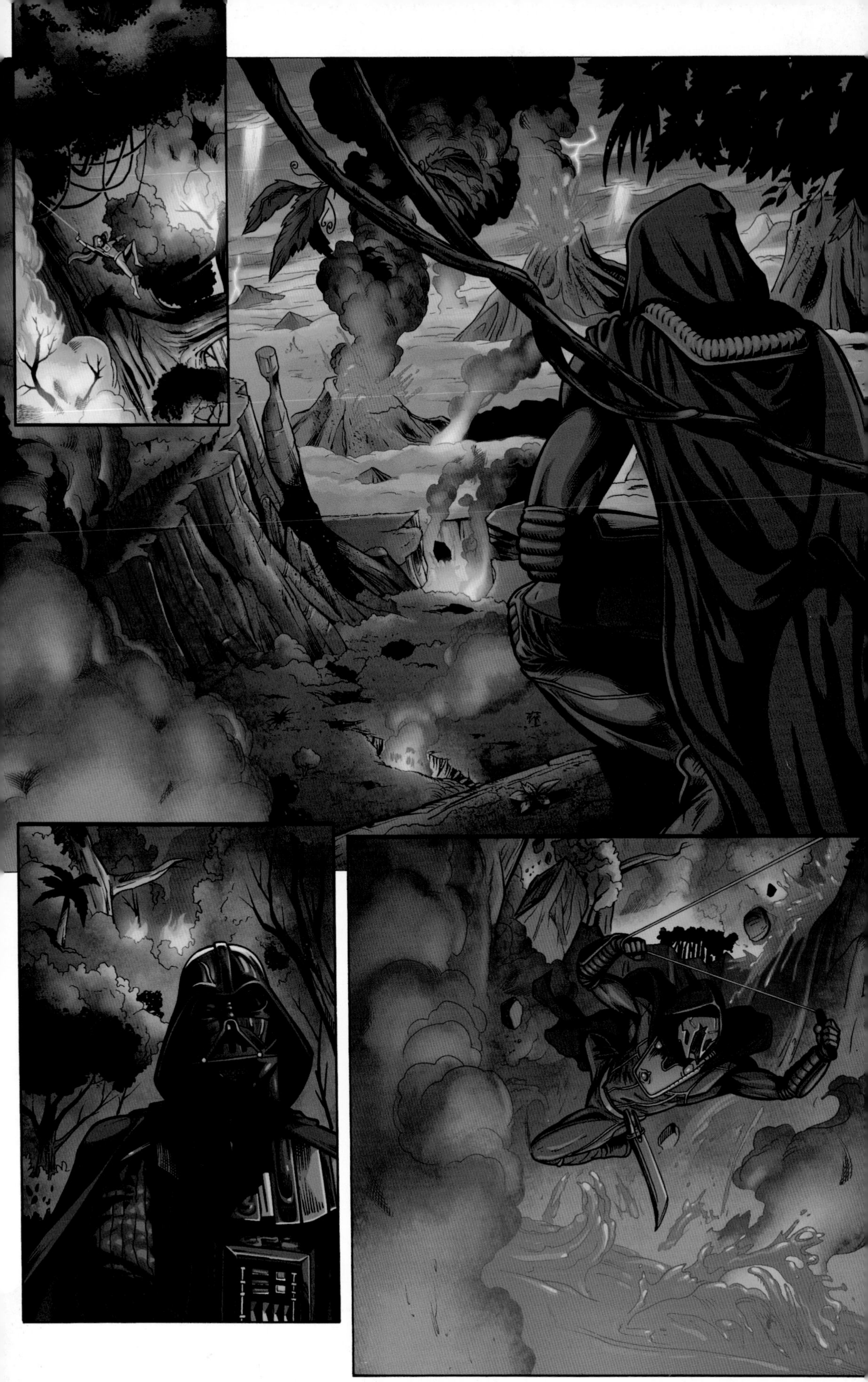

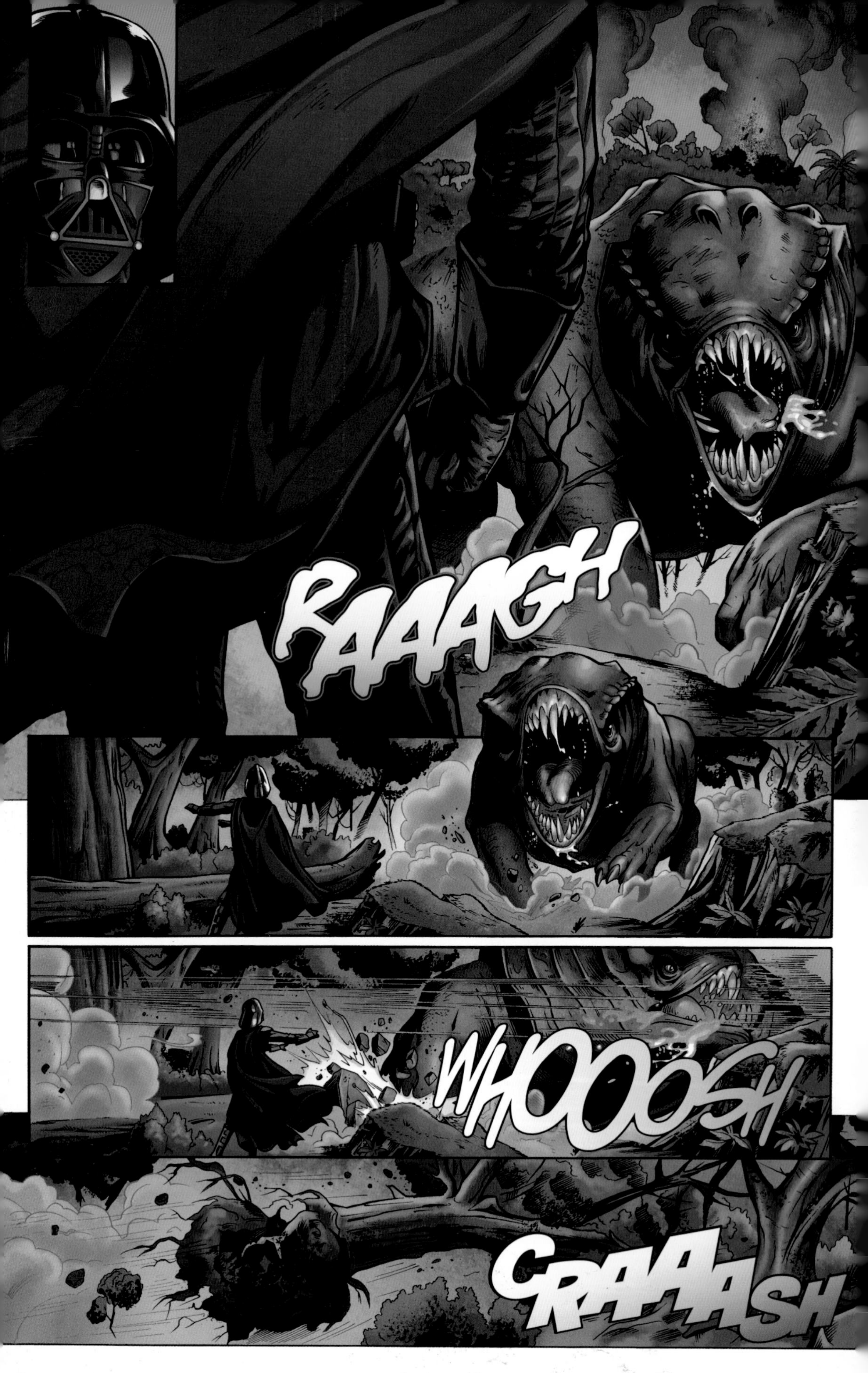
RAAAGH
WHOOOSH
CRAAAASH

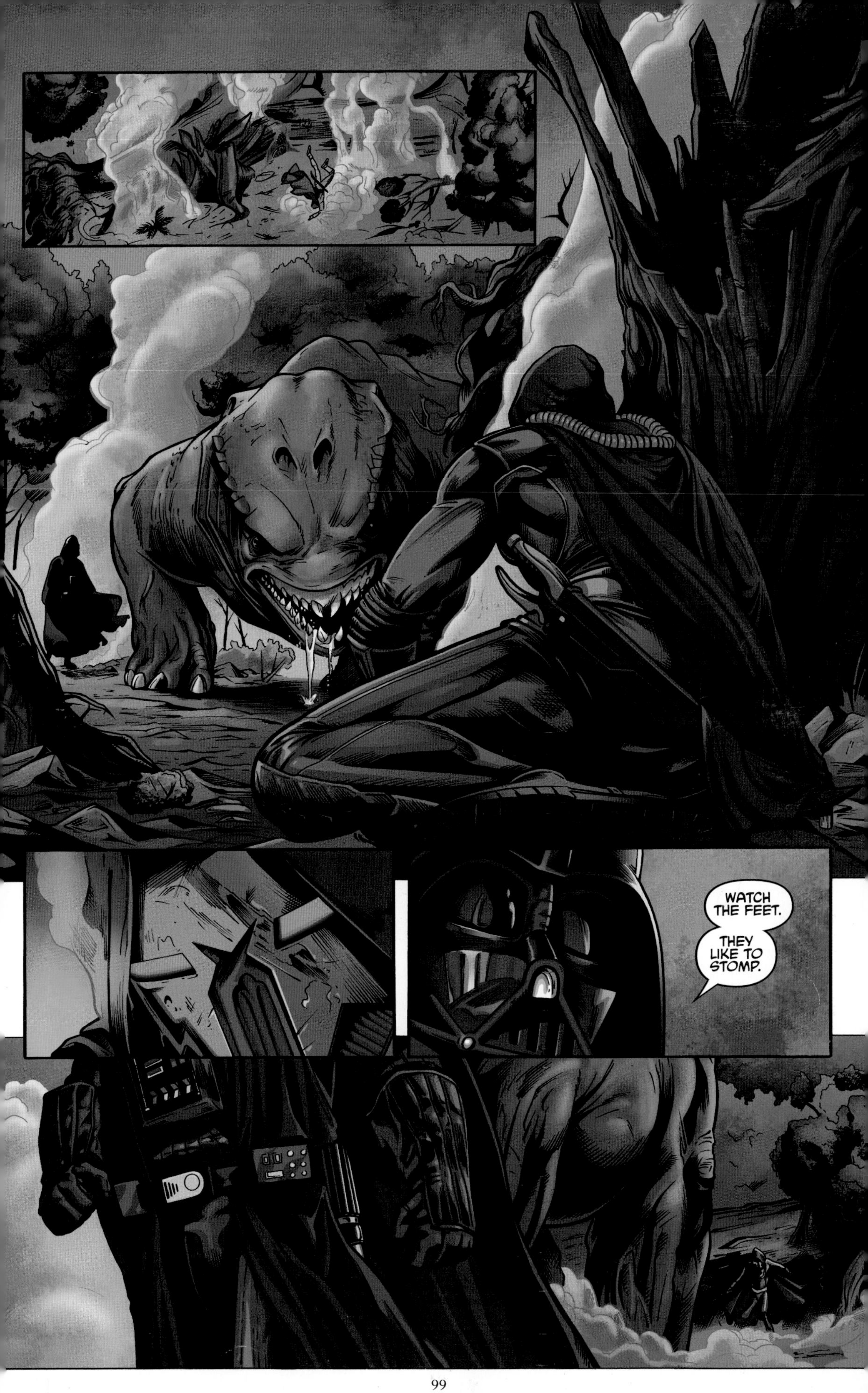
WATCH THE FEET.
THEY LIKE TO STOMP.

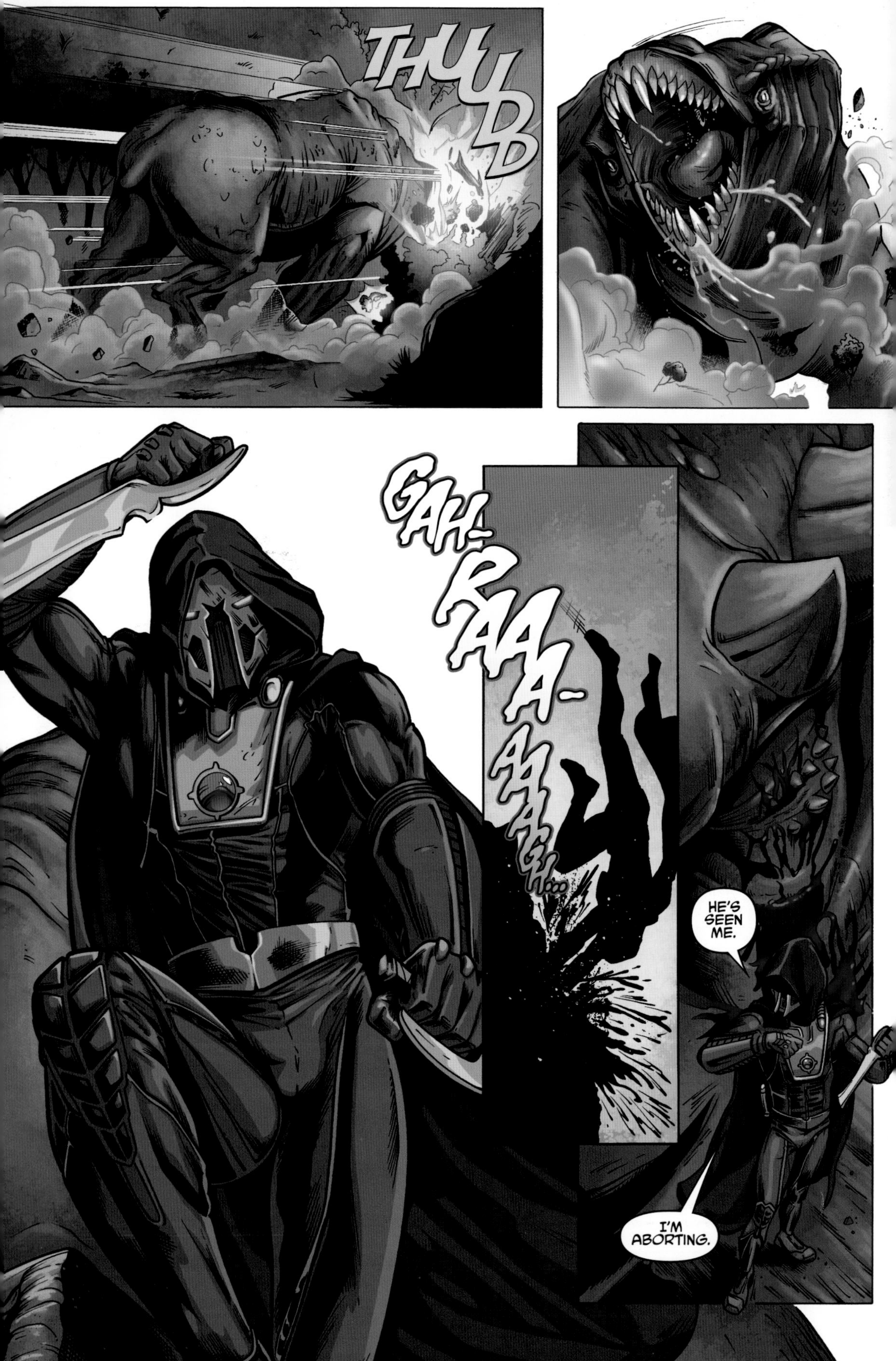
THUUDD
GAH-RAAA-AAAGH...
HE'S SEEN ME.
I'M ABORTING.

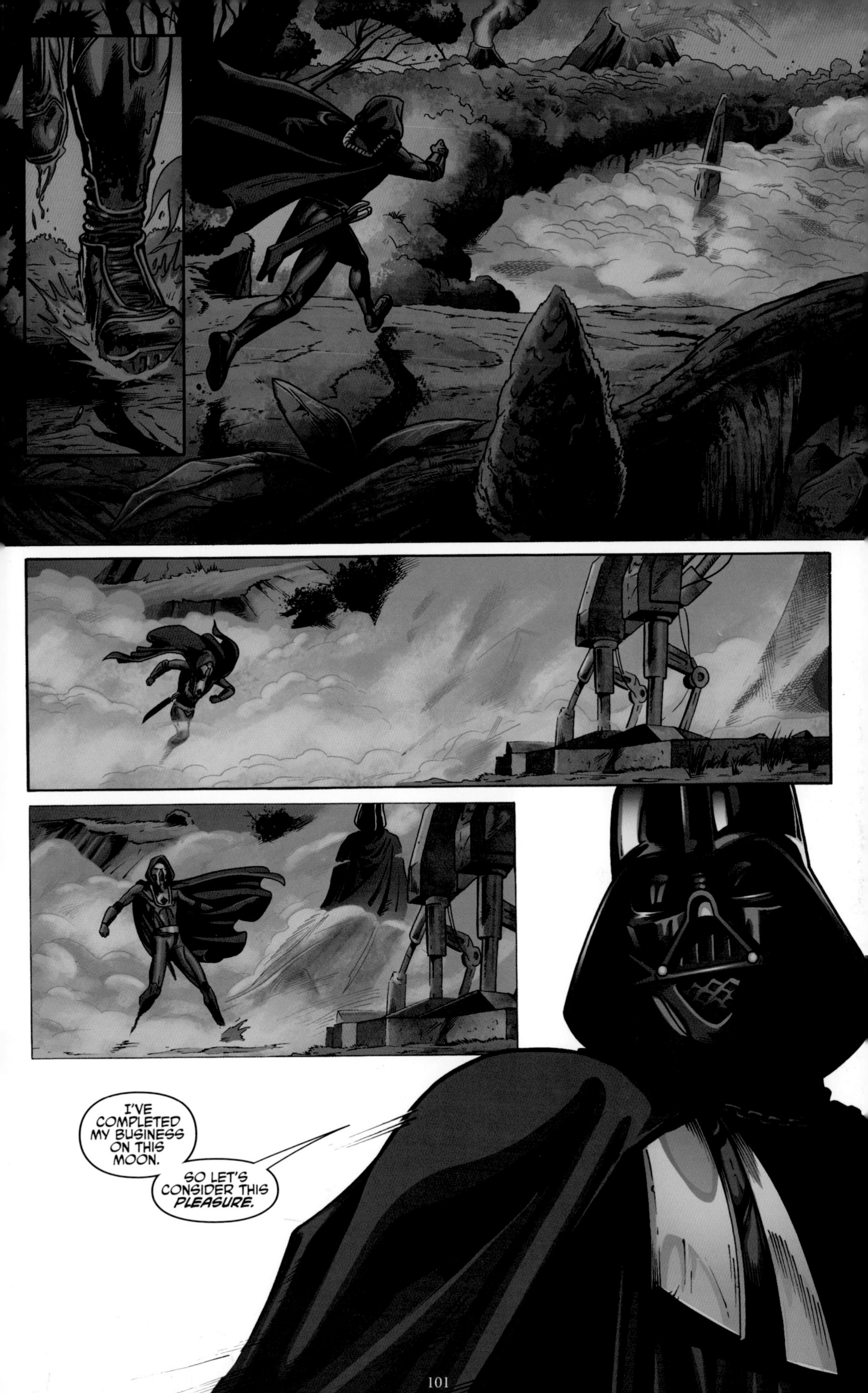
I'VE COMPLETED MY BUSINESS ON THIS MOON.
SO LET'S CONSIDER THIS *PLEASURE.*

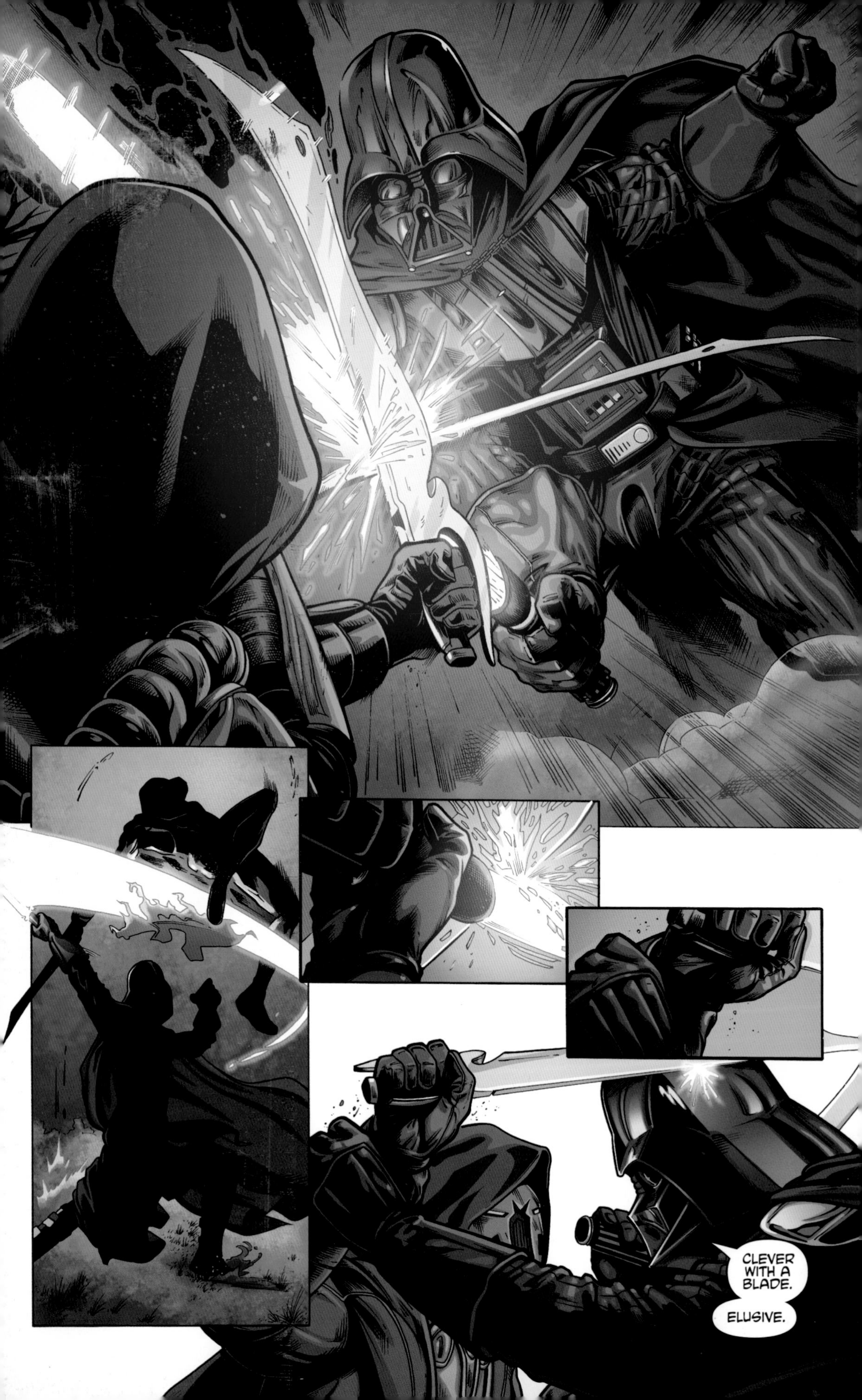
CLEVER WITH A BLADE.
ELUSIVE.

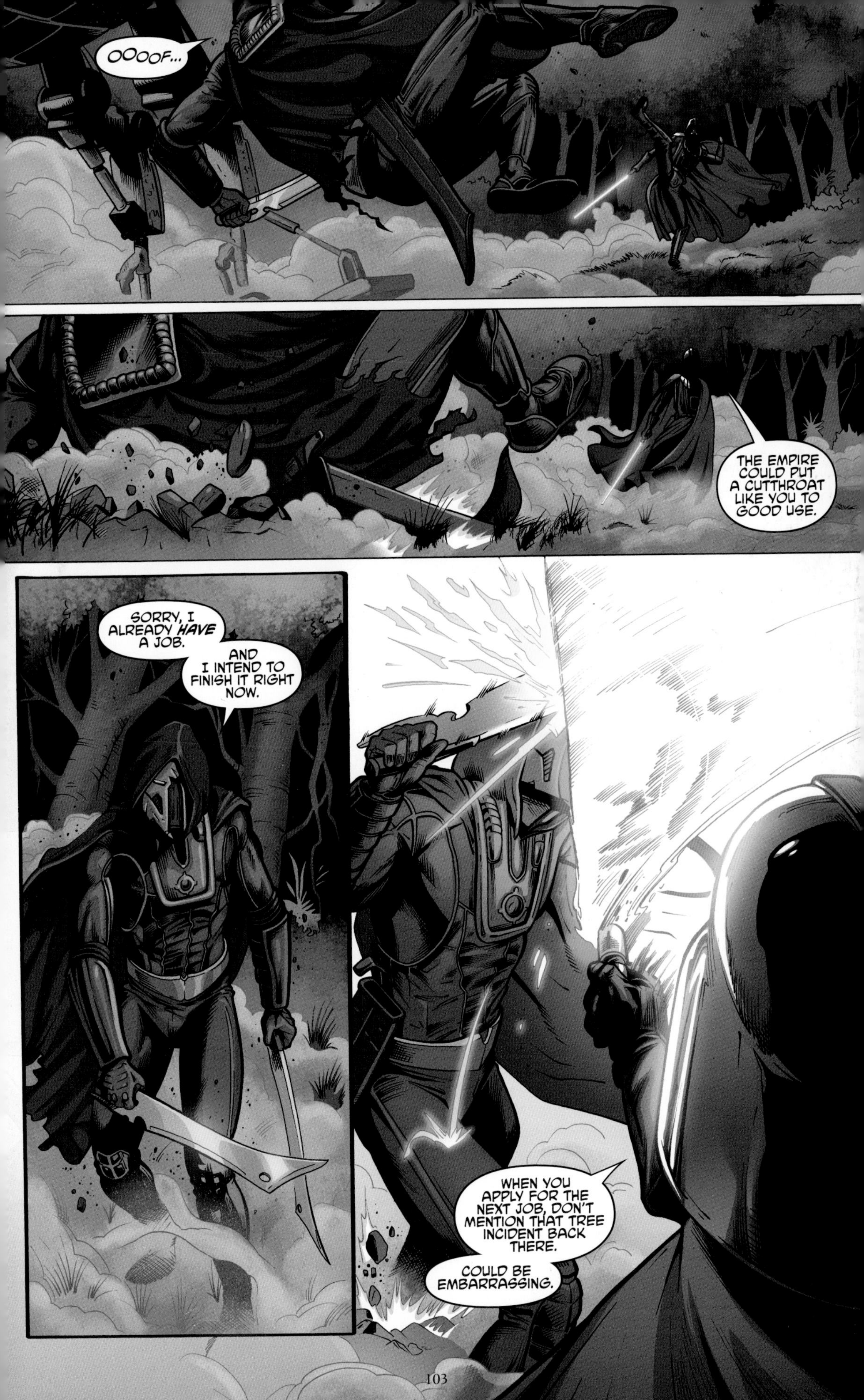
OOOOF...
THE EMPIRE COULD PUT A CUTTHROAT LIKE YOU TO GOOD USE.
SORRY, I ALREADY HAVE A JOB.
AND I INTEND TO FINISH IT RIGHT NOW.
WHEN YOU APPLY FOR THE NEXT JOB, DON'T MENTION THAT TREE INCIDENT BACK THERE.
COULD BE EMBARRASSING.

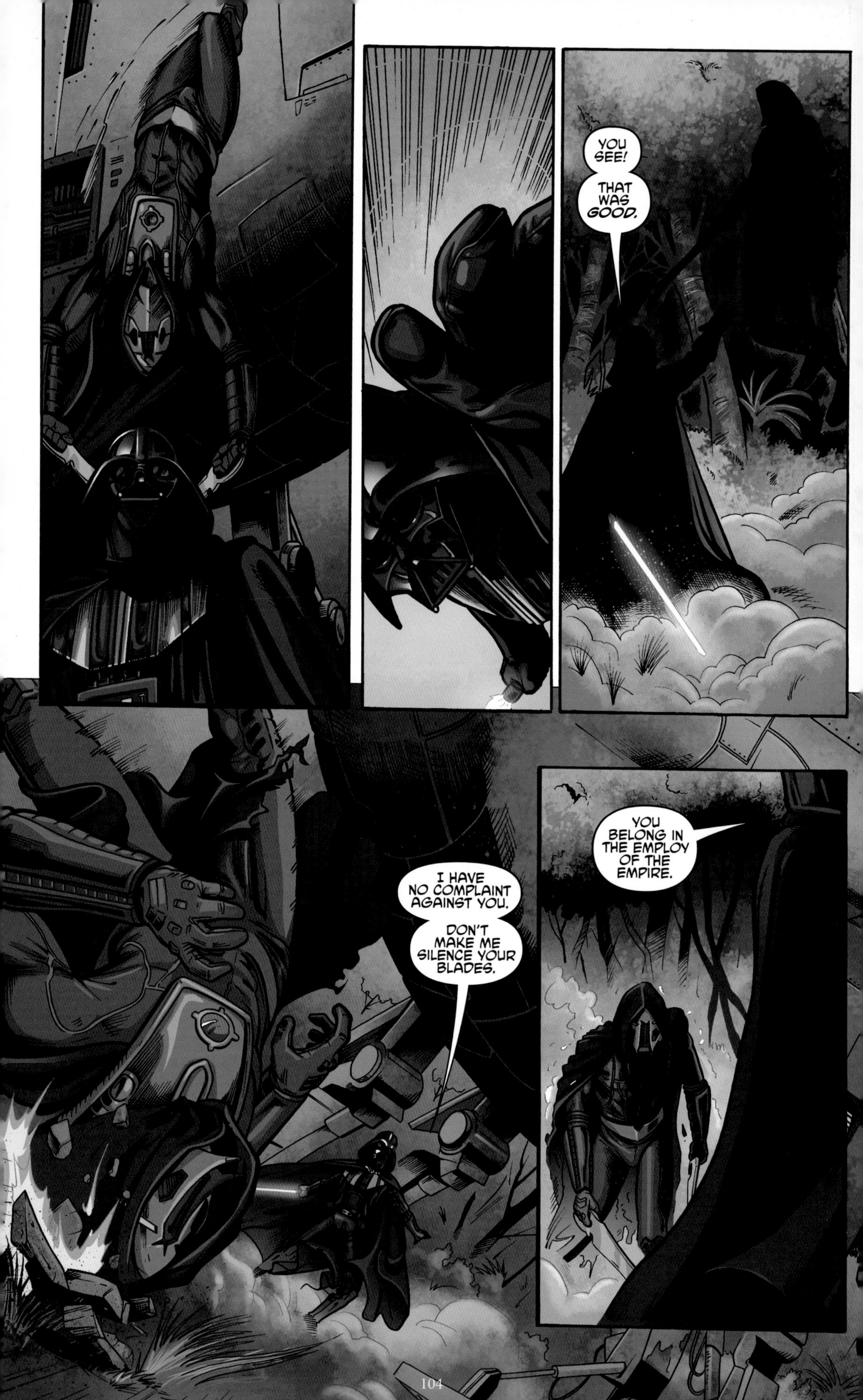

YOU SEE!
THAT WAS GOOD.
I HAVE NO COMPLAINT AGAINST YOU.
DON'T MAKE ME SILENCE YOUR BLADES.
YOU BELONG IN THE EMPLOY OF THE EMPIRE.

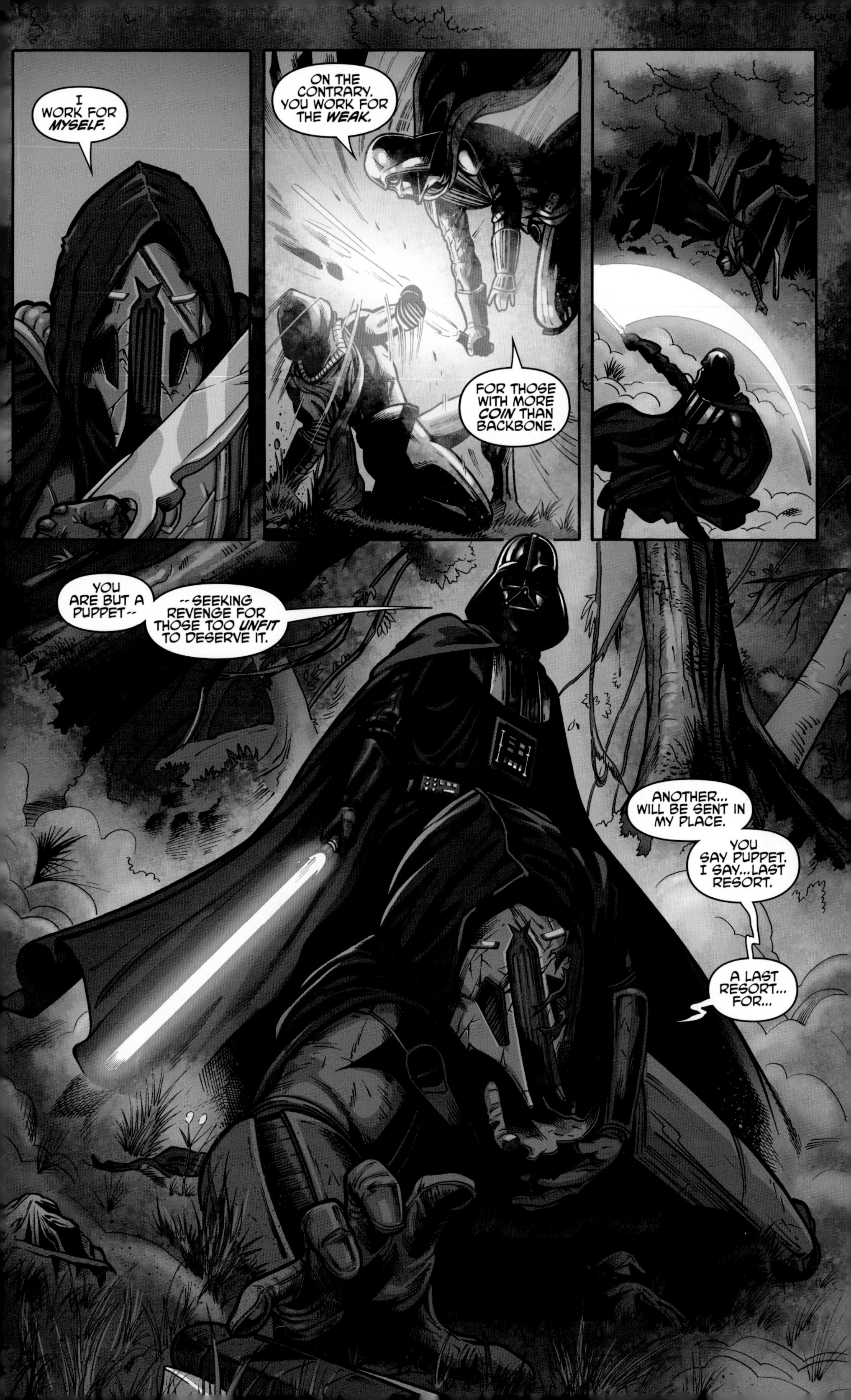

I WORK FOR *MYSELF.*
ON THE CONTRARY. YOU WORK FOR THE *WEAK.*
FOR THOSE WITH MORE *COIN* THAN BACKBONE.
YOU ARE BUT A PUPPET--
--SEEKING REVENGE FOR THOSE TOO *UNFIT* TO DESERVE IT.
ANOTHER... WILL BE SENT IN MY PLACE.
YOU SAY PUPPET. I SAY...LAST RESORT.
A LAST RESORT... FOR...

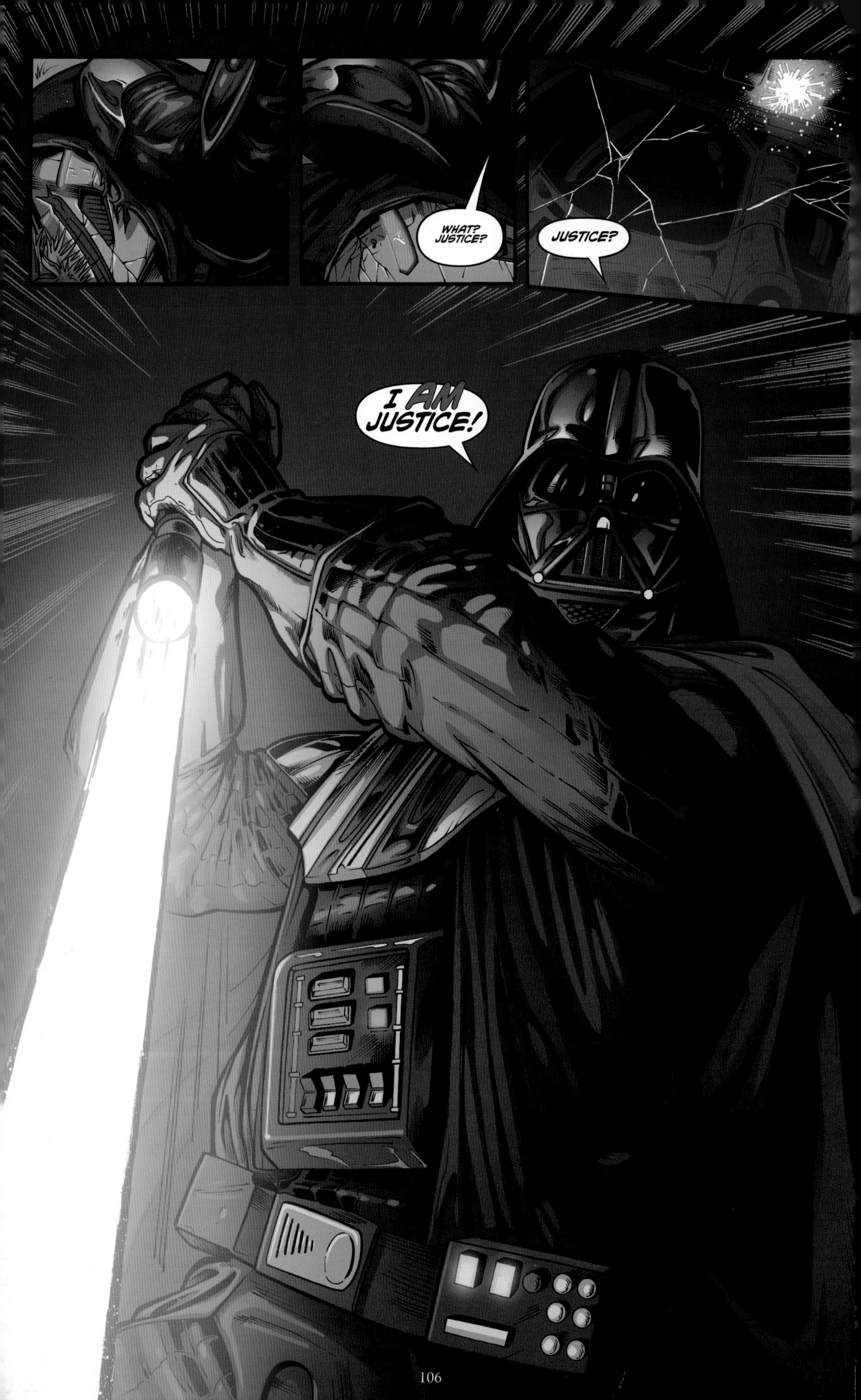
WHAT? JUSTICE?
JUSTICE?
I AM JUSTICE!

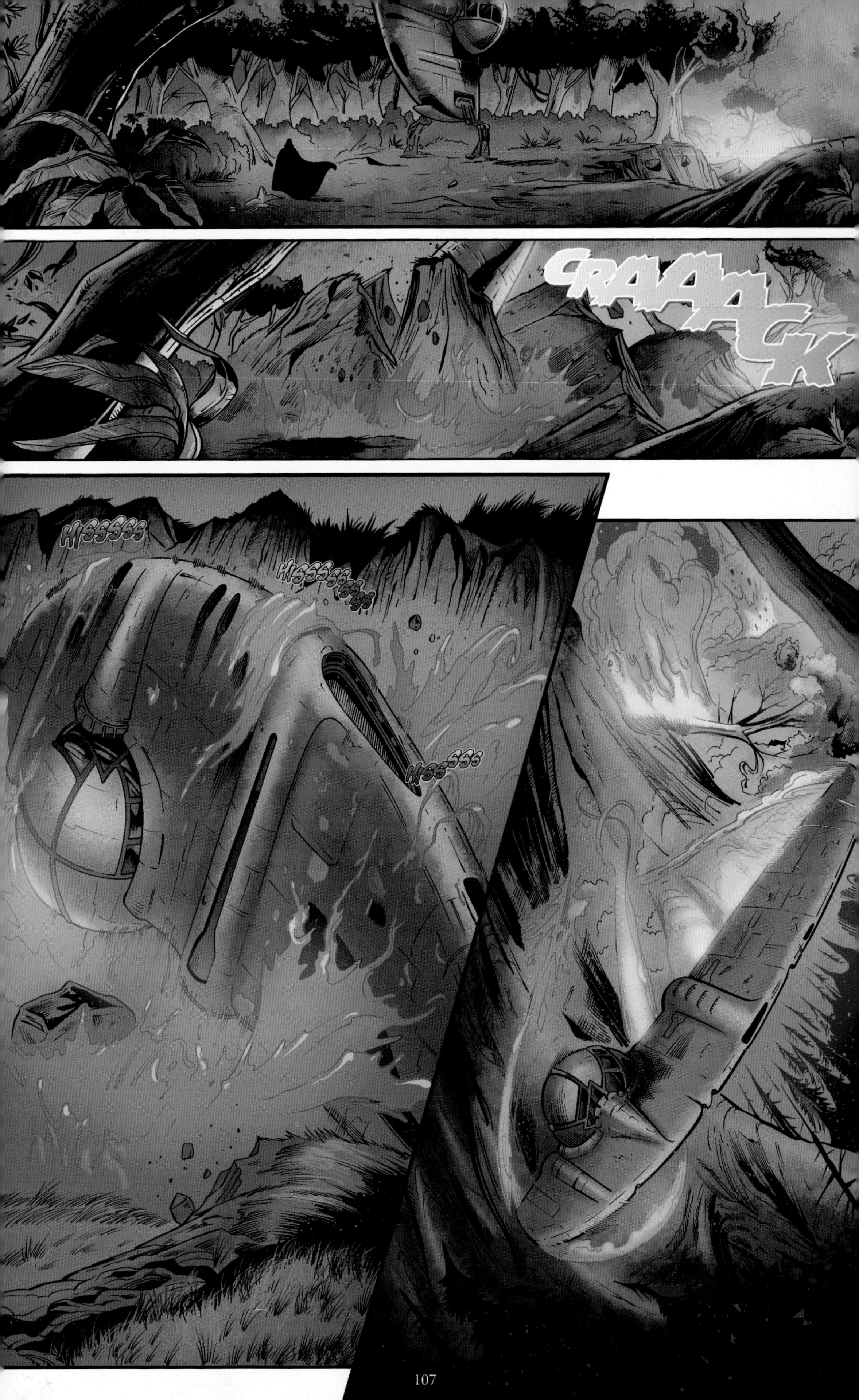
CRAAAACK
HISSSSS
HISSSSSSSSS
HISSSSS

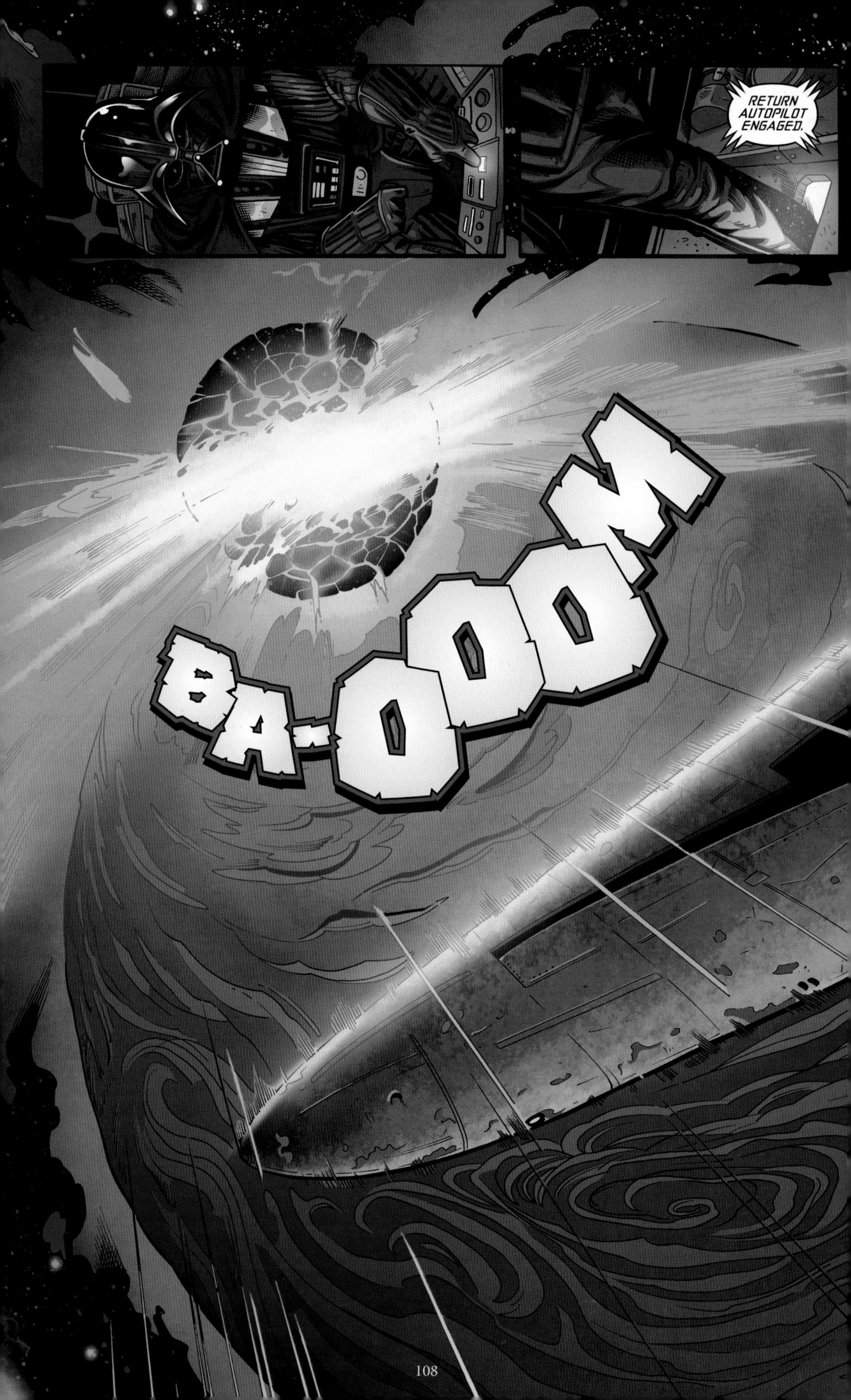
RETURN AUTOPILOT ENGAGED.
BA-OOOM

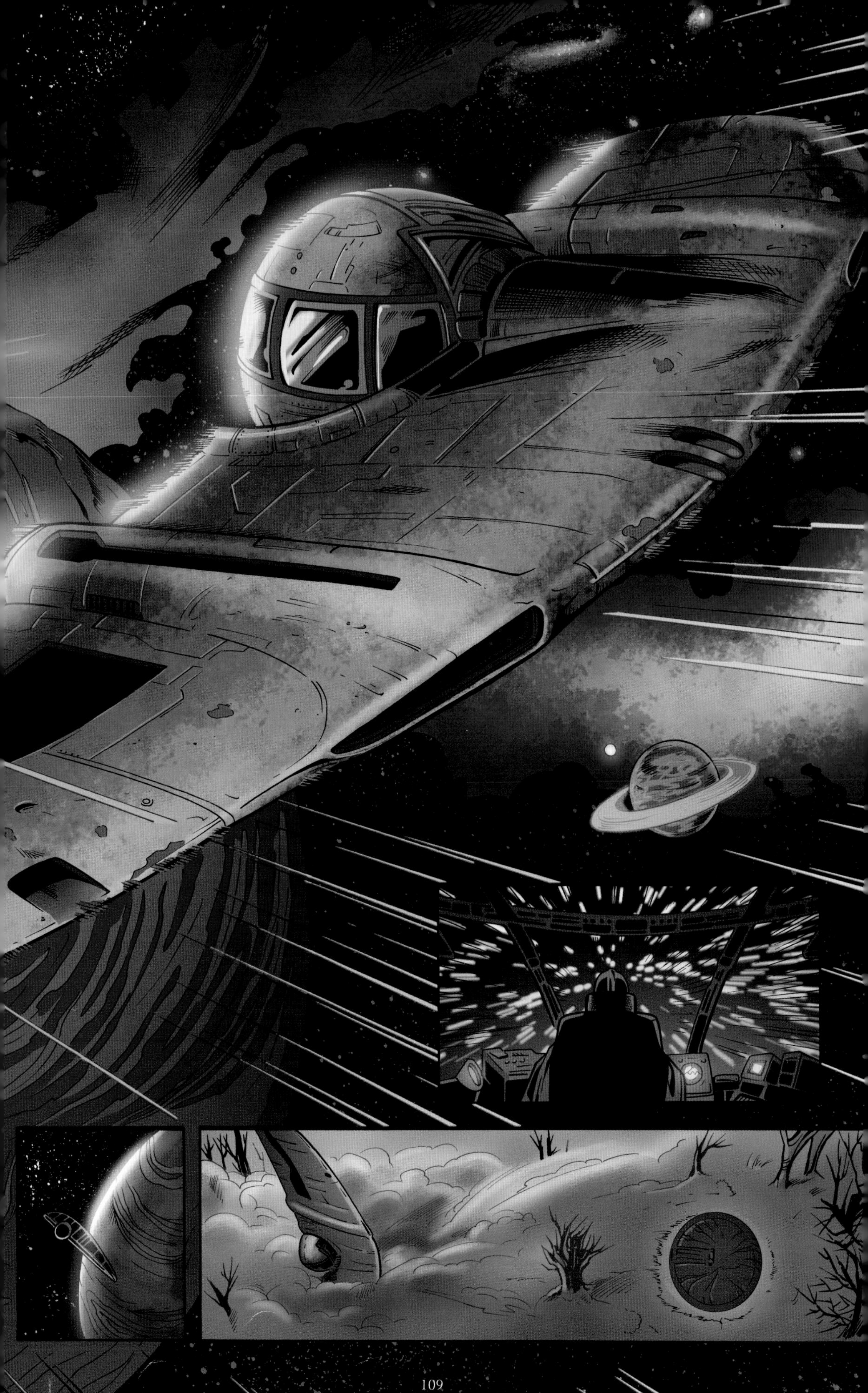

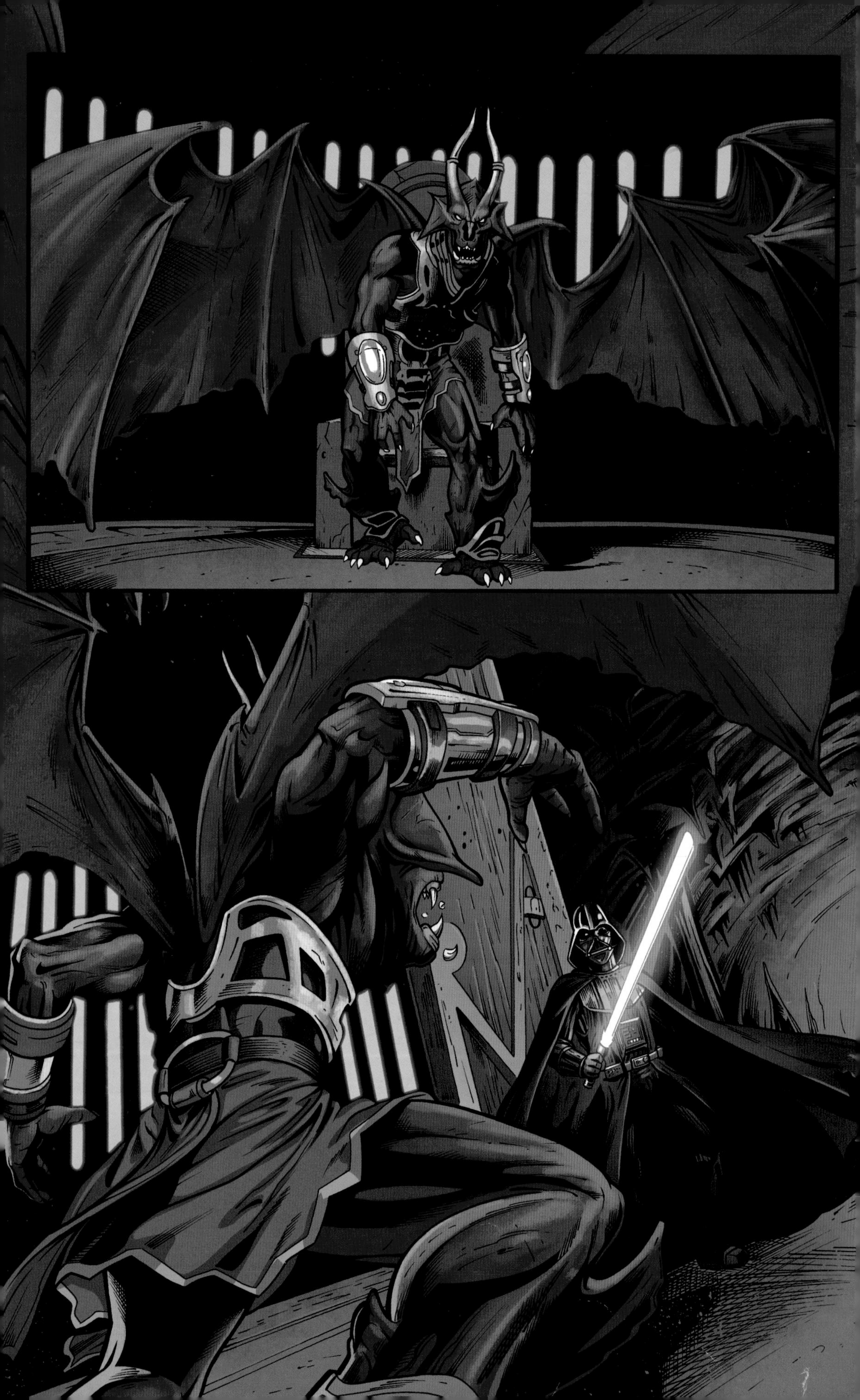

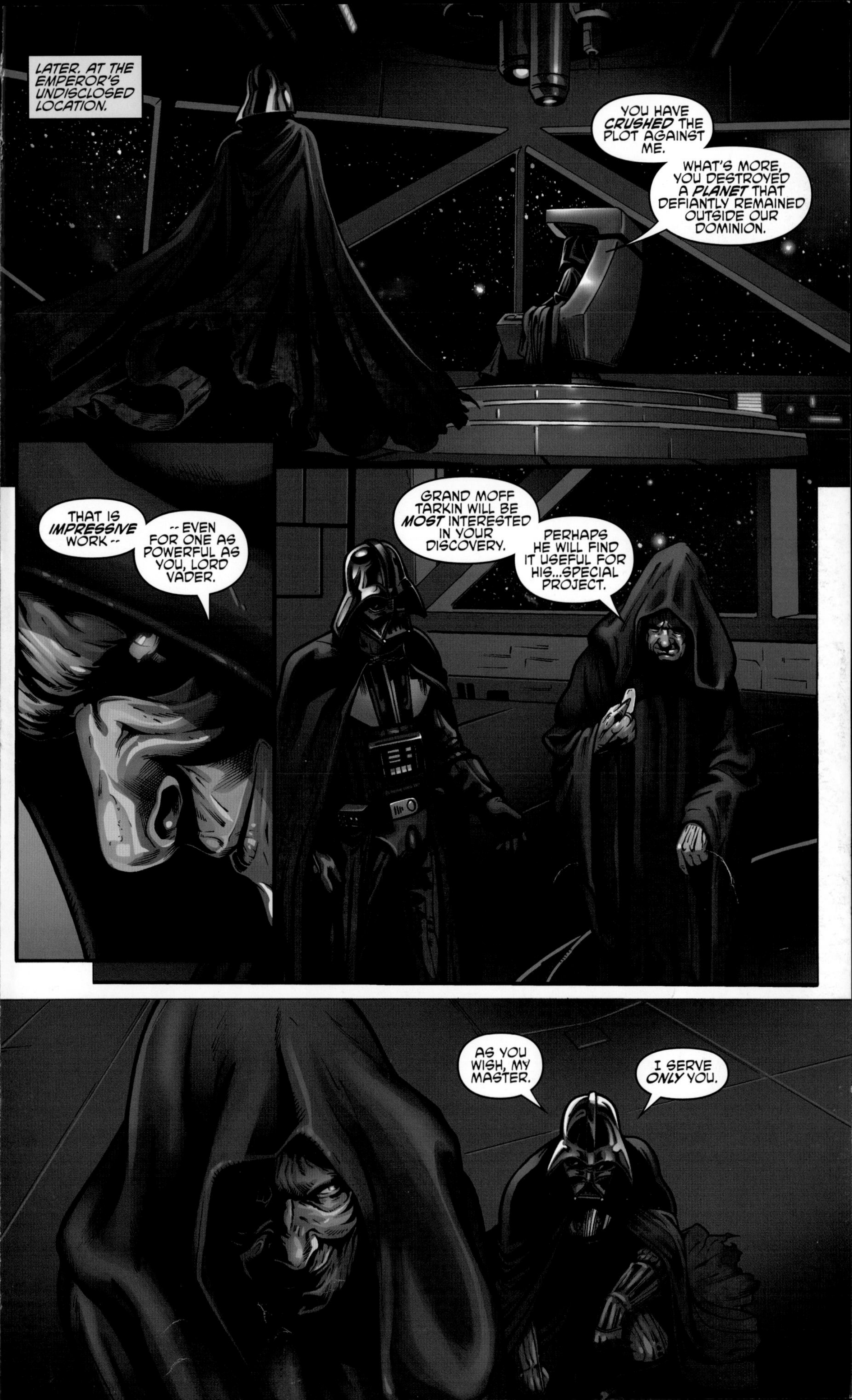
LATER. AT THE EMPEROR'S UNDISCLOSED LOCATION.
YOU HAVE CRUSHED THE PLOT AGAINST ME.
WHAT'S MORE, YOU DESTROYED A PLANET THAT DEFIANTLY REMAINED OUTSIDE OUR DOMINION.
THAT IS IMPRESSIVE WORK --
-- EVEN FOR ONE AS POWERFUL AS YOU, LORD VADER.
GRAND MOFF TARKIN WILL BE MOST INTERESTED IN YOUR DISCOVERY.
PERHAPS HE WILL FIND IT USEFUL FOR HIS...SPECIAL PROJECT.
AS YOU WISH, MY MASTER.
I SERVE ONLY YOU.

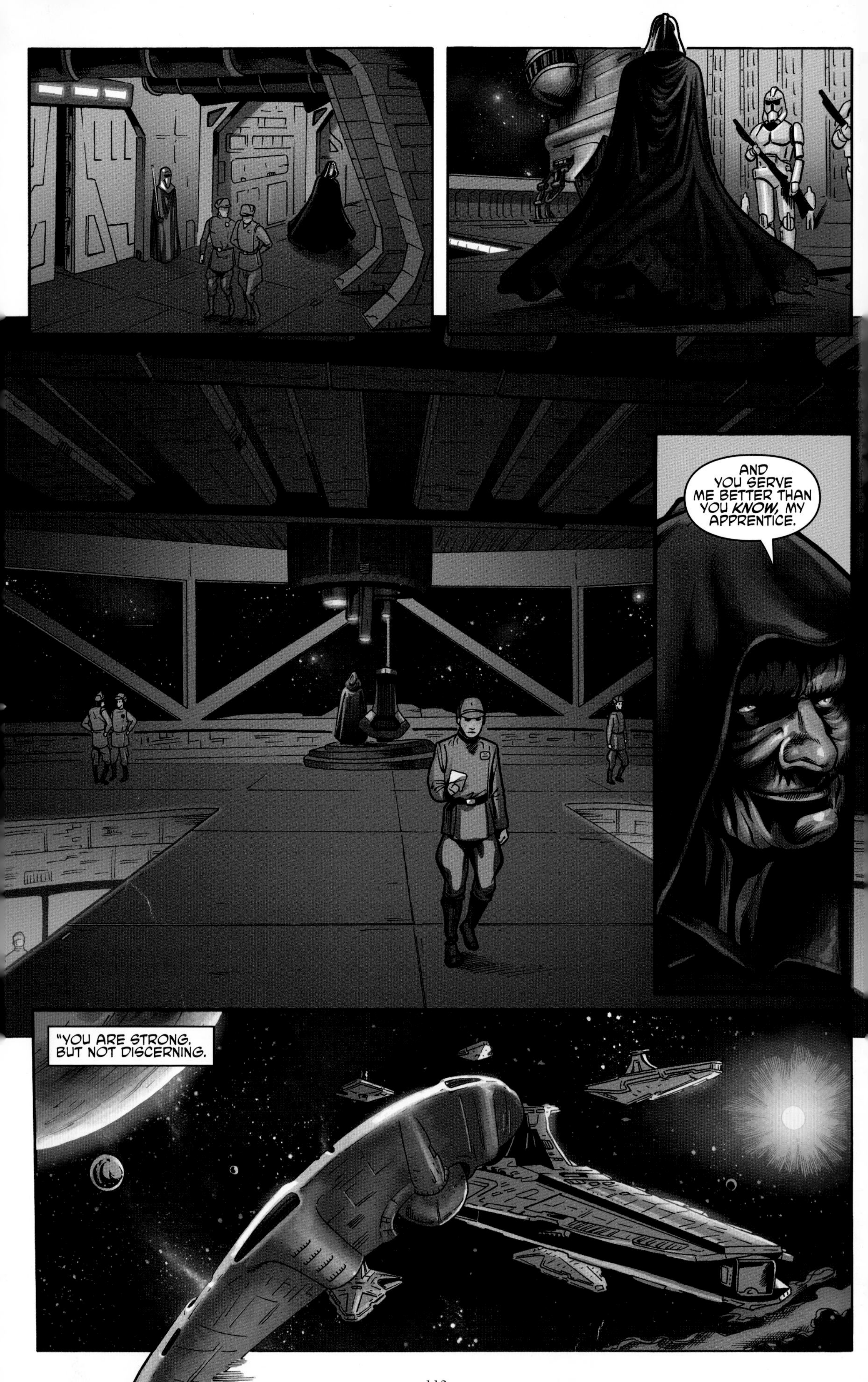
AND YOU SERVE ME BETTER THAN YOU KNOW, MY APPRENTICE.
"YOU ARE STRONG. BUT NOT DISCERNING.

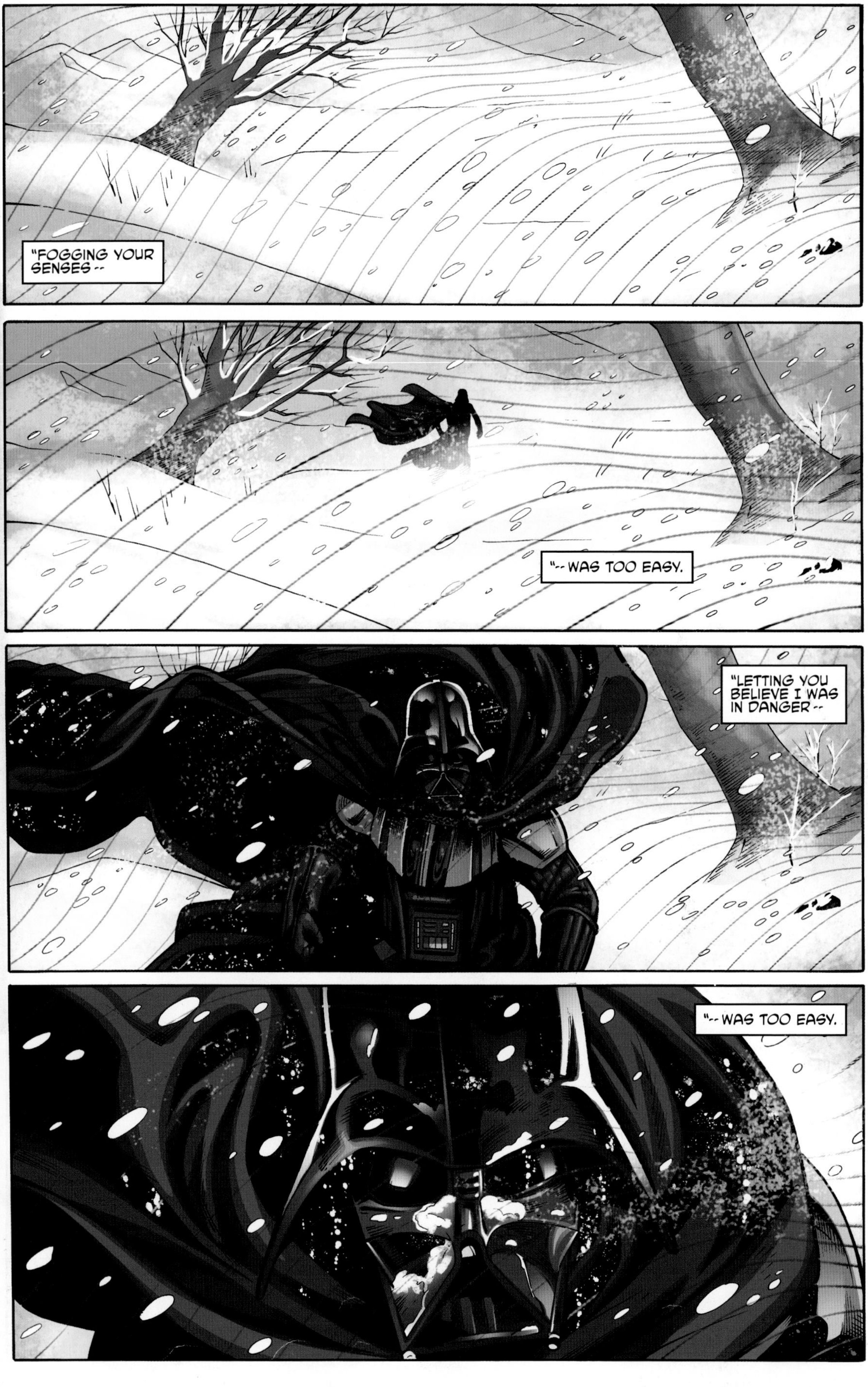
"FOGGING YOUR SENSES --
"-- WAS TOO EASY.
"LETTING YOU BELIEVE I WAS IN DANGER --
"-- WAS TOO EASY.

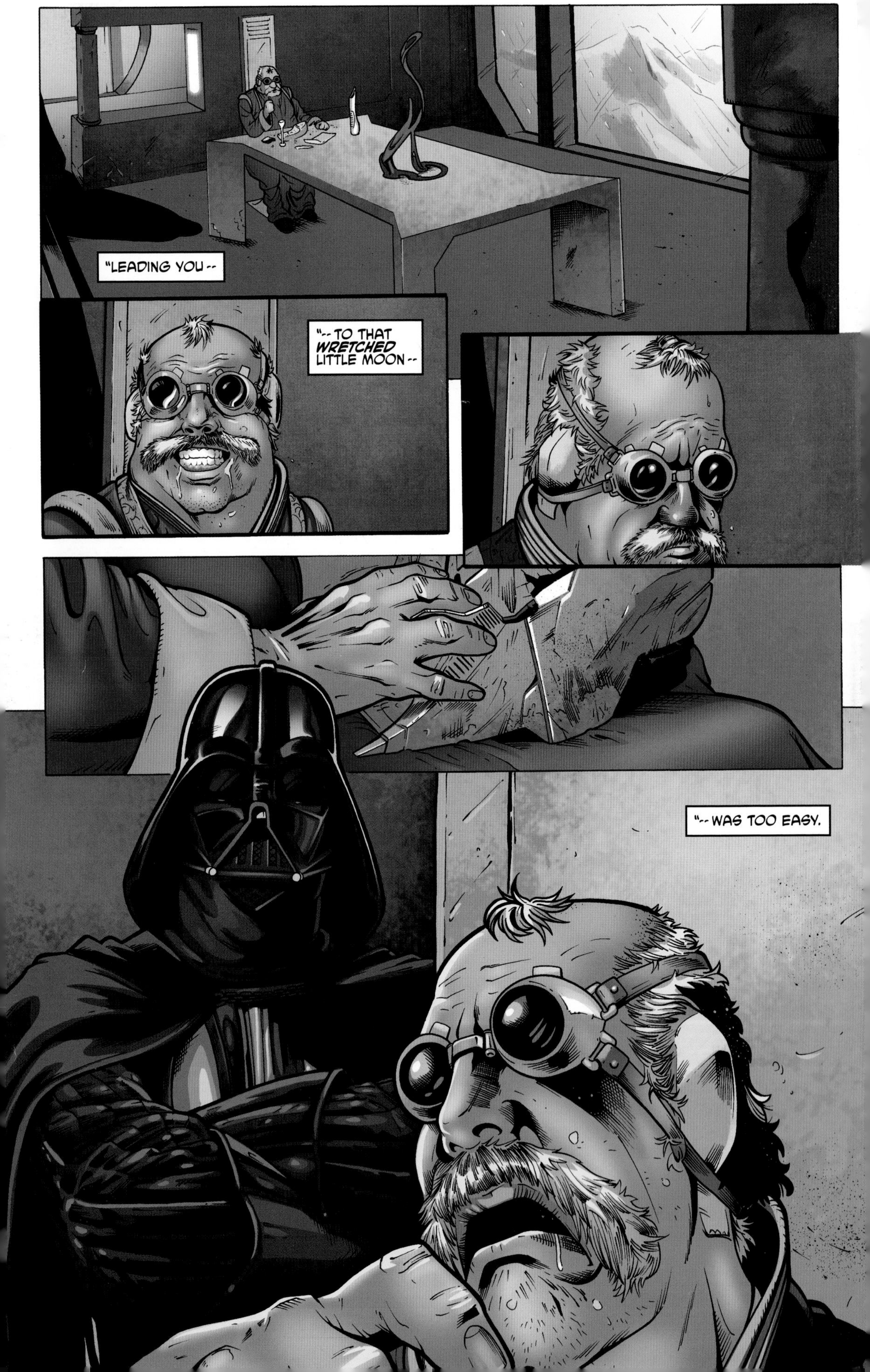
"LEADING YOU --
"-- TO THAT *WRETCHED* LITTLE MOON --
"-- WAS TOO EASY.

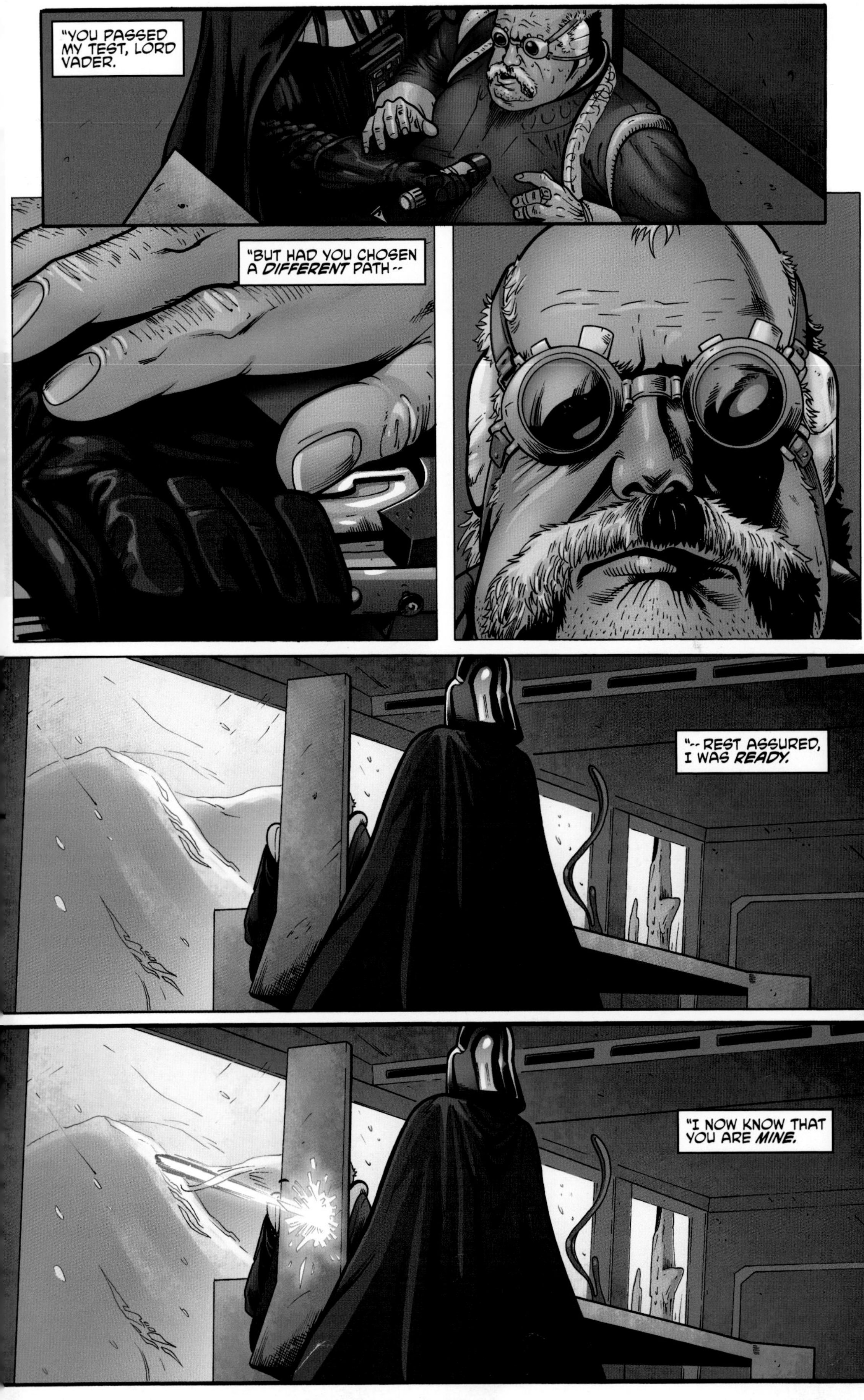
"YOU PASSED MY TEST, LORD VADER.
"BUT HAD YOU CHOSEN A *DIFFERENT* PATH--
"--REST ASSURED, I WAS *READY.*
"I NOW KNOW THAT YOU ARE *MINE.*

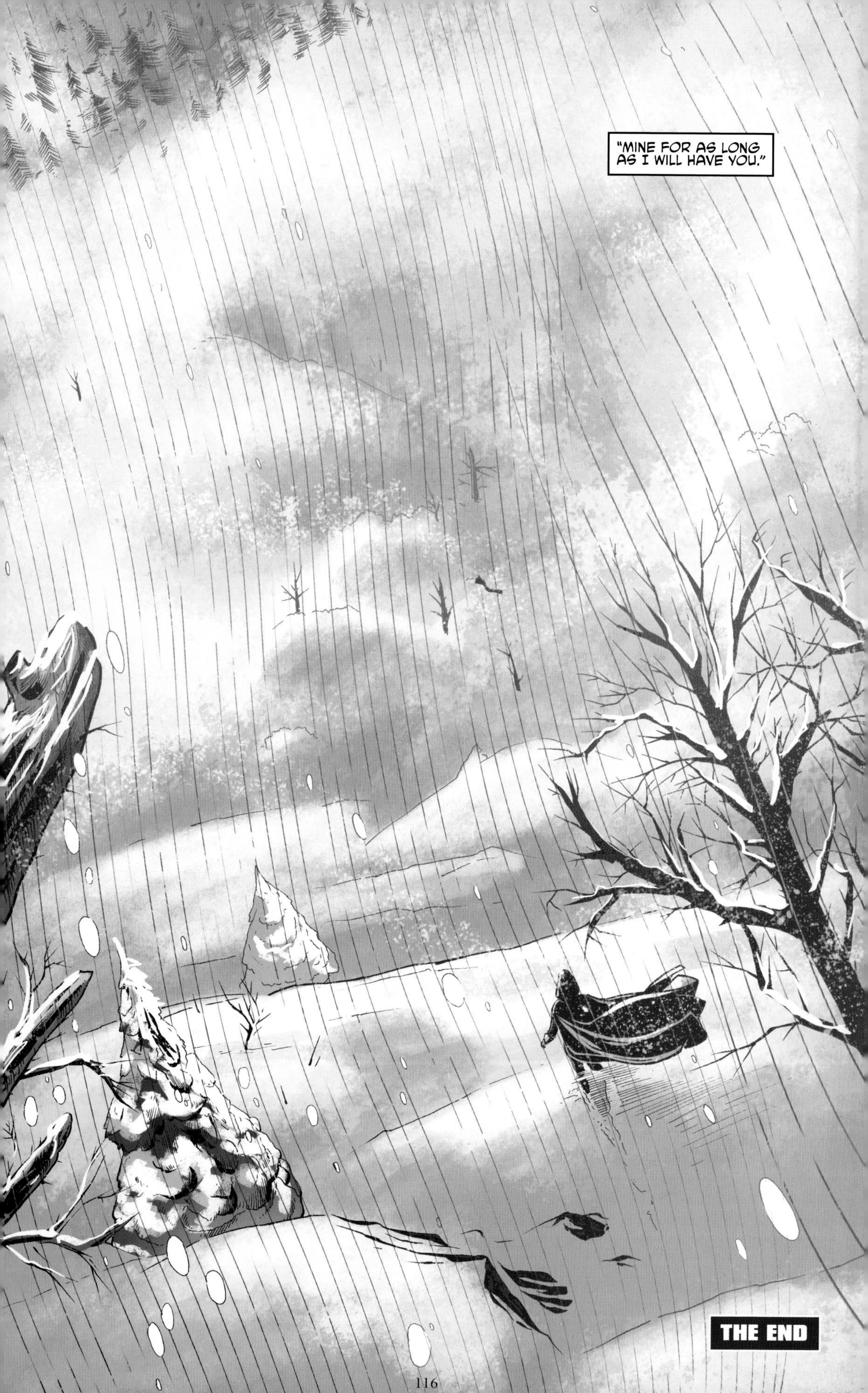
"MINE FOR AS LONG AS I WILL HAVE YOU."
THE END

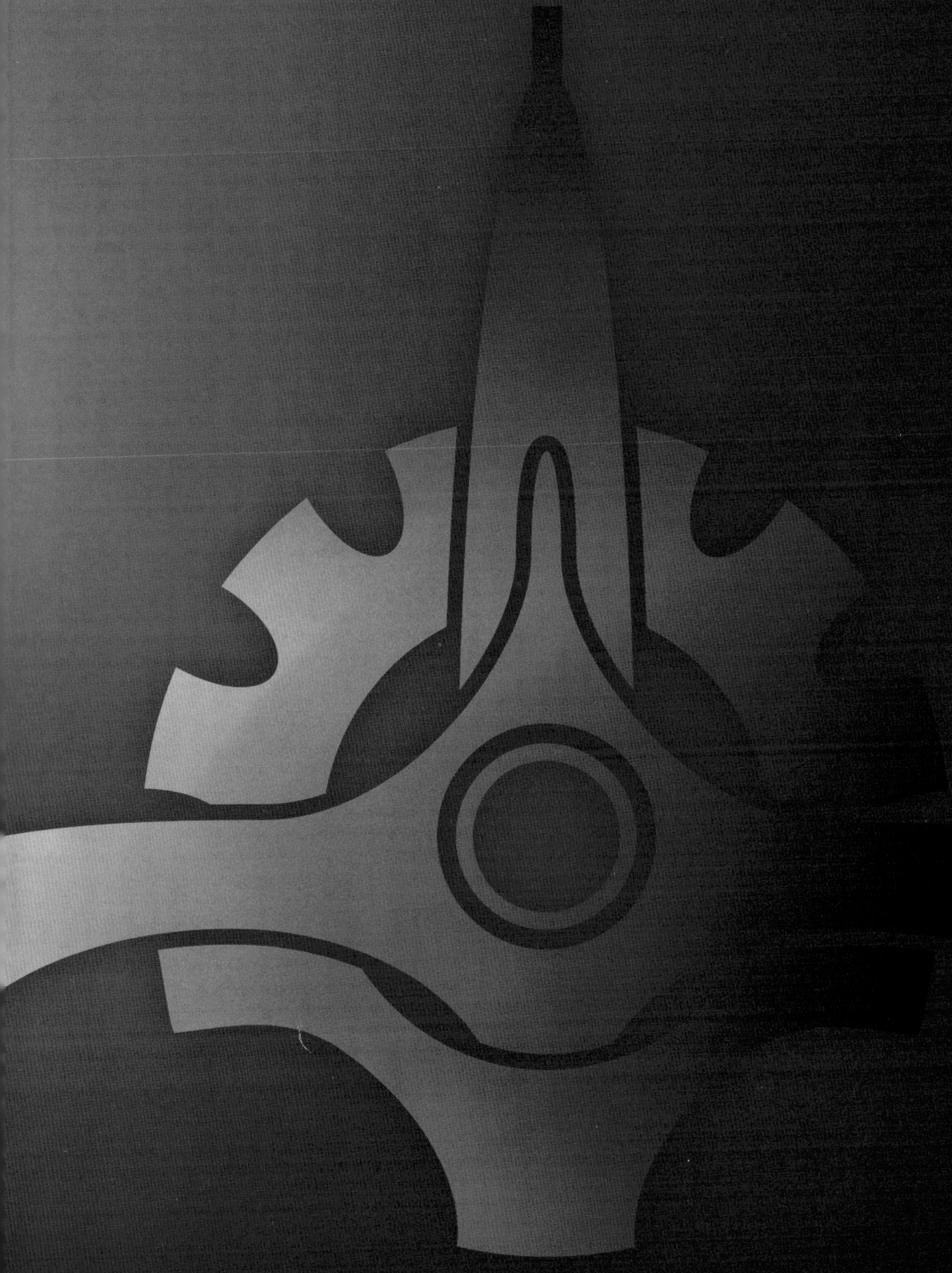

STAR WARS GRAPHIC NOVEL TIMELINE (IN YEARS)

Dawn of the Jedi—36,000 BSW4

Omnibus: Tales of the Jedi—5,000–3,986 BSW4

Knights of the Old Republic—3,964–3,963 BSW4

The Old Republic—3678, 3653, 3600 BSW4

Lost Tribe of the Sith—2974 BSW4

Knight Errant—1,032 BSW4

Jedi vs. Sith—1,000 BSW4

Jedi: The Dark Side—53 BSW4

Omnibus: Rise of the Sith—33 BSW4

Episode I: The Phantom Menace—32 BSW4

Omnibus: Emissaries and Assassins—32 BSW4

Omnibus: Quinlan Vos—Jedi in Darkness—31–30 BSW4

Omnibus: Menace Revealed—31–22 BSW4

Honor and Duty—22 BSW4

Blood Ties—22 BSW4

Episode II: Attack of the Clones—22 BSW4

Clone Wars—22–19 BSW4

Omnibus: Clone Wars—22–19 BSW4

Clone Wars Adventures—22–19 BSW4

Darth Maul: Death Sentence—20 BSW4

Episode III: Revenge of the Sith—19 BSW4

Purge—19 BSW4

Dark Times—19 BSW4

Omnibus: Droids and Ewoks—15 BSW4–3.5 ASW4

Omnibus: Droids—5.5 BSW4

Omnibus: Boba Fett—3 BSW4–10 ASW4

Agent of the Empire—3 BSW4

The Force Unleashed—2 BSW4

Omnibus: At War with the Empire—1 BSW4

Episode IV: A New Hope—SW4

Star Wars—0 ASW4

Classic Star Wars—0–3 ASW4

Omnibus: A Long Time Ago. . . .—0–4 ASW4

Omnibus: Wild Space—0–4 ASW4

Empire—0 ASW4

Omnibus: The Other Sons of Tatooine—0 ASW4

Omnibus: Early Victories—0–3 ASW4

Jabba the Hutt: The Art of the Deal—1 ASW4

Episode V: The Empire Strikes Back—3 ASW4

Omnibus: Shadows of the Empire—3.5–4.5 ASW4

Episode VI: Return of the Jedi—4 ASW4

Omnibus: X-Wing Rogue Squadron—4–5 ASW4

The Thrawn Trilogy—9 ASW4

Dark Empire—10 ASW4

Crimson Empire—11 ASW4

Jedi Academy: Leviathan—12 ASW4

Union—19 ASW4

Chewbacca—25 ASW4

Invasion—25 ASW4

Legacy—130–138 ASW4

Dawn of the Jedi
36,000 years before
Star Wars: A New Hope

Old Republic Era
25,000–1000 years before
Star Wars: A New Hope

Rise of the Empire Era
1000–0 years before Star
Wars: A New Hope

Rebellion Era
0–5 years after
Star Wars: A New Hope

New Republic Era
5–25 years after
Star Wars: A New Hope

New Jedi Order Era
25+ years after
Star Wars: A New Hope

Legacy Era
130+ years after
Star Wars: A New Hope

Vector
Crosses four eras in timeline

Volume 1 contains:
Knights of the Old Republic Volume 5
Dark Times Volume 3
Volume 2 contains:
Rebellion Volume 4
Legacy Volume 6

Infinities
Does not apply to timeline

Sergio Aragones Stomps Star Wars
Star Wars Tales
Omnibus: Infinities
Tag and Bink
Star Wars Visionaries

BSW4 = before *Episode IV: A New Hope*. ASW4 = after *Episode IV: A New Hope*.

STAR WARS HARDCOVER VOLUMES

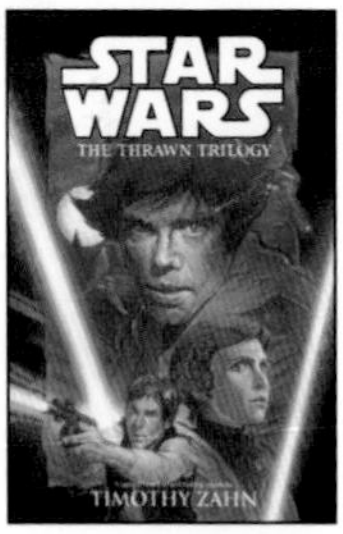
STAR WARS
THE THRAWN TRILOGY
TIMOTHY ZAHN

STAR WARS: THE THRAWN TRILOGY

Collects the comics adaptations of Timothy Zahn's best-selling novels *Heir to the Empire*, *Dark Force Rising*, and *The Last Command*. Years after the fall of the Empire, the last of the Emperor's warlords, Admiral Thrawn, is ready to destroy the New Republic—and the odds are stacked against Luke, Leia, and Han!

ISBN 978-1-59582-417-2 | $34.99

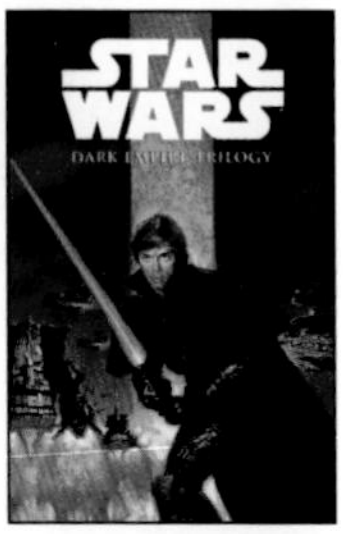
STAR WARS

STAR WARS: DARK EMPIRE TRILOGY

Six years after the fall of the Empire in *Return of the Jedi*, the battle for the galaxy's freedom rages on. The Empire has been mysteriously reborn . . . Princess Leia and Han Solo struggle to hold together the New Republic while Luke Skywalker fights an inner battle as he is drawn to the dark side . . .

ISBN 978-1-59582-612-1 | $29.99

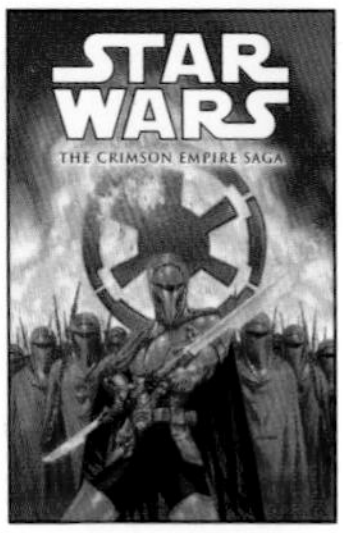
STAR WARS
THE CRIMSON EMPIRE SAGA

STAR WARS: THE CRIMSON EMPIRE SAGA

The blood-soaked tale of the last surviving member of Emperor Palpatine's Royal Guard is now complete! From revenge to redemption, the story of Kir Kanos takes him from the deserts of Yinchorr, to the halls of Imperial power, and to the inner circle of the New Republic.

ISBN 978-1-59582-947-4 | $34.99

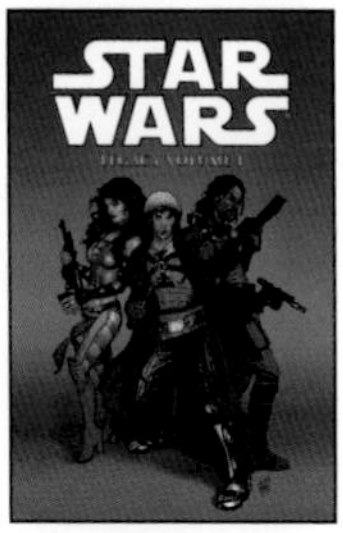
STAR WARS

STAR WARS: LEGACY

The future of Star Wars and the future of the Skywalkers is told in John Ostrander and Jan Duursema's acclaimed *Star Wars: Legacy*. A Sith legion has conquered the Empire, the Jedi have been scattered, and the galaxy is divided. Into this comes Cade Skywalker, heir to the Skywalker legacy . . .

Book 1: ISBN 978-1-61655-178-0 | $34.99

Book 2: ISBN 978-1-61655-209-1 | $34.99

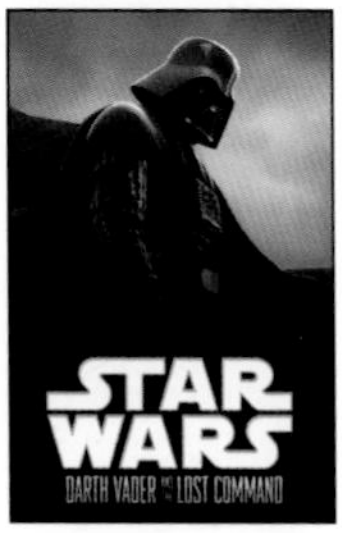
STAR WARS

STAR WARS: DARTH VADER AND THE LOST COMMAND

Still haunted by the death of Anakin Skywalker's beloved Padmé, Darth Vader is tasked with a mission to locate a lost Imperial expeditionary force—led by the son of Vader's rising nemesis, Moff Tarkin. Vader's journey is compounded by traitors among his crew and the presence of the mysterious Lady Saro.

ISBN 978-1-59582-778-4 | $24.99

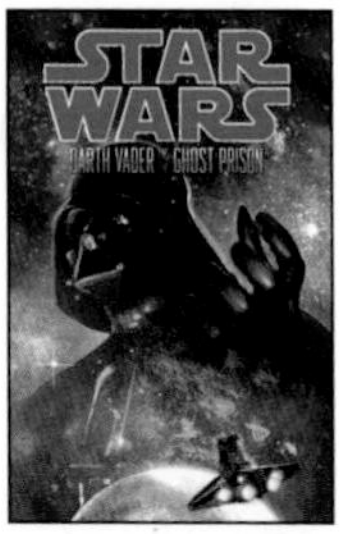
STAR WARS

STAR WARS: DARTH VADER AND THE GHOST PRISON

A traitorous uprising against the Galactic Empire leaves Emperor Palpatine close to death. Saving the Emperor—and the Empire—appears to be a lost cause . . . unless Darth Vader and a young lieutenant can uncover the secrets of the Jedi Council and locate the mysterious "Ghost Prison."

ISBN 978-1-61655-059-2 | $24.99

AVAILABLE AT YOUR LOCAL COMICS SHOP OR BOOKSTORE!

To find a comics shop in your area, call 1-888-266-4226

For more information or to order direct: • On the web: DarkHorse.com • E-mail: mailorder@darkhorse.com • Phone: 1-800-862-0052 Mon.–Fri. 9 AM to 5 PM Pacific Time

STAR WARS®
DARK TIMES

In the wake of the Clone Wars and the destruction of the Jedi Order, the dark times have begun; this is the beginning of the era of Darth Vader and Emperor Palpatine. The future is grim, evil is on the rise, and there are no more safe places in the galaxy.

Dark Times Volume 1:
The Path to Nowhere
ISBN 978-1-59307-792-1 | $17.95

Dark Times Volume 2:
Parallels
ISBN 978-1-59307-945-1 | $17.95

Dark Times Volume 3
is in Vector Volume 1
ISBN 978-1-59582-226-0 | $17.99

Dark Times Volume 4:
Blue Harvest
ISBN 978-1-59582-264-2 | $17.99